G000243409

ROUGH GUIDES **PHRASEBOOK**

GREEK

ROUGH GUIDES

Contacting the Editors

Every effort has been made to provide accurate information in this publication, but changes are inevitable. The publisher cannot be responsible for any resulting loss, inconvenience or injury.
We would appreciate it if readers would call our attention to any errors or outdated information. We also welcome your suggestions; if you come across a relevant expression not in our phrase book, please contact us at: **mail@uk.roughguides.com**

All Rights Reserved
© 2019 APA Publications (UK) Ltd.

Cover & Interior Design: Slawomir Krajewski
Head of Production: Rebeka Davies
Production Manager: Rebecca Hancock
Picture Researcher: Slawomir Krajewski
Cover Photo: all shutterstock

Interior Photos: all shutterstock

CONTENTS

LEISURE TIME

SAFE TRAVEL

FOOD

PEOPLE

DICTIONARY

PRONUNCIATION

This section is designed to make you familiar with the sounds of Greek using our simplified phonetic transcription. You'll find the pronunciation of the Greek letters explained below, together with their 'imitated' equivalents. This system is used throughout the phrase book; simply read the pronunciation as if it were English, noting any special rules below.

Stress is important in Greek, as often the meaning of the word changes depending upon which syllable is stressed. In written Greek, stress is indicated by a small mark (΄) on the syllable to be stressed. In the Greek phonetic transcription, stress is indicated with an underline.

Over the last 25 years, the Greek language has been greatly simplified, with the number of stress and breathing marks reduced; however, one may still encounter words written with the more elaborate stress marks, mainly in older Greek texts.

Please note that the question mark is indicated by the semi-colon (;) in Greek.

CONSONANTS

Letter	Approximate Pronunciation	Symbol	Example	Pronunciation
β	like v in voice	v	βάζο	<u>vah</u> • zoh
δ	voiced th, like th in then	TH	δεν	THehn
ζ	like z in zoo	z	ζω	zoh
θ	unvoiced th, like th in thing	th	θέλω	<u>theh</u> • loh
κ	like k in key	k	κότα	<u>koh</u> • tah
λ	like l in lemon	l	λεμόνι	leh • <u>moh</u> • nee
μ	like m in man	m	μαμά	mah • <u>mah</u>
ν	like n in net	n	νέο	<u>neh</u> • oh
ξ	like x in fox	ks	ξένος	<u>kseh</u> • nohs
π	like p in pen	p	πένα	<u>peh</u> • nah
ρ	trilled like a Scottish r	r	ώρα	<u>oh</u> • rah

σ	like s in sit	s	σε	seh
ç*	like s in slim	s	ήλιος	<u>ee</u> • liohs
τ	like t in tea	t	τι	tee
φ	like f in fun	f	φως	fohs
x	like ch in Scottish loch	kh	χαρά	khah • <u>rah</u>
ψ	like ps in tops	ps	ψάρι	<u>psah</u> • ree
γ	like g + h	gh	γάλα	<u>ghah</u> • lah
γγ, γκ	like g in go, but in some cases a more nasal ng as in sing	g	γκαρσόν	gahr • <u>sohn</u>
μπ	like b in bath, but in some cases more like mp as in lamp	b	μπαρ	bahr
ντ	like d in do, but in some cases more like nd as in end	d	ντομάτα	doh • <u>mah</u> • tah
τζ	like j in jazz	j	τζατζίκι	jah • jee • kee
τσ	like ts in lets	ts	τσάντα	<u>tsahn</u> • dah

* This character is used instead of **σ**, when the latter falls at the end of a word.

VOWELS

Letter	Approximate Pronunciation	Symbol	Example	Pronunciation
α	like a in father	ah	μα	mah
ε	like e in ten	eh	θέλω	<u>theh</u> • loh
η, ι, υ	like ee in keen	ee	πίνω	<u>pee</u> • noh
o, ω	like o in top	oh	πότε	<u>poh</u> • teh
αι	like e in ten	eh	μπαίνω	<u>beh</u> • noh
οι, ει, υι	like ee in keen	ee	πλοίο	<u>plee</u> • oh

VOWEL COMBINATIONS

Letter	Approximate Pronunciation	Symbol	Example	Pronunciation
αυ	1) when followed by θ, κ, ξ, π, σ, τ, φ, χ, ψ, like af in after	**ahf**	αυτός	ahf • <u>tohs</u>
	2) in all other cases, like av in avocado	**ahv**	αύρα	<u>ahv</u> • rah
ευ	1) when followed by θ, κ, ξ, π, σ, τ, φ, χ, ψ, like ef in effect	**ehf**	λευκός	lehf • <u>kohs</u>
	2) in all other cases, like ev in ever	**ehv**	νεύρο	<u>nehv</u> • roh
ου	like oo in zoo	**oo**	ούζο	<u>oo</u> • zoh
για, γεια	like yah in yard	**yah**	για	yah
γε, γιε	like ye in yet	**yeh**	γερό	yeh • <u>roh</u>
ειο,γιο	like yo in yogurt	**yoh**	γιος	yohs
γι, γυ, γη	like yea in yeast	**yee**	γύρω	<u>yee</u> • roh
ια, οια	like ia in piano	**iah**	ποια	piah

Greek is a language with a long history. The language has developed over the centuries into the modern Greek spoken today by approximately 11 million people in Greece and Cyprus, as well as Greek-speaking communities within other countries. It is a phonetic language; the sound of each letter does not usually change with its position. The characters may appear confusing at first; don't be put off by this. With a bit of practice most people can read Greek in just a few hours.

HOW TO USE THE APP

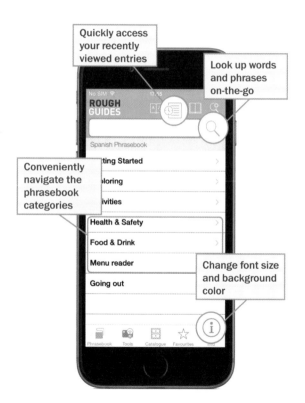

Quickly access your recently viewed entries

Look up words and phrases on-the-go

Conveniently navigate the phrasebook categories

Change font size and background color

Save the most useful everyday words and phrases to your Favorites

Use the Flash Cards Quiz to learn and memorize new words easily

Spanish Phrasebook

Can you recommend a good restaurant/ bar?
¿Puede recomend... buen

restaurante/bar?
_pweh•deh reh•koh•mehn•dahr•meh
oon bwehn rehs•taw•rahn•teh/bahr_

Take all digital advantages of the app: listen to words and phrases pronounced by native speakers

Is there a t...

Phrasebook   Tools   Catalogue   Favourites   Info

To learn how to Activate the app, see the inside back cover of this phrasebook.

GRAMMAR

Greeks generally use **εσείς** *(eh • sees)* the plural form of 'you' with people they do not know well. The familiar, singular form **εσύ** *(eh • see)*, is used among friends and with children, but don't worry too much - you will not be considered rude, just friendly!

REGULAR VERBS

Below are three of the main categories of regular verbs in the present tense. Using the endings indicated after the dash, you can use a large number of verbs competently.

Greek verbs are divided in categories that are formed by using certain endings and are conjugated accordingly. Some of the most popular endings are:

– ω *oh*	**– έρνω** <u>*ehr*</u> *• noh*
– νω *noh*	**– αίνω** <u>*eh*</u> *• noh*
– άζω <u>*ah*</u> *• zoh*	**– ένω** <u>*eh*</u> *• noh*
– άω <u>*ah*</u> *• oh*	**– άσκω** <u>*as*</u> *• koh*
– ήνω <u>*ee*</u> *• noh*	**– όμαι** <u>*oh*</u> *• meh*
– ώνω <u>*oh*</u> *• noh*	**– άμαι** <u>*ah*</u> *• meh*
– έλνω <u>*ehl*</u> *• noh*	**– έμαι** <u>*eh*</u> *• meh*

Είμαι (to be)	Present
I am	**Εγώ είμαι** *eh • <u>goh</u> <u>ee</u> • meh*
You are	**Εσύ είσαι** *eh • <u>see</u> <u>ee</u> • seh*
He is	**Αυτός είναι** *ahf • <u>tohs</u> <u>ee</u> • neh*
She is	**Αυτή είναι** *ahf • <u>tee</u> <u>ee</u> • neh*
We are	**Εμείς είμαστε** *eh • <u>mees</u> <u>eem</u> • ah • steh*
You are	**Εσείς είστε** *eh • <u>sees</u> <u>ee</u> • steh*
They are	**Αυτοί είναι** *ahf • <u>tee</u> <u>ee</u> • neh*

Αφήνω (to let)	Present
I let	**Εγώ αφήνω** ah • <u>fee</u> • noh
You let	**Εσύ αφήνεις** ah • <u>fee</u> • nees
He lets	**Αυτός αφήνει** ah • <u>fee</u> • nee
She lets	**Αυτή αφήνει** ah • <u>fee</u> • nee
We let	**Εμείς αφήνουμε** ah • <u>fee</u> • noo • meh
You let	**Εσείς αφήνετε** ah • <u>fee</u> • neh • teh
They let	**Αυτοί αφήνουν** ah • <u>fee</u> • noon

Φέρνω (to bring)	Present
I bring	**Εγώ φέρνω** <u>fehr</u> • noh
You bring	**Εσύ φέρνεις** <u>fehr</u> • nees
He brings	**Αυτός φέρνει** <u>feh</u> • rnee
She brings	**Αυτή φέρνει** <u>fehr</u> • nee
We bring	**Εμείς φέρνουμε** <u>feh</u> • rnoo • meh
You bring	**Εσείς φέρνετε** <u>feh</u> • neh • teh
They bring	**Αυτοί φέρνουν** <u>fehr</u> • noon

The infinitive/first person of most Greek verbs end in **ω**:
to do   **κάνω** <u>kah</u> • noh
To conjugate this verb, drop the final **ω**, and add the appropriate ending:

Κάνω (to do)	Present
I do	**Εγώ κάνω** eh • <u>goh</u> <u>kahn</u> • oh
You do	**Εσύ κάνεις** eh • <u>see</u> <u>kahn</u> • ees
(familiar or sing.)	
He does	**Αυτός κάνει** ahf • <u>tohs</u> <u>kahn</u> • ee
She does	**Αυτή κάνει** ahf • <u>tee</u> <u>kahn</u> • ee
We do	**Εμείς κάνουμε** eh • <u>mees</u> <u>kahn</u> • oo • meh
You do *(form., pl.)*	**Εσείς κάνετε** eh • <u>sees</u> <u>kahn</u> • eh • teh
They do	**Αυτοί κάνουν** ahf • <u>tee</u> <u>kahn</u> • oun

So, by applying this rule you can conjugate another verb ending in **ω**:

Γράφω (to write)	Present
I write	**Εγώ γράφω**
	eh • _goh_ _grahf_ • oh
You write	**Εσύ γράφεις**
	eh • _see_ _grahf_ • ees
He writes	**Αυτός γράφει**
	ahf • _tohs_ _grahf_ • ee
She writes	**Αυτή γράφει**
	ahf • _tee_ _grahf_ • ee
We write	**Εμείς γράφουμε**
	eh • _mees_ _grahf_ • oo • meh
You write	**Εσείς γράφετε**
	eh • _sees_ _grahf_ • eh • teh
They write	**Αυτοί γράφουν**
	ahf • _ee_ _grahf_ • oon

WORD ORDER

Syntax in Greek, especially in everyday spoken language, is very flexible. The standard word order is subject-verb-object, but you can change the order of sentence components to shift emphasis.

Example:

Το τρένο φεύγει τώρα. toh _treh_ • noh _fehv_ • ghee _toh_ • rah
The train leaves now.

You can say the same thing by placing the verb at the beginning of the sentence:

Φεύγει το τρένο τώρα. _fehv_ • ghee toh _treh_ • noh _toh_ • rah
The train leaves now.

Also, use an interrogatory intonation to turn this sentence into a question. The question form can work both with the verb in the beginning and at the end of the sentence.

Τώρα φεύγει το τραίνο; _toh_ • _rah fehv_ • _ghee toh_ _treh_ • _noh_
Is the train leaving now?
Note that, in Greek, the equivalent of a semi-colon (;) is used in
place of a question mark.

NEGATION

To form a negative sentence in Greek, add the word **δεν** (THehn)
before the verb.
Example:
Θέλω _theh_ • _loh_   I want
Δεν Θέλω THehn _theh_ • _loh_   I don't want

IMPERATIVES

Imperative sentences are formed by adding the appropriate
ending to the stem of the verb. The endings used to form the
imperative of a verb are mainly:
α (ah), **ε** (eh), **ήσου** (_ee_ • soo), **άσου** (_ah_ • soo).

Examples:		
πηγαίνω	pee • _yeh_ • noh	to go
Πήγαινε!	_pee_ • yeh • neh	Go!
βιάζομαι	_viah_ • zoh • meh	to hurry
Βιάσου!	_viah_ • soo	Hurry!

NOUNS & ARTICLES

There are three genders in Greek: masculine, feminine and
neuter; all nouns in Greek are assigned a specific gender. The
gender of the article changes based on the gender of the noun it
modifies.
For example:
She is tall.   **Είναι ψηλή.** _ee_ • neh psee • _lee_
He is tall.   **Είναι ψηλός.** _ee_ • neh psee • _lohs_

The article **o** (oh) is used with masculine nouns, **η** (ee) with feminine nouns and **το** (toh) with neuter nouns.

masculine	**ο καφές** oh kah • _fehs_	the coffee
feminine	**η μπίρα** ee _bee_ • rah	the beer
neuter	**το τρένο** toh _treh_ • noh	the train

Greek nouns have four cases: nominative, genitive, accusative and vocative. A simple way to explain their use would be that the nominative indicates the subject, the genitive indicates possession, the accusative indicates the object and the vocative is used to address someone. Don't worry too much about this. In most cases, people will understand what you are saying even if you use a noun with the wrong case. The words in the dictionary are in nominative.

There is no easy way to form the plural. Beginner speakers of Greek should clearly state the number along with the noun to be easily understood.

ADJECTIVES

Adjectives agree with the noun they describe in gender, case and number. The most common ending for a feminine adjective is **−η** (ee), for a masculine adjective it is **−ος** (ohs) and for the neuter **o** (oh).

Example:

Είναι γρήγορος οδηγός.　　_ee_ • neh _ghree_ • ghoh • rohs
He is a fast driver.　　　　　oh • THee • _ghohs_

Είναι γρήγορη οδηγός.　　_ee_ • neh _ghree_ • ghoh • ree
She is a fast driver.　　　　　oh • THee • _ghohs_

Είναι γρήγορο αυτοκίνητο.　_ee_ • neh _ghree_ • ghoh • roh
This is a fast car.　　　　　　ah • ftoh • _kee_ • nee • toh

COMPARATIVES & SUPERLATIVES

The comparative form of adjectives is usually formed by adding the word **πιο** (pioh) before the adjective. Also, in certain cases, the comparative may be formed by adding the ending **–ερος** m (eh • rohs), **–ερη** f (eh • ree), **–ερο** (eh • roh) n to the stem of an adjective, respectively. To form the superlative of an adjective, add the ending **–ατος** m (ah • tohs), **–ατη** f (ah • tee), **–ατο** (ah • tee) n to the stem of the adjective.

POSSESSIVE PRONOUNS

mine	**μου** *moo*	
yours	**σου** *soo*	
his/her/its	**του/της/του** *too/tees/too*	
ours	**μας** *mahs*	
yours	**σας** *sahs*	
theirs	**τους** *toos*	

Example:
Το βιβλίο είναι δικό μου. *toh veev • <u>lee</u> • oh ee • neh*
This book is mine.   *thee • <u>koh</u> moo*

ADVERBS

Adverbs are used to describe the action of verbs. Almost all adverbs are formed by adding the ending **α** (ah) to the stem of the adjective.
Example:
Οδηγεί γρήγορα. *oh • THee • <u>yee</u> <u>ghree</u> • ghoh • rah*
He drives quickly.

PRACTICALITIES

THE BASICS

NUMBERS

NEED TO KNOW

0	**μηδέν**	mee • _THehn_
1	**ένας**	_eh_ • nahs
2	**δύο**	_THee_ • oh
3	**τρεις**	trees
4	**τέσσερις**	_teh_ • seh • rees
5	**πέντε**	_pehn_ • deh
6	**έξι**	_eh_ • ksee
7	**επτά**	eh • _ptah_
8	**οκτώ**	oh • _ktoh_
9	**εννέα**	eh • _neh_ • ah
10	**δέκα**	_THeh_ • kah
11	**έντεκα**	_ehn_ • deh • kah
12	**δώδεκα**	_THoh_ • THeh • kah

13	**δεκατρία**
	THeh • kah • <u>tree</u> • ah
14	**δεκατέσσερα**
	THeh • kah • <u>teh</u> • seh • rah
15	**δεκαπέντε**
	THeh • kah • <u>pehn</u> • deh
16	**δεκαέξι**
	THeh • kah • <u>eh</u> • ksee
17	**δεκαεπτά**
	THeh • kah • eh • <u>ptah</u>
18	**δεκαοκτώ**
	THeh • kah • oh • <u>ktoh</u>
19	**δεκαεννέα**
	THeh • kah • eh • <u>neh</u> • ah
20	**είκοσι**
	<u>ee</u> • koh • see
21	**είκοσι ένα**
	<u>ee</u> • koh • see <u>eh</u> • nah
22	**είκοσι δύο**
	<u>ee</u> • koh • see <u>THee</u> • oh
30	**τριάντα**
	tree • <u>ahn</u> • dah
31	**τριάντα ένα**
	tree • <u>ahn</u> • dah <u>eh</u> • nah
40	**σαράντα**
	sah • <u>rahn</u> • dah
50	**πενήντα**
	peh • <u>neen</u> • dah
60	**εξήντα**
	eh • <u>kseen</u> • dah
70	**εβδομήντα**
	ehv • THoh • <u>meen</u> • dah

80	**ογδόντα**
	ohgh • THohn • dah
90	**ενενήντα**
	eh • neh • neen • dah
100	**εκατό**
	eh • kah • toh
101	**εκατόν ένα**
	eh • kah • tohn eh • nah
200	**διακόσια**
	THee • ah • koh • siah
500	**πεντακόσια**
	pehn • dah • koh • siah
1,000	**χίλια**
	khee • liah
10,000	**δέκα χιλιάδες**
	THeh • kah khee • liah • THehs
1,000,000	**ένα εκατομμύριο**
	eh • nah eh • kah • toh • mee • ree • oh

ORDINAL NUMBERS

first	**πρώτος** _proh_ • tohs
second	**δεύτερος** _THehf_ • teh • rohs
third	**τρίτος** _tree_ • tohs
fourth	**τέταρτος** _teh_ • tahr • tohs
fifth	**πέμπτος** _pehm_ • ptohs
once	**μια φορά** miah foh • _rah_
twice	**δύο φορές** _THee_ • oh foh • _rehs_
three times	**τρεις φορές** trees foh • _rehs_

TIME

NEED TO KNOW

What time is it?	**Τι ώρα είναι;**
	tee <u>oh</u> • rah <u>ee</u> • neh
It's noon [midday].	**Είναι μεσημέρι.**
	ee • neh meh • see • <u>meh</u> • ree
At midnight.	**Τα μεσάνυχτα.**
	tah meh • <u>sah</u> • neekh • tah
From nine o'clock. to five o'clock	**Από τις εννέα ως τις πέντε.**
	ah • <u>poh</u> tees eh • <u>neh</u> • ah ohs tees <u>pehn</u> • deh
Twenty after [past] four.	**Τέσσερις και είκοσι.**
	<u>teh</u> • seh • rees keh <u>ee</u> • koh • see
A quarter to nine.	**Εννέα παρά τέταρτο.**
	eh • <u>neh</u> • ah pah • <u>rah</u> teh • tahr • toh
5:30 a.m./p.m.	**Πεντέμιση π.μ./μ.μ.**
	pehn • <u>deh</u> • mee • see proh meh • seem • <u>vree</u> • ahs/meh • <u>tah</u> meh • seem • <u>vree</u> • ahs

DAYS

NEED TO KNOW

Monday	**Δευτέρα**	
	THehf • teh • rah	
Tuesday	**Τρίτη**	
	tree • tee	
Wednesday	**Τετάρτη**	
	teh • tahr • tee	
Thursday	**Πέμπτη**	
	pehm • tee	
Friday	**Παρασκευή**	
	pah • rahs • keh • vee	
Saturday	**Σάββατο**	
	sah • vah • toh	
Sunday	**Κυριακή**	
	keer • yah • kee chóo nat	

DATES

yesterday	**χτες**
	khtehs
today	**σήμερα**
	see • meh • rah
tomorrow	**αύριο**
	ahv • ree • oh
day	**ημέρα**
	ee • meh • rah
week	**εβδομάδα**
	ehv • THoh • mah • THah
month	**μήνας**
	mee • nahs
year	**χρόνος**
	khroh • nohs

Greece follows a day-month-year format instead of the month-day-year format used in the U.S.
E.g.: July 25, 2008; 25/07/08 = 7/25/2008 in the U.S.

MONTHS

January	**Ιανουάριος**
	ee • ah • noo • <u>ah</u> • ree • ohs
February	**Φεβρουάριος**
	fehv • roo • <u>ah</u> • ree • ohs
March	**Μάρτιος**
	<u>mahr</u> • tee • ohs
April	**Απρίλιος**
	ahp • <u>ree</u> • lee • ohs
May	**Μάιος**
	<u>mah</u> • ee • ohs
June	**Ιούνιος**
	ee • <u>oo</u> • nee • ohs
July	**Ιούλιος**
	ee • <u>oo</u> • lee • ohs
August	**Αύγουστος**
	<u>ahv</u> • ghoo • stohs
September	**Σεπτέμβριος**
	sehp • <u>tehm</u> • vree • ohs
October	**Οκτώβριος**
	ohk • <u>toh</u> • vree • ohs
November	**Νοέμβριος**
	noh • <u>ehm</u> • vree • ohs
December	**Δεκέμβριος**
	THeh • <u>kehm</u> • vree • ohs

SEASONS

| spring | **η άνοιξη** |
| | *ee <u>ah</u> • nee • ksee* |

summer	**το καλοκαίρι**
	toh kah • loh • keh • ree
fall [autumn]	**το φθινόπωρο**
	toh fthee • noh • poh • roh
winter	**ο χειμώνας**
	oh khee • moh • nahs

HOLIDAYS

January 1, New Year's Day	**Πρωτοχρονιά**
	proh • toh • hroh • niah
January 6, Epiphany	**Θεοφάνεια**
	theh • oh • fah • nee • ah
March 25, Annunciation	**Ευαγγελισμός**
	eh • vahn • geh • lee • smohs
March 25, National Holiday Proclamation of the Greek War of Independence	**Εθνική εορτή**
	ehth • nee • kee eh • ohr • tee
May 1, May Day	**Πρωτομαγιά**
	proh • toh • mah • yah

August 15, Assumption	**Κοίμηση της Θεοτόκου** _kee • mee • see tees_ _theh • oh • toh • koo_
October 28, the OXI day	**Εθνική εορτή** _ehth • nee • kee eh • ohr • tee_
December 25, Christmas	**Χριστούγεννα** _khrees • too • yeh • nah_
Moveable Holidays: Easter	**Πάσχα** _pahs • khah_
Shrove Monday (Greek Orthodox)	**Καθαρή Δευτέρα** _kah • thah • ree_ _THeh • fteh • rah_
Pentecost	**Αγίου Πνεύματος** _ah • yee • oo pnehv • mah • tohs_

Each city and town has a patron saint. The saint's holy day, also known as a name day, is a local public holiday.

The most important holidays in Greece are religious celebrations such as Easter and Christmas, with Easter being the most sacred holiday. The traditional celebrations usually start on Good Friday with a procession of the Epitaph (Bier) symbolizing the tomb of Christ. On Holy Saturday evening, the resurrection mass takes place when everyone goes to church at around 11:00 p.m. with unlit candles. At midnight the bells are rung and the priest comes out of the church to pass the Holy Light to the congregation. This is the largest religious gathering.

In most places, the crowds fill the streets outside the church, traffic is blocked and there are usually fireworks right after midnight. After this, it is customary to eat a soup called **μαγειρίτσα** *(mah • ghee • ree • tsah)*, made from the lamb's internal organs.

On Sunday the celebration is usually taken outdoors. Whole families come together to roast a lamb on the spit, a big feast lasting the whole day. If you are in the countryside you will see large parties of people roasting the lamb and you may even be invited to join them. Even in the big cities, don't be surprised if you see people doing the same on their rooftops!

Another major holiday is March 25th, which is a day of remembrance of the start of the Greek War of Independence. On this day there is a military parade in every major city.

ARRIVAL & DEPARTURE

NEED TO KNOW

I'm here on vacation [holiday]/business.	**Είμαι εδώ για διακοπές/δουλειά.**
	ee • meh eh • _THoh_ yah
	THiah • koh • _pehs_/THoo • _liah_
I'm going to…	**Θα…**
	thah…
I'm staying at the…Hotel.	**Μένω στο…ξενοδοχείο.**
	meh • _noh_ stoh…
	kseh • noh • THoh • _khee_ • oh

BORDER CONTROL

I'm just passing through.	**Απλώς περνώ από εδώ.**
	ahp • _lohs_ pehr • _noh_ ah • _poh_ eh • _THoh_
I would like to declare…	**Θα ήθελα να δηλώσω…**
	thah _ee_ • theh • _lah_ nah THee • _loh_ • soh…
I have nothing to declare.	**Δεν έχω να δηλώσω τίποτα.**
	THehn _eh_ • khoh
	nah THee • _loh_ • soh _tee_ • poh • tah

YOU MAY HEAR...

Το εισιτήριο/διαβατήριό σας, παρακαλώ.
toh ee • see • tee • ree • oh/
THee • ah • vah • tee • ree • oh
sahs pah • rah • kah • loh

Your ticket/
passport,
please.

Ποιος είναι ο σκοπός του ταξιδιού σας;
piohs ee • neh oh skoh • pohs too
tah • ksee • THee • oo sahs

What's the
purpose of
your visit?

Πού μένετε;
poo meh • neh • teh

Where are you
staying?

Πόσο καιρό θα μείνετε;
poh • soh keh • roh thah mee • neh • teh

How long are you
staying?

Με ποιον είστε εδώ;
meh piohn ee • steh eh • THoh

Who are you
with?

Έχετε τίποτα να δηλώσετε;
eh • kheh • the tee • poh • tah nah
THee • loh • seh • teh

Do you have
anything to
declare?

Πρέπει να πληρώσετε φόρο για αυτό.
preh • pee nah plee • roh • seh • teh
foh • roh yah ahf • toh

You must pay
duty on this.

Παρακαλώ ανοίξτε αυτή την τσάντα.
pah • rah • kah • loh ah • nee • ksteh
ahf • tee teen tsah • ndah

Please open this
bag.

YOU MAY SEE...

ΤΕΛΩΝΕΙΟ *teh • loh • nee • oh*	customs
ΑΦΟΡΟΛΟΓΗΤΑ ΕΙΔΗ *ah • foh • roh • loh • yee • tah ee • THee*	duty-free goods
ΕΙΔΗ ΓΙΑ ΔΗΛΩΣΗ *ee • THee yah THee • loh • see*	goods to declare
ΤΙΠΟΤΑ ΓΙΑ ΔΗΛΩΣΗ *tee • poh • tah yah THee • loh • see*	nothing to declare
ΕΛΕΓΧΟΣ ΔΙΑΒΑΤΗΡΙΩΝ *eh • leh • ghohs THee • ah • vah • tee • ree • ohn*	passport control
ΑΣΤΥΝΟΜΙΑ *ah • stee • noh • mee • ah*	police

MONEY

NEED TO KNOW

Where is…?	**Πού είναι…;**
	poo ee • neh…
the ATM	**το αυτόματο μηχάνημα ανάληψης**
	toh ahf • toh • mee • khah • nee • mah ah • nah • lee • psees
the bank	**η τράπεζα**
	ee trah • peh • zah
the currency exchange office	**γραφείο ανταλλαγής συναλλάγματος**
	ghrah • fee • oh ahn • dah • lah • ghees see • nah • lahgh • mah • tohs
What time does the bank open/close?	**Τι ώρα ανοίγει/κλείνει η τράπεζα;**
	tee oh • rah ah • nee • ghee/klee • nee ee trah • peh • zah
I'd like to change dollars/pounds into euros.	**Θα ήθελα να αλλάξω μερικά δολάρια/ λίρες σε ευρώ.**
	thah ee • theh • lah nah ah • lah • ksoh meh • ree • kah THoh • lah • ree • ah/ meh • ree • kehs lee • rehs seh ehv • roh
I want to cash some traveler's checks [cheques].	**Θα ήθελα να εξαργυρώσω μερικές ταξιδιωτικές επιταγές.**
	thah ee • theh • lah nah eh • ksahr • yee • roh • soh meh • ree • kehs tah • ksee THee • oh • tee • kehs eh • pee • tah • yehs

AT THE BANK

Can I exchange foreign currency/ get a cash advance here?	**Μπορώ να αλλάξω συνάλλαγμα εδώ;/να πάρω μετρητά προκαταβολικά εδώ;**
	boh • roh nah ah • lah • ksoh
	see • nah • lahgh • mah eh • THoh/nah
	pah • roh meh • tree • tah
	proh • kah • tah • voh lee • kah eh • THoh
What's the exchange rate?	**Ποια είναι η τιμή συναλλάγματος;**
	piah ee • neh
	ee tee • mee see • nah • lahgh • mah • tohs
How much is the fee?	**Πόση προμήθεια χρεώνετε;**
	poh • see proh • mee • thee • ah
	khreh • oh • neh • teh
I think there's a mistake.	**Νομίζω έγινε λάθος.**
	noh • mee • zoh eh • ghee • neh lah • thohs
I've lost my traveler's checks.	**Έχασα τις ταξιδιωτικές επιταγές μου.**
	eh • khah • sah tees
	tah • ksee • THee • oh • tee • kehs
	eh • pee • tah • yehs moo
My card was lost.	**Χάθηκε η κάρτα μου.**
	khah • thee • keh ee kahr • tah moo

YOU MAY SEE…

In 2002, the Greek drachma was replaced with the
European Union currency, euro, € (**ευρώ** *ehv • roh*), which is
divided into 100 cents (**λεπτό** *lehp • toh*).
Coins: 1, 2, 5, 10, 20, 50 cents; €1, 2
Notes: €5, 10, 20, 50, 100, 200, 500

My credit cards have been stolen.	**Μου έκλεψαν τις πιστωτικές μου κάρτες.**
	moo ehk • leh • psahn tees pees • toh • tee • kehs moo kahr • tehs
My card doesn't work.	**Η κάρτα μου δεν λειτουργεί.**
	ee kahr • tah moo THehn lee • toor • ghee
The ATM ate my card.	**Το ATM κράτησε την κάρτα μου.**
	toh ATM krah • tee • seh teen kahr • tah moo

For Numbers, see page 20.

YOU MAY SEE...

ΕΙΣΑΓΕΤΕ ΤΗΝ ΚΑΡΤΑ	insert card
ee • sah • yeh • teh teen kahr • tah	
ΑΚΥΡΩΣΗ	cancel
ah • kee • roh • see	
ΔΙΑΓΡΑΦΗ	clear
THee • ahgh • rah • fee	
ΕΙΣΑΓΕΤΕ	enter
ee • sah • yeh • teh	
PIN	PIN
peen	
ΑΝΑΛΗΨΗ	withdraw
ah • nah • lee • psee	
ΑΠΟ ΛΟΓΑΡΙΑΣΜΟ ΟΨΕΩΣ	from checking [current] account
ah • poh loh • ghahr • yahz • moh oh • pseh • ohs	
ΑΠΟ ΛΟΓΑΡΙΑΣΜΟ ΤΑΜΙΕΥΤΗΡΙΟΥ	from savings account
ah • poh loh • ghahr • yahz • moh tah • mee • ehf • tee • ree • oo	
ΑΠΟΔΕΙΞΗ	receipt
ah • poh • THee • ksee	

CONVERSATION

LANGUAGE DIFFICULTIES

Do you speak English?	**Μιλάτε Αγγλικά;**
	mee • lah • teh ahng • lee • kah
Does anyone here speak English?	**Μιλάει κανείς εδώ Αγγλικά;**
	mee • lah • ee kah • nees eh • THoh ahng • lee • kah
I don't speak Greek.	**Δεν μιλώ Ελληνικά.**
	THehn mee • loh eh • lee • nee • kah

All major foreign currencies, traveler's checks and Eurocheques are widely accepted at banks and currency exchange offices throughout Greece. In addition, ATMs can be found outside most main banks; these accept VISA, MasterCard, American Express, Eurocard and a variety of other international bank and credit cards.
Banks are generally open Monday through Friday from 7:30 a.m. or 8:00 a.m. to 2:30 p.m. (1:30 p.m. on Friday). Centrally located banks are also open on Saturday. Currency exchange offices usually stay open until late evening.

Could you speak more slowly?	**Μπορείτε να μιλάτε πιο αργά;** *boh • ree • the nah mee • lah • teh pioh ahr • ghah*

NEED TO KNOW

Hello.	**Χαίρετε.** *kheh • reh • teh*
How are you?	**Πώς είστε;** *pohs ee • steh*
Fine, thanks. And you?	**Καλά, ευχαριστώ. Εσείς;** *kah • lah ehf • khah • ree • stoh eh • sees*
Excuse me!	**Συγγνώμη!** *seegh • noh • mee*
Do you speak English?	**Μιλάτε Αγγλικά;** *mee • lah • the ahng • lee • kah*
What's your name?	**Πώς λέγεστε;** *pohs leh • yeh • steh*
My name is…	**Λέγομαι…** *leh • ghoh • meh…*
Nice to meet you.	**Χαίρω πολύ.** *kheh • roh poh • lee*
Where are you from?	**Από πού είστε;** *ah • poh poo ee • steh*
I'm from the U.S./U.K.	**Είμαι από τις Ηνωμένες Πολιτείες/το Ηνωμένο Βασίλειο.** *ee • meh ah • poh tees ee • noh • meh • nehs poh • lee • tee • ehs/toh ee • noh • meh • noh vah • see • lee • oh*
What do you do?	**Τι δουλειά κάνετε;** *tee THoo • liah kah • neh • teh*
I work for…	**Δουλεύω για…** *THoo • leh • voh yah…*

I'm a student.	**Είμαι φοιτητής** m **/φοιτήτρια** f. _ee_ • meh fee • tee • _tees/_ fee • _tee_ • tree • ah
I'm retired.	**Είμαι συνταξιούχος.** _ee_ • meh seen • dah • ksee • _oo_ • khohs
Do you like…?	**Σου αρέσει…;** soo ah • _reh_ • see…
Goodbye.	**Γεια σας.** yah sahs
See you later.	**Τα λέμε αργότερα.** tah _leh_ • meh ahr • _ghoh_ • teh • rah

In Greek, Mrs. is **κυρία** (kee • _ree_ • ah), Mr. is **κύριος**
(kee • _ree_ • ohs) and Miss is **δεσποινίς** (THehs • pee • _nees_).
Greek has a formal and an informal form of 'you': **γεια σας**
(yah sahs) and **γεια σου** (yah soo), respectively. The informal
is used between friends or when addressing children. Use
the formal **γεια σας** unless prompted to do otherwise.

Could you repeat that?	**Μπορείτε να το επαναλάβετε;** boh • _ree_ • the nah toh eh • pah • nah • _lah_ • veh • teh
Excuse me!	**Συγγνώμη!** seegh • _noh_ • mee
What was that?	**Τι είπατε;** tee _ee_ • pah • teh
Can you spell it?	**Μπορείς να το συλλαβίσεις;** boh • _rees_ nah toh see • lah • _vee_ • sees
Can you write it down, please?	**Μου το γράφετε παρακαλώ;** moo toh _ghrah_ • feh • teh pah • rah • kah • _loh_

Can you translate this for me?	**Μπορείτε να μου μεταφράσετε αυτό;** *boh • <u>ree</u> • teh nah moo meh • tahf • <u>rah</u> • seh • teh ahf • <u>toh</u>*
What does this/ that mean?	**Τι σημαίνει αυτό/εκείνο;** *tee see • <u>meh</u> • nee ahf • <u>toh</u>/eh • <u>kee</u> • noh*
I (don't) understand.	**(Δεν) Καταλαβαίνω.** *(THehn) kah • tah • lah • <u>veh</u> • noh*
Do you understand?	**Καταλαβαίνετε;** *kah • tah • lah • <u>veh</u> • neh • teh*

MAKING FRIENDS

Hello.	**Χαίρετε.** *<u>kheh</u> • reh • teh*
Good morning.	**Καλημέρα.** *kah • lee • <u>meh</u> • rah*
Good afternoon/ evening.	**Καλησπέρα.** *kah • lee • <u>speh</u> • rah*
Good night.	**Καληνύχτα.** *kah • lee • <u>neekh</u> • tah*
My name is…	**Λέγομαι…** *<u>leh</u> • ghoh • meh…*
What's your name?	**Πώς λέγεστε;** *pohs <u>leh</u> • yehs • teh*

YOU MAY HEAR…

Μιλώ (μόνο) λίγα Αγγλικά.
mee • <u>loh</u> (<u>moh</u> • noh) lee • ghah ahng • lee • <u>kah</u>

I speak (only) a little English.

Δεν μιλώ Αγγλικά.
THehn mee • <u>loh</u> ahng • lee • <u>kah</u>

I don't speak English.

I'd like to introduce you to…	**Θα ήθελα να σας συστήσω τον** m **/την** f **…** *thah ee • theh • lah nah sahs* *sees • tee • soh tohn/teen…*
Pleased to meet you.	**Χαίρω πολύ.** *kheh • roh poh • lee*
How are you?	**Πώς είστε;** *pohs ees • teh*
Fine, thanks.	**Καλά, ευχαριστώ.** *kah • lah ehf • khah • rees • toh*
And you?	**Εσείς;** *eh • sees*

TRAVEL TALK

I'm here…	**Είμαι εδώ…** *ee • meh eh • THoh…*
on business	**για δουλειά** *yah THoo • lee • ah*
vacation [holiday]	**για διακοπές** *yah THiah • koh • pehs*
studying	**για σπουδές** *yah spoo • THehs*
I'm staying here for…	**Μένω εδώ για…** *meh • noh eh • THoh yah…*

i

Greeks shake hands when they meet for the first time
and on subsequent meetings. With close friends,
it is customary to exchange kisses on both cheeks when
meeting and parting. It is polite to address people you meet
for the first time by their surname until prompted to use their
first name.

I've been here…	**Είμαι εδώ…**
	_ee_ • meh eh • _THoh_…
a day	**μια ημέρα**
	miah _meh_ • rah
a week	**μια εβδομάδα**
	miah ehv • THoh • _mah_ • THah
a month	**ένα μήνα**
	eh • nah _mee_ • nah
Where are you from?	**Από πού είστε;**
	ah • _poh_ poo _ee_ • steh
I'm from…	**Είμαι από…**
	_ee_ • meh ah • _poh_…

For Numbers, see page 20.

PERSONAL

Who are you with?	**Με ποιον/ποιαν είστε;**
	meh piohn/piahn <u>ee</u> • steh
I'm on my own.	**Είμαι μόνος** m **/μόνη** f **μου.**
	<u>ee</u> • meh <u>moh</u> • nohs/moh • <u>nee</u> moo
I'm with…	**Είμαι με…**
	<u>ee</u> • meh meh…
my husband/wife	**τον σύζυγο/την σύζυγό μου**
	tohn <u>see</u> • zee • ghoh/teen
	<u>see</u> • zee • <u>ghoh</u> moo
my boyfriend/ girlfriend	**τον φίλο/την κοπέλα μου**
	tohn <u>fee</u> • loh/teen koh • <u>peh</u> • lah moo
a friend	**ένα φίλο** m **/μια φίλη** f
	<u>eh</u> • nah <u>fee</u> • loh/miah <u>fee</u> • lee
a colleague	**έναν συνάδελφο**
	<u>eh</u> • nahn see • <u>nah</u> • THehl • foh
When's your birthday?	**Πότε είναι τα γενέθλιά σου;**
	<u>poh</u> • teh <u>ee</u> • neh tah
	gheh • <u>nehth</u> • lee • <u>ah</u> soo
How old are you?	**Πόσο χρονών είσαι;**
	<u>poh</u> • soh khroh • <u>nohn</u> ee • seh
I'm…	**Είμαι…**
	<u>ee</u> • meh…

Are you married?	**Είστε παντρεμένος;**
	_ee_ • steh pah • dreh • _meh_ • nohs
I'm...	**Είμαι...**
	_ee_ • meh...
single	**ελεύθερος** m /**ελεύθερη** f
	eh • _lehf_ • theh • rohs/eh • _lehf_ • theh • ree
in a relationship	**δεσμευμένος** m /**δεσμευμένη** f
	THehs • mehv • _meh_ • nohs/
	THehs • mehv • _meh_ • nee
engaged	**αρραβωνιασμένος**
	ah • rah • voh • niah • _zmeh_ • nohs
married	**παντρεμένος** m /**παντρεμένη** f
	pahn • dreh • _meh_ • nohs/
	pahn • dreh • _meh_ • nee
divorced	**διαζευγμένος** m /**διαζευγμένη** f
	THee • ah • zehv • _ghmeh_ • nohs/
	THee • ah • zehv • _ghmeh_ • ee
separated	**σε διάσταση**
	seh THee • _ah_ • stah • see
I'm widowed.	**Είμαι χήρος** m /**χήρα** f.
	ee • meh khee • _rohs/khee_ • rah
Do you have children/grandchildren?	**Έχετε παιδιά/εγγόνια;**
	_eh_ • kheh • the peh • _THyah_/
	eh • _goh_ • niah

WORK & SCHOOL

What do you do?	**Τι δουλειά κάνετε;**
	tee THoo • _liah kah_ • neh • teh
What are you studying?	**Τι σπουδάζετε;**
	tee spoo • _THah_ • zeh • teh
I'm studying...	**Σπουδάζω...**
	spoo • _THah_ • zoh...
I...	**Εγώ...**
	Eh • _ghoh_

work full-/part-time	**δουλεύω με πλήρη/μερική απασχόληση**
	THoo • lehv • oh meh plee • ree/
	meh • ree • kee ah • pah • skhoh • lee • see
am unemployed	**δεν δουλεύω**
	THehn THoo • lehv • oh
work at home	**δουλεύω στο σπίτι**
	THoo • lehv • oh stoh spee • tee
Who do you work for...?	**Για ποιον δουλεύετε...;**
	yah piohn THoo • leh • veh • teh...
I work for...	**Δουλεύω για...**
	THoo • leh • voh yah...
Here's my business card.	**Ορίστε η κάρτα μου.**
	oh • ree • steh ee kahr • tah moo

WEATHER

What's the weather forecast for tomorrow?	**Τι λέει η πρόβλεψη του καιρού για αύριο;**
	tee leh • ee ee proh • vleh • psee too
	keh • roo yah ah • vree • oh
What beautiful/ terrible weather!	**Τι ωραίος/απαίσιος καιρός!**
	tee oh • reh • ohs/
	ah • peh • see • ohs keh • rohs
It's cool/warm.	**Έχει δροσιά/ζέστη.**
	eh • khee roh • siah/zeh • stee

It's cold/hot.	**Κάνει κρύο/ζέστη.**
	kah • nee <u>kree</u> • oh/<u>zeh</u> • stee
It's rainy/sunny.	**Ο καιρός είναι βροχερός/ηλιόλουστος.**
	oh keh • <u>rohs</u> <u>ee</u> • neh vroh • kheh • <u>rohs</u>/ ee • <u>lioh</u> • loo • stohs
It's snowy/icy.	**Έχει παγωνιά.**
	eh • khee pah • ghoh • <u>niah</u>
Do I need a jacket/ an umbrella?	**Να πάρω ζακέτα/ομπρέλα;**
	nah <u>pah</u> • roh zah • <u>keh</u> • tah/ ohm • <u>breh</u> • lah

For Seasons, see page 26.

ON THE WAY

GETTING AROUND

NEED TO KNOW

How do I get to town?	**Πώς μπορώ να πάω στην πόλη;** *pohs boh • roh nah pah • oh steen poh • lee*
Where's...?	**Πού είναι...;** *poo ee • neh...*
the airport	**το αεροδρόμιο** *toh ah • eh • roh • THroh • mee • oh*
the train [railway] station	**ο σταθμός των τρένων** *oh stahth • mohs ton treh • nohn*
the bus station	**ο σταθμός των λεωφορείων** *oh stahth • mohs tohn leh • oh • foh • ree • ohn*
the metro station	**ο σταθμός του μετρό** *oh stahth • mohs too meh • troh*
How far is it?	**Πόσο απέχει;** *poh • soh ah • peh • khee*
Where can I buy tickets?	**Από πού μπορώ να αγοράσω εισιτήρια;** *ah • poh poo boh • roh nah ah • ghoh • rah • soh ee • see • tee • ree • ah*

A one-way/ return-trip ticket.	**Ένα απλό εισιτήριο/εισιτήριο με επιστροφή;**
	_eh_ • _nah ahp_ • _loh_ ee • _see_ • _tee_ • _ree_ • _oh_/ ee • _see_ • _tee_ • _ree_ • _oh meh_
	_eh_ • _pees_ • _troh_ • _fee_
How much?	**Πόσο;**
	poh • _soh_
Is there a discount?	**Υπάρχει μειωμένο εισιτήριο;**
	ee • _pahr_ • _khee mee_ • _oh_ • _meh_ • _noh_
	ee • _see_ • _tee_ • _ree_ • _oh_
Which…?	**Ποια…;**
	piah…
gate	**είσοδος**
	_ee_ • _soh_ • _THohs_
line	**γραμμή**
	ghrah • _mee_
platform	**πλατφόρμα**
	plaht • _fohr_ • _mah_
Where can I get a taxi?	**Πού μπορώ να βρω ταξί;**
	poo boh • _roh nah vroh_
	tah • _ksee_
Please take me to this address.	**Παρακαλώ πηγαίνετέ με σε αυτή τη διεύθυνση.**
	pah • _rah_ • _kah_ • _loh_ pee • _yeh_ • _neh_ • _the_ meh seh ahf • _tee_ tee
	THee • _ehf_ • _theen_ • _see_
Where can I rent a car?	**Πού μπορώ να νοικιάσω ένα αυτοκίνητο;**
	poo boh • _roh_ nah nee • _kee_ • _ah_ • _soh_ _eh_ • _nah ahf_ • _toh_ • _kee_ • _nee_ • _toh_
Can I have a map?	**Μπορώ να έχω ένα χάρτη;**
	boh • _roh_ nah eh • _khoh eh_ • _nah_ _khahr_ • _tee_

TICKETS

When's...to Athens?	**Πότε αναχωρεί...για Αθήνα;** _poh • the ah • nah • khoh • ree...yah_ _ah • thee • nah_
the (first) bus	**το (πρώτο) λεωφορείο** _toh (proh • toh) leh • oh • foh • ree • oh_
the (next) flight	**η (επόμενη) πτήση** _ee (eh • poh • meh • nee) ptee • see_
the (last) train	**το (τελευταίο) τρένο** _toh (teh • lehf • teh • oh) treh • noh_
Where can I buy tickets?	**Από πού μπορώ να αγοράσω εισιτήρια;** _ah • poh poo boh • roh nah_ _ah • ghoh • rah • soh ee • see • tee • ree • ah_
One ticket./Two tickets.	**Ένα εισιτήριο./Δύο εισιτήρια.** _eh • nah ee • see • tee • ree • oh/THee • oh_ _ee • see • tee • ree • ah_
For today/tomorrow.	**Για σήμερα/αύριο.** _yah see • meh • rah/ahv • ree • oh_
A first/economy class ticket.	**Ένα πρώτης/οικονομικής θέσης εισιτήριο.** _eh • nah proh • tees/_ _ee • koh • noh • mee • kees theh • sees_ _ee • see • tee • ree • oh_
A...ticket.	**Ένα εισιτήριο....** _eh • nah ee • see • tee • ree • oh_
one-way	**χωρίς επιστροφή** _khoh • rees eh • pee • stroh • fee_
return trip	**με επιστροφή** _meh eh • pee • stroh • fee_
business class	**για θέση business** _yah theh • see business_
How much?	**Πόσο;** _poh • soh_

Is there a discount for...?	**Υπάρχει μειωμένο εισιτήριο για...;**
	ee • pahr • khee mee • oh • meh • noh
	ee • see • tee • ree • oh yah...
children	**παιδιά**
	peh • THyah
students	**φοιτητές**
	fee • tee • tehs
senior citizens	**ηλικιωμένοι**
	ee • lee • kee • oh • meh • nee
tourists	**τουρίστες**
	too • ree • stehs
The express bus/ express train, please.	**Το λεωφορείο express/ τρένο express, παρακαλώ.**
	toh leh • oh • foh • ree • oh express/
	treh • noh express, pah • rah • kah • loh
The local bus/train, please.	**Το τοπικό λεωφορείο/τρένο, παρακαλώ.**
	toh toh • pee • koh leh • oh • foh • ree • oh/
	treh • noh, pah • rah • kah • loh
I have an e-ticket.	**Έχω e-ticket.**
	eh • khoh ee tee • keht
Can I buy a ticket on the bus/train?	**Μπορώ να αγοράσω εισιτήριο στο λεωφορείο/ τρένο;**
	boh • roh nah ah • ghoh • rah • soh
	ee • see • tee • ree • oh stoh
	leh • oh • foh • ree • oh/treh • noh
Do I have to stamp the ticket before boarding?	**Πρέπει να σφραγίσω το εισιτήριο πριν ανέβω;**
	preh • pee nah sfrah • yee • soh toh
	ee • see • tee • ree • oh preen ah • neh • voh
Can I return on the same ticket?	**Μπορώ να επιστρέψω με το ίδιο εισιτήριο;**
	boh • roh nah eh • pee • streh • pso meh toh
	ee • THioh ee • see • tee • ree • oh
I'd like to...my reservation	**Θα ήθελα να...την κράτησή μου.**
	Thah ee • theh • lah nah...teen
	krah • tee • see moo

cancel	**ακυρώσω**
	ah • kee • roh • soh
change	**αλλάξω**
	ah • lah • ksoh
confirm	**επιβεβαιώσω**
	eh • pee • veh • veh • oh • soh

For Days, see page 25.

AIRPORT TRANSFER

How much is a taxi to the airport?	**Πόσο κοστίζει το ταξί ως το αεροδρόμιο;**
	poh • soh kohs • tee • zee toh tah • ksee ohs toh ah • eh • roh • THroh • mee • oh
To...Airport, please.	**Στο...αεροδρόμιο, παρακαλώ.**
	stoh...ah • eh • roh • THroh • mee • oh pah • rah • kah • loh
My airline is...	**Πετάω με την εταιρία...**
	peh • tah • oh meh teen eh • teh • ree • ah...
My flight leaves at...	**Η πτήση μου φεύγει στις...**
	ee ptee • see moo fehv • ghee stees...
I'm in a rush.	**Βιάζομαι.**
	vee • ah • zoh • meh
Can you take an alternate route?	**Μπορείτε να πάτε από άλλο δρόμο;**
	boh • ree • teh nah pah • teh ah • poh ah • loh THroh • moh
Can you drive faster/slower?	**Μπορείτε να πάτε πιο γρήγορα/αργά;**
	boh • ree • teh nah pah • teh pioh ghree • ghoh • rah/ahr • ghah

For Time, see page 24.

YOU MAY SEE...

ΑΦΙΞΕΙΣ *ah • fee • ksees*	arrivals
ΑΝΑΧΩΡΗΣΕΙΣ *ah • nah • khoh • ree • sees*	departures
ΠΑΡΑΛΑΒΗ ΑΠΟΣΚΕΥΩΝ *pah • rah • lah • vee ah • pohs • keh • vohn*	baggage claim
ΑΣΦΑΛΕΙΑ *ah • sfah • lee • ah*	security
ΠΤΗΣΕΙΣ ΕΣΩΤΕΡΙΚΟΥ *ptee • sees eh • soh • teh • ree • koo*	domestic flights
ΠΤΗΣΕΙΣ ΕΞΩΤΕΡΙΚΟΥ *ptee • sees eh • ksoh • teh • ree • koo*	international flights
ΕΛΕΓΧΟΣ ΑΠΟΣΚΕΥΩΝ *eh • legh • khos ah • pos • keh • vohn*	check-in
E-TICKET CHECK-IN *ee • tee • keht tsehk • een*	e-ticket check-in
ΠΥΛΕΣ ΕΠΙΒΙΒΑΣΗΣ *pee • lehs eh • pee • vee • vah • sees*	boarding gates

YOU MAY HEAR...

Με ποια εταιρία πετάτε;
meh piah eh • teh • ree • ah peh • tah • teh
What airline are you flying?

Τοπική ή Διεθνή;
toh • pee • kee ee THee • ehth • nee
Domestic or International?

Σε ποιον τερματικό σταθμό;
seh piohn tehr • mah • tee • koh stahth • moh
What terminal?

CHECKING IN

Where is the check-in desk for flight...?	**Πού είναι το γραφείο παράδοσης αποσκευών για την πτήση...;**
	poo <u>ee</u> • neh toh ghrah • <u>fee</u> • oh ah • <u>rah</u> • THoh • sees ah • poh • skeh • <u>vohn</u> yah teen <u>tee</u> • see...
My name is...	**Λέγομαι...**
	<u>leh</u> • ghoh • meh...
I'm going to...	**Πηγαίνω...**
	pee • <u>gheh</u> • noh...
I have...	**Έχω...**
	<u>eh</u> • khoh
one suitcase	**μία βαλίτσα**
	<u>mee</u> • ah vah • <u>lee</u> • tsah
two suitcases	**δύο βαλίτσες**
	<u>THee</u> • oh vah • <u>lee</u> • tsehs
one piece of hand luggage	**μία χειραποσκευή**
	<u>mee</u> • ah khee • rah • poh • skehv • <u>ee</u>
How much luggage is allowed?	**Πόσο είναι το επιτρεπόμενο βάρος;**
	<u>poh</u> • soh <u>ee</u> • neh toh eh • pee • treh • <u>poh</u> • meh • noh <u>vah</u> • rohs
Is that pounds or kilos?	**Είναι σε λίβρες ή σε κιλά;**
	<u>ee</u> • neh seh <u>lee</u> • vrehs ee seh kee • <u>lah</u>
Which terminal?	**Σε ποιο τέρμιναλ;**
	seh pi • <u>oh teh</u> • rmee • nahl
Which gate does flight...leave from?	**Από ποια έξοδο φεύγει η πτήση...;**
	ah • <u>poh</u> piah eh • ksoh • THoh <u>fehv</u> • yee ee <u>ptee</u> • see...
I'd like a window/ an aisle seat.	**Θα ήθελα μια θέση στο παράθυρο/ διάδρομο.**
	thah <u>ee</u> • theh • lah mee • <u>ah theh</u> • see toh pah • <u>rah</u> • thee • roh/THee • <u>ah</u> • THroh • moh
When do we leave/ arrive?	**Πότε φεύγουμε/φθάνουμε;**
	<u>poh</u> • the <u>fehv</u> • ghoo • meh/<u>fthah</u> • noo • meh

YOU MAY HEAR...

Ο επόμενος!
oh eh • <u>poh</u> • meh • nohs
Next!

Το εισιτήριο/διαβατήριο σας, παρακαλώ.
toh ee • see • <u>tee</u> • ree • oh/
THee • ah • vah • <u>tee</u> • ree • <u>oh</u>
sahs pah • rah • kah • <u>loh</u>
Your ticket/
passport, please.

Πόσες αποσκευές έχετε;
<u>poh</u> • sehs ah • poh • skeh • <u>vehs</u>
<u>eh</u> • kheh • teh
How much
luggage
do you have?

Έχετε υπέρβαρο.
<u>eh</u> • kheh • teh ee • <u>pehr</u> • vah • roh
You have excess
baggage.

**Αυτό είναι πολύ βαρύ/μεγάλο για
αποσκευή χειρός.**
ahf • <u>toh ee</u> • neh poh • <u>lee</u>
vah • <u>ree</u>/meh • <u>gha</u> • loh yah
ah • pohs • keh • <u>vee</u> khee • <u>rohs</u>
That's too heavy/
large for
a carry-on
[to carry on
board].

Φτιάξατε τις βαλίτσες σας μόνος σας
m/**μόνη σας** f**;**
ftee • <u>ah</u> • ksah • teh tees vah • <u>lee</u> • tses
sahs <u>moh</u> • nohs sahs/<u>moh</u> • nee sahs
Did you pack
these bags
yourself?

Σας έδωσε κανείς να μεταφέρετε κάτι;
sahs eh • THoh seh kah • <u>nees</u> nah
meh • tah • <u>feh</u> • reh • the <u>kah</u> • tee
Did anyone give
you anything
to carry?

Αδειάστε τις τσέπες σας.
ah • THiah • steh tees <u>tseh</u> • pehs sahs
Empty your
pockets.

Βγάλτε τα παπούτσια σας.
<u>vghahl</u> • teh tah pah • <u>poo</u> • tsiah sahs
Take off your
shoes.

Τώρα αρχίζει η επιβίβαση για την πτήση...
<u>toh</u> • rah ahr • <u>khee</u> • zee ee
eh • pee • <u>vee</u> • vah • see yah teen <u>ptee</u> • see...
Now boarding
flight...

Is flight...delayed?	**Υπάρχει καθυστέρηση στην πτήση...;**
	e • pahr • khee kah • thee • steh • ree • see
	steen tee • see...
How late will it be?	**Πόσο θα αργήσει;**
	poh • soh thah ahr • ghee • see

LUGGAGE

Where is/are...?	**Πού είναι...;**
	poo ee • neh...
the luggage carts [trolleys]	**τα καροτσάκια αποσκευών**
	tah kah • roh • tsah • kee • ah ah • pohs • keh • vohn
the luggage lockers	**οι θυρίδες**
	ee thee • ree • THehs
the luggage claim	**η φύλαξη αποσκευών**
	ee fee • lah • ksee h • poh • skeh • vohn
I've lost my luggage.	**Έχασα τις αποσκευές μου.**
	eh • khah • sah tees ah • pohs • keh • vehs moo
My luggage has been stolen.	**Μου έκλεψαν τις αποσκευές.**
	moo ehk • leh • psahn tees ah • pohs • keh • vehs
My suitcase was damaged.	**Η βαλίτσα μου χάλασε στη μεταφορά.**
	ee vah • lee • tsah moo khah • lah • seh stee eh • tah • foh • rah

FINDING YOUR WAY

Where is/are...?	**Πού είναι...;**
	poo ee • neh...
the currency exchange office	**το γραφείο ανταλλαγής συναλλάγματος**
	toh ghrah • fee • oh ahn • dah • lah • ghees ee • nah • lahgh • mah • tohs

the car hire	**το γραφείο ενοικιάσεως αυτοκινήτων**
	toh ghrah • fee • oh
	eh • nee • kee • ah • seh • ohs
	ahf • toh • kee • nee • tohn
the exit	**η έξοδος**
	ee eh • ksoh • THohs
the taxis	**τα ταξί**
	tah tah • ksee
Is there...into town?	**Υπάρχει...για την πόλη;**
	ee • pahr • khee...yah teen poh • lee
a bus	**λεωφορείο**
	leh • oh • foh • ree • oh
a train	**τρένο**
	treh • noh
a metro	**μετρό**
	meh • troh

For Asking Directions, see page 69.

TRAIN

How do I get to the (main) train station?	**Πώς πάνε στον (κεντρικό) σιδηροδρομικό σταθμό;**
	pohs pah • neh stohn (kehn • dree • koh)
	see • THee • roh • THroh • mee • koh
	stahth • moh
How far is it?	**Πόσο απέχει;**
	poh • soh ah • peh • khee
Where is/are...?	**Πού είναι...;**
	poo ee • neh...
the ticket office	**το γραφείο εισιτηρίων**
	toh ghrah • fee • oh
	ee • see • tee • ree • ohn
the information desk	**το γραφείο πληροφοριών**
	toh ghrah • fee • oh plee • roh • foh • ree • ohn

the luggage lockers	**οι θυρίδες**
	ee thee • <u>ree</u> • THehs
the platform	**η αποβάθρα**
	ee ah • poh • <u>vahth</u> • rah
Could I have a schedule [timetable]?	**Μπορώ να έχω ένα πρόγραμμα δρομολογίων;**
	boh • <u>roh</u> nah eh • <u>khoh</u> eh • nah
	<u>proh</u> • ghrah • mah
	THroh • moh • loh • <u>yee</u> • ohn
How long is the trip?	**Πόση ώρα διαρκεί το ταξίδι;**
	<u>poh</u> • see <u>oh</u> • rah
	THee • ahr • <u>kee</u> toh tah • <u>ksee</u> • THee
Is it a direct train?	**Είναι απευθείας τρένο;**
	ee • neh ah • pehf • <u>thee</u> • ahs <u>treh</u> • noh
Do I have to change trains?	**Χρειάζεται να αλλάξω τρένο;**
	khree • <u>ah</u> • zeh • the
	nah ah • <u>lah</u> • ksoh <u>treh</u> • noh
Is the train on time?	**Το τρένο είναι στην ώρα του;**
	toh <u>treh</u> • noh ee • <u>neh</u> steen <u>oh</u> • rah too

For Tickets, see page 50.

YOU MAY SEE...	
ΠΡΟΣ ΑΠΟΒΑΘΡΕΣ	to the
prohs ah • poh • <u>vahth</u> • rehs	platforms
ΠΛΗΡΟΦΟΡΙΕΣ	information
plee • roh • foh • <u>ree</u> • ehs	
ΚΡΑΤΗΣΕΙΣ	reservations
krah • <u>tee</u> • sees	
ΑΙΘΟΥΣΑ ΑΝΑΜΟΝΗΣ	waiting room
<u>eh</u> • thoo • sah ah • nah • moh • <u>nees</u>	
ΑΦΙΞΕΙΣ	arrivals
ah • <u>fee</u> • ksees	
ΑΝΑΧΩΡΗΣΕΙΣ	departures
ah • nah • khoh • <u>ree</u> • sees	

DEPARTURES

When is the train to...?	**Πότε φεύγει το τρένο για...;**
	poh • teh <u>fehv</u> • ghee toh <u>treh</u> • noh yah...
Is this the right platform for...?	**Είναι αυτή η σωστή αποβάθρα για το τρένο για...;**
	<u>ee</u> • neh ahf • <u>tee</u> ee sohs • <u>tee</u>
	ah • poh • <u>vahth</u> • rah yah toh <u>treh</u> • noh yah...
Where is platform...?	**Πού είναι η αποβάθρα...;**
	poo <u>ee</u> • neh ee
	ah • poh • <u>vahth</u> • rah...
Where do I change for...?	**Πού αλλάζω για...;**
	poo ah • <u>lah</u> • zoh yah...

ON BOARD

Can I sit here/open the window?	**Μπορώ να καθίσω εδώ/ ανοίξω το παράθυρο;**
	boh • <u>roh</u> nah kah • <u>thee</u> • soh eh • <u>THoh</u>/

ah • nee • ksoh toh pah • rah • thee • roh

That's my seat. **Νομίζω αυτή είναι η θέση μου.**
*noh • mee • zoh ahf • tee ee • neh
ee theh • see moo*

Here's my **Να η κράτησή μου.**
reservation. *nah ee krah • tee • see moo*

The Greek train system is operated by OSE
(**ΟΣΕ, Οργανισμός Σιδηροδρόμων Ελλάδος** *oh • seh,
ohr • ghah • neez • mohs see • THee • roh • THroh • mohn
eh • lah • THohs*). The network is quite limited and, though
the journey is scenic, is usually quite slow.
The I/C, Intercity (**Υπερταχεία** *ee • pehr • tah • khee • ah*),
makes few stops, but is more expensive. Make sure
you reserve a seat in advance. All trains have bars and
a sleeping car for longer journeys.

BUS

Where's the bus **Πού είναι ο σταθμός λεωφορείων;**
station? *poo ee • neh oh stahth • mohs
leh • oh • foh • ree • ohn*

How far is it? **Πόσο απέχει;**
poh • soh ah • peh • khee

How do I get to...? **Πώς πάνε σε...;**
pohs pah • neh seh...

Is this the bus to...? **Είναι αυτό το λεωφορείο για...;**
*ee • neh ahf • toh toh leh • oh • foh • ree • oh
yah...*

Could you tell me **Μπορείτε να μου πείτε πού να κατέβω;**
when to get off? *boh • ree • teh nah moo pee • teh poo nah
kah • teh • voh*

Do I have to change buses?	**Χρειάζεται να αλλάξω λεωφορείο;**
	khree • <u>ah</u> • zeh • teh nah ah • <u>lah</u> • ksoh leh • oh • foh • <u>ree</u> • oh
Stop here, please!	**Σταματείστε εδώ, παρακαλώ!**
	stah • mah • <u>tees</u> • teh eh • <u>THoh</u> pah • rah • kah • <u>loh</u>

For Tickets, see page 50.

YOU MAY SEE...

ΣΤΑΣΗ ΛΕΩΦΟΡΕΙΩΝ	bus stop
<u>stah</u> • see leh • oh • foh • <u>ree</u> • ohn	
ΕΙΣΟΔΟΣ/ΕΞΟΔΟΣ	enter/exit
ee • soh • THohs/eh • ksoh • THohs	
ΑΚΥΡΩΣΤΕ ΤΟ ΕΙΣΙΤΗΡΙΟ ΣΑΣ	validate your
ah • kee • <u>roh</u> • steh toh ee • see • <u>tee</u> • ree • oh sahs	ticket

---

YOU MAY HEAR...

Επιβιβαστείτε!	All aboard!
eh • pee • vee • vahs • <u>tee</u> • teh	
Τα εισιτήριά σας, παρακαλώ.	Tickets, please.
tah ee • see • <u>tee</u> • ree • <u>ah</u> sahs pah • rah • kah • <u>loh</u>	
Πρέπει να αλλάξετε σε...	You have to
<u>preh</u> • pee nah ah • <u>lah</u> • kseh • teh seh...	change at...
Επόμενη στάση...	Next stop...
eh • <u>poh</u> • meh • nee <u>stah</u> • see...	

METRO

Where's the nearest metro station?	**Πού είναι ο κοντινότερος σταθμός του μετρό;**
	poo ee • neh oh koh • ndee • noh • teh • rohs stahth • mohs too meh • troh
Could I have a map of the metro?	**Μπορώ να έχω ένα χάρτη του μετρό;**
	boh • roh nah eh • khoh eh • nah khahr • tee too meh • troh
Which line should I take for...?	**Ποια γραμμή πρέπει να πάρω για...;**
	piah ghrah • mee preh • pee nah pah • roh yah...
Which direction?	**Προς ποια κατεύθυνση;**
	prohs piah kah • tehf • theen • see
Where do I change for...?	**Πού αλλάζω για...;**
	poo ah • lah • zoh yah...
Is this the right train for...?	**Είναι αυτό το σωστό τρένο για...;**
	ee • neh ahf • toh toh sohs • toh treh • noh yah...
How many stops to...?	**Πόσες στάσεις μέχρι...;**
	poh • sehs stah • sees meh • khree
Where are we?	**Πού είμαστε;**
	poo ee • mahs • the

For Finding your Way, see page 56.

Athens is the only Greek city currently served by a **μετρό** *(meh • troh)*, subway. Before boarding public transportation you need to buy a ticket at the special kiosks or automatic ticketing machines marked **ΕΙΣΙΤΗΡΙΑ** *(ee • see • tee • ree • ah)*. Validate your ticket in the machine, found by the platform, before you get on. In Athens, tickets are valid for 90 minutes and can be used for buses, metro, trolleybuses, trams and part of the suburban railway. Daily, weekly or monthly tickets and reduced fares are available.

BOAT & FERRY

When is the ferry to…?	**Πότε φεύγει το φέρρυ-μπωτ για…;**
	poh • the fehv • ghee toh feh • ree boht yah…
Can I take my car onboard?	**Μπορώ να επιβιβάσω το αυτοκίνητό μου;**
	boh • roh nah eh • pee • vee • vah • soh toh ahf • toh kee • nee • toh moo
What time is the next sailing?	**Πότε είναι ο επόμενος απόπλους;**
	poh • teh ee • nehoh eh • poh • meh • nohs ah • poh • ploos
Can I book a seat/cabin?	**Μπορώ να κλείσω θέση/καμπίνα;**
	boh • roh nah klee • soh theh • see/kah • bee • nah
How long is the crossing?	**Πόσο διαρκεί το πέρασμα;**
	poh • soh THee • ahr • kee toh peh • rah • smah
Where are the life jackets?	**Πού είναι τα σωσίβια;**
	poo ee • neh tah soh • see • vee • ah

For Weather, see page 44.

YOU MAY SEE…

ΝΑΥΑΓΟΣΩΣΤΙΚΗ ΛΕΜΒΟΣ	life boats
nah • vah • ghoh • sohs • tee • kee lehm • vohs	
ΣΩΣΙΒΙΑ	life jackets
soh • see • vee • ah	

It is likely that after your arrival in Athens, you will be heading straight for the port of Piraeus to catch a ferry. The harbor front is lined with ticket agents; ferry prices are fixed. Each agent tends to sell tickets for one company serving a particular route. A window display (usually in Greek and English) will tell you exactly what islands that ferry goes to. Sleeping on the deck is allowed, but make sure to take a sleeping bag and wear warm clothes, even in July! Once on an island, you may decide to go on an island tour. Several converted fishing boats run daily trips. Note that throwing anything into the sea off a boat deck is an offense in Greece, and you will be fined if caught.

TAXI

Where can I get a taxi?	**Πού μπορώ να βρω ταξί;** *poo boh • roh nah vroh tah • ksee*
Can you send a taxi?	**Μπορείτε να στείλετε ταξί;** *boh • ree • teh nah stee • leh • te tah • ksee*
Do you have the number for a taxi?	**Έχετε το τηλέφωνο για ταξί;** *eh • kheh • teh toh tee • leh • foh • noh yah tah • ksee*
I'd like a taxi now/ for tomorrow at…	**Θα ήθελα ένα ταξί τώρα/για αύριο στις…** *thah ee • theh • lah eh • nah tah • ksee toh • rah/yah ahv • ree • oh stees…*
Pick me up at (place/time)…	**Ελάτε να με πάρετε από/στις…** *eh • lah • the nah meh pah • reh • teh ah • poh/stees…*
I'm going to…	**Πηγαίνω…** *pee • gheh • noh…*
this address	**σε αυτή τη διεύθυνση** *seh ahf • tee tee THee • ehf • theen • see*

the airport	**στο αεροδρόμιο**
	stoh ah • eh • roh • <u>THroh</u> • mee • oh
the train [railway] station	**στον σιδηροδρομικό σταθμό**
	stohn see • THee • roh • THroh • mee • <u>koh</u> stahth <u>moh</u>
I'm late.	**Έχω αργήσει.**
	<u>eh</u> • hoh ahr • <u>ghee</u> • see
Can you drive faster/slower?	**Μπορείτε να πάτε πιο γρήγορα/αργά;**
	boh • <u>ree</u> • teh nah <u>pah</u> • teh pioh <u>gree</u> • ghoh • rah/ahr • <u>ghah</u>
Stop/Wait here.	**Σταματήστε/Περιμένετε εδώ.**
	stah • mah • <u>tee</u> • steh/ peh • ree • <u>meh</u> • neh • teh eh • <u>THoh</u>
How much?	**Πόσο;**
	<u>poh</u> • soh
You said it would cost...euros.	**Είπατε ότι θα κόστιζε...ευρώ.**
	<u>ee</u> • pah • the <u>oh</u> • tee thah <u>kohs</u> • tee • zeh...ehv • <u>roh</u>
Keep the change.	**Κρατείστε τα ρέστα.**
	krah • <u>tees</u> • teh tah <u>rehs</u> • tah
A receipt, please.	**Μια απόδειξη, παρακαλώ.**
	miah ah • <u>poh</u> • THee • ksee pah • rah • kah • <u>loh</u>

In Athens, licensed taxis are yellow with a blue stripe. In all major cities, fares are fixed. For longer distances you should agree to a fare before the trip. Tipping is not compulsory, but it is common to round up the amount due.

YOU MAY HEAR...

Πού μπορώ να;
poo boh • roh nah

Where to?

Πού είναι η διεύθυνση;
poo ee • neh ee THee • ehf • theen • see

What's the address?

BICYCLE & MOTORBIKE

I'd like to hire...	**θα ήθελα να νοικιάσω...** *thah ee • theh • lah nah nee • kiah • soh...*
a bicycle	**ένα ποδήλατο** *eh • nah poh • THee • lah • toh*
a moped	**ένα μοτοποδήλατο** *eh • nah moh • toh • poh • THee • lah • toh*
a motorbike	**μία μοτοσικλέτα** *mee • ah moh • toh • see • kleh • tah*
How much per day/week?	**Πόσο κοστίζει την ημέρα/την εβδομάδα;** *poh • soh koh • stee • zee teen ee • meh • rah/tee ehv • THoh • mah • THah*
Can I have a helmet/lock?	**Μπορώ να έχω ένα κράνος/μία κλειδαριά;** *boh • roh nah eh • khoh eh • nah krah • nohs/mee • ah klee • THah • riah*

CAR HIRE

Where can I hire a car?	**Πού μπορώ να νοικιάσω ένα αυτοκίνητο;**
	poo boh•roh nah nee•kiah•soh eh•nah ahf•toh•kee•nee•toh
I'd like to hire...	**Θα ήθελα να νοικιάσω ένα...**
	thah ee•theh•lah nah nee•kiah•soh eh•nah...
a cheap/small car	**ένα φτηνό/μικρό αυτοκίνητο**
	eh•nah ftee•noh/mee•kroh ahf•toh•kee•nee•toh
a 2-/4-door car	**δίπορτο/τετράπορτο αυτοκίνητο**
	ee•poh•rtoh/teh•trah•poh•rtoh ahf•toh•kee•nee•toh
an automatic/ manual car	**αυτόματο αυτοκίνητο/ αυτοκίνητο με συμπλέκτη**
	ahf•toh•mah•toh ahf•toh•kee•nee•toh/ ahf•toh•kee•nee•toh meh see•bleh•ktee
a car with air-conditioning	**αυτοκίνητο με κλιματισμό**
	ahf•toh•kee•nee•toh meh klee•mah•tee•smoh
a car seat	**παιδικό κάθισμα αυτοκινήτου**
	peh•THee•koh kah•thee•smah ahf•toh•kee•nee•too
How much...?	**Πόσο κάνει...;**
	poh•soh kah•nee...
per day/week	**την ημέρα/ενδομάδα**
	teen ee•meh•rah/ehv•THoh•mah•THah
per kilometer	**το χιλιόμετρο**
	toh khee•lee•oh•meht•roh
for unlimited mileage	**για απεριόριστη απόσταση**
	yah ah•peh•ree•oh•rees•tee ah•poh•stah•see

with insurance	**με ασφάλεια**
	meh ah • sfah • lee • ah
Are there any discounts?	**Υπάρχει έκπτωση;**
	ee • pahr • khee ehk • ptoh • see

YOU MAY HEAR...

Έχετε διεθνή άδεια οδήγησης;	Do you have an international driver's license?
eh • kheh • the THee • ehth • nee ah • THee • ah oh • THee • ghee • sees	
Μπορώ να δω το διαβατήριό σας, παρακαλώ;	May I see your passport, please?
boh • roh nah THoh toh THee • ah • vah • tee • ree • oh sahs pah • rah • kah • loh	
Θέλετε ασφάλεια;	Do you want insurance?
theh • leh • teh ah • sfah • lee • ah	
Υπάρχει μία προκαταβολή των...	There is a deposit of...
ee • pahr • khee miah proh • kah • tah • voh • lee tohn...	
Παρακαλώ υπογράψτε εδώ.	Please sign here.
pah • rah • kah • loh ee • poh • ghrah • psteh eh • THoh	

FUEL STATION

Where's the next fuel station, please?	**Πού είναι το επόμενο βενζινάδικο, παρακαλώ;**
	poo ee • neh toh eh • poh • meh • noh vehn • zee • nah • THee • koh pah • rah • kah • loh
Fill it up, please.	**Γεμίστε το, παρακαλώ.**
	yeh • mee • steh toh pah • rah • kah • loh

...liters, please.	**...λίτρα βενζίνη, παρακαλώ.**
	...lee • trah vehn • zee • nee
	pah • rah • kah • loh
I'll pay in cash/by	**Θα πληρώσω τοις μετρητοίς/με πιστωτική**
credit card.	**κάρτα.**
	thah plee • roh • soh tees meh • tree • tees/
	meh pee • stoh • tee • kee kah • rtah

For Numbers, see page 20.

YOU MAY SEE...

ΑΠΛΗ	regular
ah • plee	
ΣΟΥΠΕΡ	premium [super]
soo • pehr	
ΝΤΗΖΕΛ	diesel
dee • zehl	

ASKING DIRECTIONS

Is this the right	**Είναι αυτός ο σωστός δρόμος για...;**
road to...?	*ee • neh ahf • tohs oh sohs • tohs*
	THroh • mohs yah...
How far is it to...?	**Πόσο μακριά είναι για...;**
	poh • soh mahk • ree • ah ee • neh yah...
Where's...?	**Πού είναι...;**
	poo ee • neh...
...Street	**η οδός...**
	ee oh • THohs...
this address	**αυτή η διεύθυνση**
	ahf • tee ee THee • ehf • theen • see
the highway	**η εθνική οδός**
[motorway]	*ee ehth • nee • kee oh • THohs*

Can you show me on the map?	**Μπορείτε να μου δείξετε στο χάρτη;**
	boh • ree • the nah moo THee • kseh • teh
	stoh khahr • tee
I'm lost.	**Έχω χαθεί.**
	eh • hoh khah • thee

PARKING

Can I park here?	**Μπορώ να παρκάρω εδώ;**
	boh • roh nah pahr • kah • roh eh • THoh
Is there a parking lot [car park] nearby?	**Υπάρχει χώρος στάθμευσης εδώ κοντά;**
	ee • pahr • khee khoh • rohs
	stath • mehf • sees eh • THoh kohn • dah
Where's…?	**Πού είναι…;**
	poo ee • neh
the parking garage	**το πάρκινγκ**
	toh pah • rkee • ng
the parking meter	**το παρκόμετρο**
	toh pah • rkoh • meh • troh
How much…?	**Πόσο κοστίζει…;**
	poh • soh koh • stee • zee…
per hour	**την ώρα**
	teen oh • rah
per day	**την ημέρα**
	teen ee • meh • rah
overnight	**τη νύχτα**
	tee neeh • khtah

Parking in large cities, particularly Athens, can be a problem as spaces are limited. It is likely that you will need to park in an indoor or outdoor parking lot. Prices vary greatly, depending on your location.

YOU MAY HEAR...

ευθεία/ίσια	straight ahead
ehf • <u>thee</u> • ah/<u>ee</u> • see • ah	
στα αριστερά	on the left
stah ah • rees • teh • <u>rah</u>	
στα δεξιά	on the right
stah THeh • ksee • <u>ah</u>	
στη/μετά τη γωνία	on/around the corner
stee/meh • <u>tah</u> tee ghoh • <u>nee</u> • ah	
απέναντι	opposite
ah • <u>peh</u> • nahn • dee	
πίσω	behind
<u>pee</u> • soh	
δίπλα	next to
<u>THee</u> • plah	
μετά	after
meh • <u>tah</u>	
βόρεια/νότεια	north/south
<u>voh</u> • ree • ah/<u>noh</u> • tee • ah	
ανατολικά/δυτικά	east/west
ah • nah • toh • lee • <u>kah</u>/THee • tee • <u>kah</u>	
στο φανάρι	at the traffic light
stoh fah • <u>nah</u> • ree	
στη διασταύρωση	at the intersection
stee THee • ah • <u>stahv</u> • roh • see	

YOU MAY SEE...

 ΑΠΑΓΟΡΕΥΕΤΑΙ Η ΕΠΙ ΤΟΠΟΥ ΣΤΡΟΦΗ   no u-turn
*ah • pah • ghoh • <u>reh</u> • veh • teh ee eh
<u>pee toh</u> • poo stroh • <u>fee</u>*

 **ΥΠΟΧΡΕΩΤΙΚΗ ΠΑΡΑΧΩΡΗΣΗ
ΠΡΟΤΕΡΑΙΟΤΗΤΑΣ**   yeld
*ee • pohkh • reh • oh • tee • <u>kee</u>
pah • rah • <u>khoh</u> • ree • see
proh • teh • reh • <u>oh</u> • tee • tahs*

 ΥΠΟΧΡΕΩΤΙΚΗ ΔΙΑΚΟΠΗ ΠΟΡΕΙΑΣ   stop
*ee • pohkh • reh • oh • tee • <u>kee</u>
THee • ah • koh • <u>pee</u> poh • <u>ree</u> • ahs*

 **ΠΕΡΙΟΧΗ ΑΠΑΓΟΡΕΥΣΗΣ
ΣΤΑΘΜΕΥΣΗΣ**   no parking
*peh • ree • oh • <u>khee</u>
ah • pah • <u>ghoh</u> • rehf • sees
<u>stahth</u> • mehf • sees*

 **ΑΠΑΓΟΡΕΥΕΤΑΙ Η ΣΤΑΣΗ ΚΑΙ Η
ΣΤΑΘΜΕΥΣΗ**   no stopping
*ah • pah • ghoh • <u>reh</u> • veh • teh ee
<u>stah</u> • see keh ee <u>stahth</u> • mehf • see*

 ΜΟΝΟΔΡΟΜΟΣ   one way
moh • <u>noh</u> • THroh • mohs

BREAKDOWN & REPAIR

My car broke down/won't start.	**Το αυτοκίνητό μου χάλασε/δεν παίρνει μπρος.**
	toh ahf • toh • kee • nee • toh moo khah • lah • seh/THehn pehr • nee brohs
Can you fix it today?	**Μπορείτε να το επισκευάσετε σήμερα;**
	boh • ree • teh nah toh eh • pees • keh • vah • seh • the see • meh • rah
When will it be ready?	**Πότε θα είναι έτοιμο;**
	poh • teh thah ee • neh eh • tee • moh
How much?	**Πόσο;**
	poh • soh
I have a puncture/ flat tyre (tire).	**Έχω σκασμένο λάστιχο.**
	eh • khoh skah • zmeh • noh lah • stee • khoh

For Time, see page 24.

ACCIDENTS

There's been an accident.	**Έγινε ένα ατύχημα.**
	eh • yee • neh eh • nah ah • tee • khee • mah
Call an ambulance/ the police.	**Καλέστε ένα ασθενοφόρο/την αστυνομία.**
	kah • lehs • teh eh • nah ahs • theh • noh • foh • roh/teen ahs • tee • noh • mee • ah

For Police, see page 148.

PLACES TO STAY

NEED TO KNOW

Can you recommend a hotel?	**Μπορείτε να μου συστήσετε ένα ξενοδοχείο;** *boh • ree • teh nah moo sees • tee • seh • teh eh • nah kseh • noh • THoh • khee • oh*
I have a reservation.	**Έχω κλείσει δωμάτιο.** *eh • khoh klee • see THoh • mah • tee • oh*
My name is…	**Λέγομαι…** *leh • ghoh • meh…*
Do you have a room…?	**Έχετε ελεύθερο δωμάτιο…;** *eh • kheh • the eh • lehf • theh • roh THoh • mah • tee • oh…*
for one/two	**μονόκλινο/δίκλινο** *moh • noh • klee • noh/THee • klee • noh*
with a bathroom	**με μπάνιο** *meh bah • nioh*
with air- -conditioning	**με κλιματισμό** *meh klee • mah • teez • moh*
For tonight.	**Γι' απόψε.** *yah • poh • pseh*
For two nights.	**Για δύο βράδια.** *yah THee • oh vrah • THee • ah*
For one week.	**Για μια εβδομάδα.** *yah mee • ah ev • THoh • mah • THah*
How much?	**Πόσο;** *poh • soh*

Do you have anything cheaper?	**Έχετε τίποτα φθηνότερο;** _eh • keh • the <u>tee</u> • poh • tah fthee • <u>noh</u> • teh • roh_
When's check-out?	**Τι ώρα πρέπει να αδειάσουμε το δωμάτιο;** _tee <u>oh</u> • rah <u>preh</u> • pee nah ah • THee • <u>ah</u> • soo • meh toh THoh • <u>mah</u> • tee • oh_
Can I leave this in the safe?	**Μπορώ να αφήσω αυτό στη θυρίδα;** _boh • <u>roh</u> nah ah • <u>fee</u> • soh ahf • <u>toh</u> stee thee • <u>ree</u> • THah_
Could we leave our baggage here until…?	**Μπορούμε να αφήσουμε τα πράγματά μας εδώ ως τις…;** _boh • <u>roo</u> • meh nah ah • <u>fee</u> • soo • meh tah <u>prahgh</u> • mah • <u>tah</u> mahs eh • <u>THoh</u> ohs tees…_
Could I have the bill/a receipt?	**Μπορώ να έχω τον λογαριασμό/μιααπόδειξη;** _boh • <u>roh</u> nah eh • <u>hoh</u> tohn loh • ghahr • yahs • <u>moh</u>/miah ah • <u>poh</u> • THee • ksee_
I'll pay in cash/by credit card.	**Θα πληρώσω τοις μετρητοίς/με πιστωτική κάρτα.** _thah plee • <u>roh</u> • soh tees meht • <u>ree</u> • tees/meh pees • toh • tee • <u>kee</u> <u>kahr</u> • tah_

SOMEWHERE TO STAY

Can you recommend a hotel?	**Μπορείτε να μου συστήσετε ένα ξενοδοχείο…;** _boh • <u>ree</u> • teh nah moo sees • <u>tee</u> • seh • teh <u>eh</u> • nah kseh • noh • THoh • <u>khee</u> • oh…_

Can you recommend…?	**Μπορείτε να προτείνετε…;**
	boh • ree • teh nah
	proh • tee • neh • teh
a hostel	**ένα ξενώνα**
	eh • nah kseh • noh • nah
a campsite	**ένα μέρος για κάμπινγκ;**
	eh • nah meh • rohs yah kahm • peeng
a bed and breakfast	**ένα δωμάτιο με πρωινό**
	eh • nah THoh • mah • tee • oh
	meh proh • ee • noh
What is it near?	**Πού κοντά είναι;**
	poo kohn • dah ee • neh
How do I get there?	**Πώς πάω εκεί;**
	pohs pah • oh eh • kee

AT THE HOTEL

I have a reservation.	**Έχω κλείσει δωμάτιο.**
	eh • hoh klee • see THoh • mah • tee • oh
My name is…	**Λέγομαι…**
	leh • ghoh • meh…
Do you have a room…?	**Έχετε δωμάτιο…;**
	eh • kheh • the THoh • mah • tee • oh…
with a bathroom [toilet]/shower	**με μπάνιο/ντους**
	meh bah • nioh/doo
with air--conditioning	**με κλιματισμό**
	meh klee • mah • teez • moh
that's smoking/ non-smoking	**για καπνιστές/μη καπνιστές**
	yah kahp • nees • tehs/mee
	kahp • nees • tehs
For tonight.	**Γι' απόψε.**
	yah • poh • pseh
For two nights.	**Για δύο βράδια.**
	yah THee • oh vrah • THiah

For one week.	**Για μία εβδομάδα.**
	yah mee • ah ev • THoh • mah • THah
Does the hotel have...?	**Έχει το ξενοδοχείο...;**
	eh • khee toh kseh • noh • THoh • khee • oh...
a computer	**υπολογιστή**
	ee • poh • loh • ghees • tee
an elevator [lift]	**ασανσέρ**
	ah • sahn • sehr
(wireless) internet service	**υπηρεσία (ασύρματου) internet**
	ee • pee • reh • see • ah (ah • seer • mah • too)
	een • tehr • neht
room service	**υπηρεσία δωματίου**
	ee • pee • reh • see • ah THoh • mah • tee • oo
a pool	**πισίνα**
	pee • see • nah
a gym	**γυμναστήριο**
	gheem • nahs • tee • ree • oh
I need...	**χρειάζομαι...**
	khree • ah • zoh • meh...
an extra bed	**άλλο ένα κρεβάτι**
	ah • loh eh • nah kreh • vah • tee
a cot	**ένα ράντζο**
	eh • nah rahn • joh
a crib	**ένα παιδικό κρεβάτι**
	eh • nah peh • THee • koh kreh • vah • tee

If you didn't reserve a place to stay before your trip,
visit the local tourist information office for a list of places to
stay. Booking ahead is recommended in the high season, from
July to the end of August.

Greece offers a large variety of accommodation
options: **Ξενοδοχεία** (ksehn • oh • THoh • khee • ah), hotels;
Διαμερίσματα (THee • ah • meh • reez • mah • tah), furnished
apartments; **Δωμάτια** (THoh • mah • tee • ah) furnished
rooms, with or without a private bath; **Παραδοσιακά δωμάτια**
(pah • rah • THoh • see • ah • kah THoh • mah • tee • ah),
apartments in traditional but renovated homes; **Ξενώνας
νεότητας** (kseh • noh • nahs neh • oh • tee • tahs), youth
hostels; **Κάμπιγκ** (kahm • peeng) campsites and more.

PRICE

How much per night/week?	**Πόσο κάνει τη βραδιά/την εβδομάδα;** poh • soh kah • nee tee vrah • iah/teen ehv • oh • mah • ah
Does the price include breakfast/sales tax [VAT]?	**Η τιμή συμπεριλαμβάνει πρωινό/ΦΠΑ;** ee tee • mee seem • beh • ree • lahm • vah • nee proh • ee • noh/fee pee • ah
Are there any discounts?	**Έχει έκπτωση;** eh • khee ehk • ptoh • see

PREFERENCES

Can I see the room?	**Μπορώ να δω το δωμάτιο;** boh • roh nah doh toh THoh • mah • tee • oh
I'd like a...room.	**Θα ήθελα...δωμάτιο.** tha ee • theh • lah...THoh • mah • tee • oh
better	**καλύτερο** kah • lee • teh • roh
bigger	**μεγαλύτερο** meh • ghah • lee • teh • roh

cheaper	**πιο φθηνό**
	pioh fthee • noh
quieter	**πιο ήσυχο**
	pioh ee • see • khoh
I'll take it.	**Θα το πάρω.**
	thah toh pah • roh
No, I won't take it.	**Όχι, δεν θα το πάρω.**
	oh • khee, THen thah toh pah • roh

QUESTIONS

Where's…?	**Πού είναι…;**
	poo ee • neh…
the bar	**το μπαρ**
	toh bahr
the bathroom	**το μπάνιο**
	toh bah • nioh
the elevator [lift]	**το ασανσέρ**
	toh ah • sahn • sehr
Can I have…?	**Μπορώ να έχω…;**
	boh • roh nah eh • khoh…
a blanket	**μια κουβέρτα**
	miah koo • vehr • tah
an iron	**ένα σίδερο**
	eh • nah see • THeh • roh
the room key/ key card	**το κλειδί δωματίου/την κάρτα**
	toh klee • THee THoh • mah • tee • oo/ teen kahr • tah
a pillow	**ένα μαξιλάρι**
	eh • nah mah • ksee • lah • ree
soap	**σαπούνι**
	sah • poo • nee
toilet paper	**χαρτί υγείας**
	khahr • tee ee • ghee • ahs

a towel	**μια πετσέτα μπάνιου**
	miah peh • tseh • tah bah • nee • oo
Can I use this adapter here?	**Μπορώ να χρησιμοποιήσω αυτόν τον προσαρμοστή εδώ;**
	boh • roh nah khree • see • moh • pee • ee • soh ahf • tohn tohn proh • sahr • mohs • tee eh • THoh
How do I turn on the lights?	**Πώς ανάβουν τα φώτα;**
	pohs ah • nah • voon tah foh • tah
Could you wake me at...?	**Μπορείτε να με ξυπνήσετε στις...;**
	boh • ree • teh nah meh kseep • nee • seh • teh stees...
Could I have my things from the safe?	**Μπορώ να έχω τα πράγματά μου από τη θυρίδα;**
	boh • roh nah eh • khoh tah prahgh • mah • tah moo ah • poh tee thee • ree • THah
Is there mail/ a message for me?	**Υπάρχει αλληλογραφία/κάποιο μήνυμα για μένα;**
	ee • pahr • khee ah • lee • lohgh • rah • fee • ah/ kah • pioh mee • nee • mah yah meh • nah
Do you have a laundry service?	**Έχετε υπηρεσία πλυντηρίων;**
	eh • kheh • teh ee • pee • reh • see • ah plee • dee • ree • ohn

💬

YOU MAY HEAR...

Το διαβατήριό σας/την πιστωτική σας κάρτα, παρακαλώ.	Your passport/ credit card, please.
toh ee • ah • vah • tee • ree • oh sahs/teen pees • toh • tee • kee sahs kahr • tah pah • rah • kah • loh	
Παρακαλώ συμπληρώστε αυτό το έντυπο.	Please fill out this form.
pah • rah • kah • loh seem • blee • rohs • teh ahf • toh toh ehn • dee • poh	
Υπογράψτε εδώ.	Sign here.
ee • pohgh • rahp • steh eh • THoh	

PROBLEMS

There's a problem.	**Υπάρχει ένα πρόβλημα.** *ee • pahr • hee eh • nah prohv • lee • mah*
I've lost my key/key card.	**Έχασα το κλειδί/την κάρτα μου.** *eh • hah • sah toh klee • THee/teen kahr • tah moo*
I've locked myself out of my room.	**Κλειδώθηκα έξω από το δωμάτιό μου.** *klee • THoh • thee • kah eh • ksoh ah • poh toh THoh • mah • tee • oh moo*
There's no hot water/toilet paper.	**Δεν υπάρχει ζεστό νερό/χαρτί υγείας.** *Then ee • pahr • khee zeh • stoh neh • roh/khahr • tee ee • yee • ahs*
The room is dirty.	**Το δωμάτιο είναι βρώμικο.** *Toh THoh • mah • tee • oh ee • neh vroh • mee • koh*
There are bugs in our room.	**Υπάρχουν έντομα στο δωμάτιό μας.** *ee • pahr • hoon ehn • doh • mah stoh THoh • mah • tee • oh mahs*
...is broken.	**...είναι σπασμένος m /σπασμένη f /σπασμένο n.** *...ee • neh spahs • mehn • ohs/spahs • mehn • ee/spahs • mehn • oh*
Can you fix...?	**Μπορείτε να φτιάξετε...;** *boh • ree • teh nah ftiah • kseh • teh...*
the air conditioning	**τον κλιματισμό** *tohn klee • mah • teez • moh*
the fan	**τον ανεμιστήρα** *tohn ah • neh • mee • stee • rah*
the heating	**τη θέρμανση** *tee thehr • mahn • see*
the light	**το φως** *toh fohs*
the TV	**την τηλεόραση** *teen tee • leh • oh • rah • see*

the toilet **την τουαλέτα**
teen too • ah • leh • tah

I'd like to move to **Θα ήθελα να μεταφερθώ σε άλλο δωμάτιο.**
another room. *thah ee • theh • lah nah meh • tah • fehr • thoh
she ah • loh THoh • mah • tee • oh*

YOU MAY SEE...

ΩΘΗΣΑΤΕ/ΕΛΞΑΤΕ *oh • thee • sah • teh/ehl • ksah • teh*	push/pull
ΜΠΑΝΙΟ/ΤΟΥΑΛΕΤΑ *bah • nioh/too • ah • leh • tah*	bathroom/ restroom [toilet]
ΝΤΟΥΣ *dooz*	shower
ΑΣΑΝΣΕΡ *ah • sahn • sehr*	elevator [lift]
ΣΚΑΛΑ *skah • lah*	stairs
ΠΛΥΝΤΗΡΙΟ *pleen • dee • ree • oh*	laundry
ΜΗΝ ΕΝΟΧΛΕΙΤΕ *meen eh • nohkh • lee • teh*	do not disturb
ΠΥΡΟΣΤΕΓΗΣ ΘΥΡΑ *pee • rohs • teh • ghees thee • rah*	fire door
ΕΞΟΔΟΣ ΚΙΝΔΥΝΟΥ *eh • ksoh • THohs keen • THee • noo*	emergency exit
ΥΠΗΡΕΣΙΑ ΑΦΥΠΝΙΣΗΣ *ee • pee • reh • see • ah ah • feep • nee • sees*	wake-up call

---

Tipping depends largely on your class of hotel;
the higher the class, the more generous the
tip. As a guideline, a euro or two per service rendered is
recommended in standard hotels.

CHECKING OUT

When's check-out?	**Τι ώρα πρέπει να αδειάσουμε το δωμάτιο;** tee <u>oh</u> • rah <u>preh</u> • pee nah ah • THee • <u>ah</u> • soo • meh toh THoh • <u>mah</u> • tee • oh
Could we leave our baggage here until…?	**Μπορούμε να αφήσουμε τα πράγματά μας εδώ ως τις…;** boh • <u>roo</u> • meh nah ah • <u>fee</u> • soomeh tah <u>prahgh</u> • mah • <u>tah</u> mahs eh • <u>THoh</u> ohs tees…
Can I have an itemized bill/ a receipt?	**Μπορώ να έχω έναν αναλυτικό λογαριασμό/μια απόδειξη;** boh • <u>roh</u> nah eh • khoh eh • nah nah • nah • lee • tee • <u>koh</u> loh • ghahr • yahz • <u>moh</u>/miah ah • <u>poh</u> • ee • ksee
I think there's a mistake in this bill.	**Νομίζω ότι έγινε ένα λάθος στο λογαριασμό.** noh • <u>mee</u> • zoh oh • tee eh • yee • neh eh • nah lah • thohs stoh loh • ghahr • yahz • <u>moh</u>
I'll pay in cash/by credit card.	**Θα πληρώσω τοις μετρητοίς/με πιστωτική κάρτα.** thah plee • <u>roh</u> • soh tees meht • ree • <u>tees</u>/ meh pees • toh • tee • <u>kee</u> <u>kahr</u> • tah

RENTING

I've reserved an apartment/ a room.	**Έχω κλείσει ένα διαμέρισμα/δωμάτιο.** <u>eh</u> • hoh <u>klee</u> • see <u>eh</u> • nah ee • ah • <u>meh</u> • rees • mah/ oh • <u>mah</u> • tee • oh
My name is…	**Λέγομαι…** <u>leh</u> • ghoh • meh…

Can I have the key/key card?	**Μπορώ να έχω το κλειδί/την κάρτα;**
	boh • roh nah eh • hoh toh klee • THee/teen kahr • tah
Are there...?	**Υπάρχουν...;**
	ee • pahr • khoon...
dishes	**πιάτα**
	piah • tah
pillows	**μαξιλάρια**
	mah • ksee • lah • ree • ah
sheets	**σεντόνια**
	sehn • doh • niah
towels	**πετσέτες**
	peh • tseh • tehs
kitchen utensils	**οικιακά σκεύη**
	ee • kee • ah • kah skeh • vee
When do I put out the bins/recycling?	**Πότε να βγάλω έξω τα σκουπίδια/ την ανακύκλωση;**
	poh • teh nah vghah • loh eh • ksoh tah skoo • pee • THiah/teen ah • nah • kee • kloh • see
...has broken down.	**...χάλασε.**
	...khah • lah • seh
How does...work?	**Πώς λειτουργεί...;**
	pohs lee • toor • ghee...
the air-conditioner	**το κλιματιστικό**
	toh klee • mah • tees • tee • koh
the dishwasher	**το πλυντήριο πιάτων**
	toh plee • ndee • ree • oh piah • tohn
the freezer	**ο καταψύκτης**
	oh kah • tah • psee • ktees
the heater	**ο θερμοσίφωνας**
	oh thehr • moh • see • foh • nahs
the microwave	**ο φούρνος μικροκυμάτων**
	oh foor • nohs meek • roh • kee • mah • tohn

the refrigerator	**το ψυγείο**
	toh psee • ghee • oh
the stove	**η κουζίνα**
	ee koo • zee • nah
the washing machine	**το πλυντήριο**
	toh pleen • dee • ree • oh

> In Greece the electricity supply is 220 V, with standard continental 2-pin or 3-pin plugs. A multi-adapter is recommended.

DOMESTIC ITEMS

I need...	**Χρειάζομαι...**
	khree • ah • zoh • meh...
an adapter	**έναν προσαρμοστή**
	eh • nahn proh • sahr • mohs • tee
aluminum foil	**λίγο αλουμινόχαρτο**
	lee • ghoh ah • loo • mee • noh • khahr • toh
a bottle opener	**ένα τιρμπουσόν**
	eh • nah teer • boo • sohn
a broom	**μια σκούπα**
	miah skoo • pah
a can opener	**ένα ανοιχτήρι**
	eh • nah ah • neeh • tee • ree
cleaning supplies	**μερικά καθαριστικά**
	meh • ree • kah kah • thah • rees • tee • kah
a corkscrew	**ένα τιρμπουσόν**
	eh • nah teer • boo • sohn
detergent	**λίγο απορρυπαντικό**
	lee • ghoh ah • poh • ree • pahn • dee • koh
dishwashing liquid	**λίγο υγρό πιάτων**
	lee • ghoh ee • ghroh piah • tohn

bin bags	**μερικές σακκούλες σκουπιδιών**
	meh • ree • kehs sah • koo • lehs skoo • pee • THee • ohn
a light bulb	**μια λάμπα**
	miah lah • mbah
matches	**μερικά σπίρτα**
	meh • ree • kah speer • tah
a mop	**μια σφουγγαρίστρα**
	miah sfoo • ghahr • ees • trah
napkins	**χαρτοπετσέτες**
	khah • rtoh • peh • tseh • tehs
paper towels	**χαρτοπετσέτες**
	khah • rtoh • peh • tseh • tehs
plastic wrap [cling film]	**διαφανή μεμβράνη**
	THee • ah • fah • nee mehm • vrah • nee
a plunger	**μια βεντούζα**
	miah vehn • doo • zah
scissors	**ένα ψαλίδι**
	eh • nah psah • lee • THee
a vacuum cleaner	**μια ηλεκτρική σκούπα**
	miah ee • lehk • tree • kee skoo • pah

For In the Kitchen, see page 198.

AT THE HOSTEL

Do you have any places left for tonight?	**Έχετε θέση για απόψε;**
	eh • kheh • teh theh • see yah ah • poh • pseh
Can I have…?	**Μπορώ να έχω…;**
	boh • roh nah eh • khoh…
a single/ double room	**μονό/διπλό δωμάτιο**
	moh • noh/THee • ploh THoh • mah • tee • oh

a blanket	**μια κουβέρτα**
	miah koo • vehr • tah
a pillow	**ένα μαξιλάρι**
	eh • nah mah • ksee • lah • ree
sheets	**σεντόνια**
	sehn • doh • niah
a towel	**μια πετσέτα μπάνιου**
	miah peh • tseh • tah bah • nioo
Do you have lockers?	**Έχετε ντουλάπια;**
	eh • kheh • teh doo • lah • piah
What time are the doors locked?	**Τί ώρα κλειδώνετε;**
	tee oh • rah klee • THoh • neh • the
Do I need a membership card?	**Χρειάζομαι κάρτα μέλους;**
	khree • ah • zoh • meh kahr • tah meh • loos
Here's my international student card.	**Αυτή είναι η διεθνής φοιτητική μου κάρτα.**
	ahf • tee ee • neh ee THee • eh • thnees fee • tee • tee • kee moo kahr • ta

GOING CAMPING

Can I camp here?	**Μπορώ να κάνω κάμπινγκ εδώ;**
	boh • roh nah kah • noh kahm • peeng • THoh
Is there a campsite near here?	**Υπάρχει χώρος κάμπινγκ εδώ κοντά;**
	ee • pahr • khee khoh • rohs kahm • peeng eh • THoh kohn • dah
What is the charge per day/week?	**Ποιό είναι το κόστος για την ημέρα/την εβδομάδα;**
	pioh ee • neh toh kohs • tohs yah teen ee • meh • rah/ehv • THoh • mah • THah
Are there...?	**Υπάρχουν...;**
	ee • pahr • hoon...
cooking facilities	**ηλεκτρική κουζίνα**
	ee • lehk • tree • kee koo • zee • nah

electrical outlets	**πρίζες**
	pree • zehs
laundry facilities	**πλυντήρια**
	pleen • _dee_ • ree • ah
showers	**ντους**
	dooz
tents for hire	**σκηνές για ενοικίαση**
	skee • nehs yah eh • nee • _kee_ • ah • see
Where can I empty the chemical toilet?	**Πού μπορώ να αδειάσω τη χημική τουαλέτα;**
	poo boh_roh_ nah ah • THee • _ah_ • soh tee khee • mee_kee_ too ah • _leh_ • tah

For In the Kitchen, see page 198.

YOU MAY SEE...

ΠΟΣΙΜΟ ΝΕΡΟ	drinking water
poh • see • moh neh • _roh_	
ΑΠΑΓΟΡΕΥΕΤΑΙ Η ΚΑΤΑΣΚΗΝΩΣΗ	no camping
ahpah • ghoh • _reh_ • vehteh ee kah • tahs • _kee_ • nohsee	
ΜΗΝ ΑΝΑΒΕΤΕ ΦΩΤΙΑ	no fires/
meen ah • _nah_ • veh • teh foh • tee • _ah_	barbecues

COMMUNICATIONS

NEED TO KNOW

Where's an internet cafe?	**Πού υπάρχει internet cafe;** *poo ee • pahr • khee* *een • tehr • neht kah • feh*
Can I access the internet/check e-mail here?	**Μπορώ να μπω στο internet/να ελέγξω τα e-mail μου εδώ;** *boh • roh nah boh stoh* *een • tehr • neht/nah* *eh • lehng • ksoh tah ee • meh • eel* *moo eh • THoh*
How much per hour/half hour?	**Πόσο χρεώνεται η ώρα/μισή ώρα;** *poh • soh hreh • oh • neh • teh ee* *oh • rah/mee • see oh • rah*
How do I connect/log on?	**Πώς μπορώ να συνδεθώ/μπω;** *pohs boh • roh nah* *seehn • THeh • thoh/boh*
I'd like a phone card.	**Θα ήθελα μια τηλεκάρτα.** *thah ee • theh • lah miah* *tee • leh • kahr • tah*
Can I have your phone number?	**Μπορώ να έχω τον αριθμό τηλεφώνου σας;** *boh • roh nah eh • hoh tohn* *ah • reeth • moh tee • leh • foh • noo sahs*
Here's my number/e-mail address.	**Ορίστε το τηλέφωνό μου/e-mail μου.** *oh • rees • teh toh tee • leh • foh • noh* *moo/ee • meh • eel moo*
Call me.	**Πάρτε με τηλέφωνο.** *pahr • teh meh tee • leh • foh • noh*

E-mail me.	**Στείλτε μου e-mail.**
	steel • teh moo ee • _meh_ • eel
Hello. This is…	**Εμπρός. Είμαι…**
	ehm • _brohs_ ee • _meh_…
I'd like to speak to…	**Θα ήθελα να μιλήσω με…**
	thah _ee_ • theh • lah nah mee • _lee_ • soh
	meh…
Repeat that, please.	**Επαναλάβετέ το, παρακαλώ.**
	eh • pah • nah • _lah_ • veh • _teh_ toh
	pah • rah • kah • _loh_
I'll be in touch.	**Θα επικοινωνήσω μαζί σας.**
	thah eh • pee • kee • noh • _nee_ • soh
	mah • _zee_ sahs
Bye.	**Αντίο.**
	ah • _dee_ • oh
Where is the nearest/main post office?	**Πού είναι το κοντινότερο/κεντρικό ταχυδρομείο;**
	poo _ee_ • neh toh
	koh • ndee • _noh_ • teh • roh/
	kehn • dree • _koh_
	tah • khee • THroh • _mee_ • oh
I'd like to send this to…	**Θα ήθελα να στείλω αυτό σε…**
	thah _ee_ • theh • lah nah _stee_ • loh
	ahf • _toh_ seh…

ONLINE

Where's an internet cafe?	**Πού υπάρχει ένα internet cafe;**
	poo ee • _pahr_ • khee _eh_ • nah
	een • tehr • _neht_ kah • _feh_
Does it have wireless internet?	**Έχει ασύρματο internet;**
	_eh_ • khee ah • _seer_ • mah • toh
	een • tehr • _neht_

What is the WiFi password?	**Ποιος είναι ο κωδικός πρόσβασης για το WiFi;**
	piohs ee • neh oh koh • THee • kohs proh • svah • sees yah toh WiFi
Is the WiFi free?	**Το WiFi είναι δωρεάν;**
	toh WiFi ee • neh THo • reh • ahn
Do you have bluetooth?	**Έχετε bluetooth;**
	eh • kheh • teh bluetooth
How do I turn the computer on/off?	**Πώς ανοίγει/κλείνει ο υπολογιστής;**
	pohs ah • nee • ghee/klee • nee oh ee • poh • loh • ghees • tees
Can I...?	**Μπορώ...;**
	boh • roh...
access the internet here	**να έχω πρόσβαση στο internet από εδώ**
	nah eh • hoh prohs • vah • see stoh een • tehr • neht ah • poh eh • THoh
check e-mail	**να ελέγχω τα e-mail μου**
	nah eh • leng • ksoh tah ee • meh • eel moo
print	**εκτυπώσω**
	ehk • tee • poh • soh
plug in/charge my laptop iPhone/iPad	**να συνδέσω/φορτίσω το laptop/iPhone/iPad**
	nah seen • THeh • soh toh laptop/iPhone/iPad
access Skype	**να μπω στο Skype**
	nah boh stoh Skype
How much per hour/half hour?	**Πόσο χρεώνεται η ώρα/μισή ώρα;**
	poh • soh hreh • oh • neh • teh ee oh • rah/mee • see oh • rah
How do I...?	**Πώς μπορώ να...;**
	pohs boh • roh nah
connect/disconnect	**συνδεθώ/αποσυνδεθώ**
	seen • theh • THoh/ah • poh • seen • theh • THoh

log on/off	**συνδεθώ/αποσυνδεθώ**
	seen • theh • THoh/
	ah • poh • seen • theh • THoh
type this symbol	**πληκτρολογήσω αυτό το σύμβολο**
	pleek • troh • loh • ghee • soh ahf • toh toh
	seem • voh • loh
What's your e-mail?	**Ποιο είναι το e-mail σας;**
	pioh ee • neh toh ee • meh • eel sahs
My e-mail is…	**Το e-mail μου είναι…**
	toh ee • meh • eel moo ee • neh…
Do you have a scanner?	**Έχετε σαρωτή;**
	eh • kheh • teh sah • roh • tee

YOU MAY SEE…

ΚΛΕΙΣΙΜΟ	close
klee • see • moh	
ΔΙΑΓΡΑΦΗ	delete
THee • ahgh • rah • fee	
EMAIL	e-mail
ee • meh • eel	
ΕΞΟΔΟΣ	exit
eh • ksoh • THohs	
ΒΟΗΘΕΙΑ	help
voh • ee • thee • ah	
ΕΦΑΡΜΟΓΗ ΑΜΕΣΟΥ ΜΗΝΥΜΑΤΟΣ	instant messenger
eh • fahr • moh • yee ah • meh • soo mee • nee • mah • tohs	
INTERNET	internet
een • tehr • neht	

YOU MAY SEE...

ΣΥΝΔΕΣΗ _seen • theh • see_	login
ΝΕΟ (ΜΗΝΥΜΑ) _neh • oh mee • nee • mah_	new (message)
ON/OFF _ohn/ohf_	on/off
ΑΝΟΙΧΤΟ _ah • neekh • toh_	open
ΕΚΤΥΠΩΣΗ _ehk • tee • poh • see_	print
ΑΠΟΘΗΚΕΥΣΗ _ah • poh • thee • kehf • see_	save
ΑΠΟΣΤΟΛΗ _ah • pohs • toh • lee_	send
ΟΝΟΜΑ ΧΡΗΣΤΗ _oh • noh • mah khrees • tee_	username
ΚΩΔΙΚΟΣ ΠΡΟΣΒΑΣΗΣ _koh • THee • kohs prohs • vah • sees_	password
ΑΣΥΡΜΑΤΟ INTERNET _ah • seer • mah • toh een • tehr • neht_	wireless internet

SOCIAL MEDIA

Are you on Facebook/ Twitter?	**Είστε στο Facebook/Twitter;** _ee • steh stoh Facebook/Twitter_
What's your username?	**Ποιο είναι το όνομα χρήστη;** _pioh ee • neh toh oh • noh • mah khree • stee_
I'll add you as a friend.	**Θα σε προσθέσω ως φίλο.** _thah seh proh • stheh • soh ohs fee • loh_

I'll follow you on Twitter. **Θα σε ακολουθώ στο Twitter.**
thah seh ah • koh • loo • thoh stoh Twitter

Are you following...? **Ακολουθείς...;**
ah • koh • loo • thees

I'll put the pictures on Facebook/Twitter. **Θα βάλω τις φωτογραφίες στο Facebook/Twitter.**
thah vah • loh tees foh • toh • ghrah • fee • ehs sto Facebook/Twitter

I'll tag you in the pictures. **Θα σε σημειώσω στις φωτογραφίες.**
thah seh see • mee • oh • soh stees foh • toh • ghrah • fee • ehs

---

YOU MAY HEAR...

Ποιος είστε;
piohs ee • steh
Who's calling?

Περιμένετε, παρακαλώ.
peh • ree • meh • neh • the pah • rah • kah • loh
Hold on, please.

Θα σας συνδέσω.
thah sahs seen • THeh • soh
I'll put you through.

Θέλετε να αφήσετε μήνυμα;
theh • leh • teh nah ah • fee • seh • teh mee • nee • mah
Would you like to leave a message?

Ξανακαλέστε αργότερα/σε δέκα λεπτά.
ksah • nah • kah • lehs • teh ahr • ghoh • teh • rah/she eh • kah lehp • tah
Call back later/in ten minutes.

Να σας πάρει εκείνος/εκείνη;
nah sahs pah • ree eh • kee • nohs/ eh • kee • nee
Can he/she call you back?

Ποιος είναι ο αριθμός σας;
piohs ee • neh oh ah • reeth • mohs sahs
What's your number?

PHONE

Throughout Greece, even in remote areas, there are plenty of public phones; these are mainly card operated. Phone cards can be purchased from **περίπτερα** (peh • _ree_ • pteh • rah), kiosks. You can also purchase a **κάρτα για κινητό** (kah • rtah yiah kee • nee • _toh_) prepaid card for your wireless phone from any of the conveniently located wireless phone stores.

A phone card/ prepaid phone, please.	**Μια τηλεκάρτα/χρονοκάρτα.** miah tee • leh • _kahr_ • tah/ khroh • noh • _kahr_ • tah
How much?	**Πόσο;** _poh_ • soh
Where's the pay phone?	**Πού είναι ένα καρτοτηλέφωνο;** poo ee • neh toh kahr • toh • tee • _leh_ • foh • noh
What's the area/ country code for…?	**Ποιος είναι ο κωδικός περιοχής/χώρας για…;** piohs ee • neh oh koh • THee • _kohs_ peh • ree • oh • _khees_/khoh • rahs yah…
What's the number for Information?	**Ποιος είναι ο αριθμός για Πληροφορίες;** piohs ee • neh oh ah • reeth • _mohs_ yah plee • roh • foh • _ree_ • ehs
I'd like the number for…	**Θα ήθελα έναν αριθμό για…** thah ee • theh • lah eh • nahn ah • reeth • _moh_ yah…
I'd like to call collect [reverse the charges].	**Θέλω να τηλεφωνήσω με αναστροφή χρέωσης.** _theh_ • loh nah tee • leh • foh • _nee_ • soh meh ah • nah • stroh • _fee_ khreh • oh • sees
My phone doesn't work here.	**Το τηλέφωνό μου δεν λειτουργεί εδώ.** toh tee • _leh_ • foh • _noh_ moo THehn lee • toor • _ghee_ eh • _THoh_
What network are you on?	**Σε ποιο δίκτυο είσαι;** seh pioh _THee_ • ktee • oh ee • seh

Is it 3G?	**Είναι 3G;**
	ee • neh 3G
I have run out of credit/minutes.	**Δεν έχω μονάδες/λεπτά.**
	THehn eh • khoh moh • <u>nah</u> • THehs/ leh • ptah
Can I buy some credit?	**Μπορώ να αγοράσω μονάδες;**
	boh • <u>roh</u> nah ah • ghoh • <u>rah</u> • soh moh • <u>nah</u> • THehs
Do you have a phone charger?	**Έχετε φορτιστή για τηλέφωνο;**
	eh • kheh • teh foh • rtee • <u>stee</u> yah tee • <u>leh</u> • foh • noh
Can I have your number?	**Μπορώ να έχω τον αριθμό τηλεφώνου σας;**
	boh • <u>roh</u> nah eh • khoh tohn ah • reeth • <u>moh</u> tee • leh • <u>foh</u> • noo sahs
Here's my number.	**Ορίστε ο αριθμός τηλεφώνου μου.**
	oh • <u>ree</u> • steh oh ah • reeth • <u>mohs</u> tee • leh • <u>foh</u> • noo moo
Please text me.	**Παρακαλώ, στείλτε μου μήνυμα.**
	pah • rah • kah • <u>loh</u> <u>steel</u> • teh moo <u>mee</u> • nee • mah
I'll call you.	**Θα σας πάρω τηλέφωνο.**
	thah sahs <u>pah</u> • rohtee • <u>leh</u> • foh • noh

For Numbers, see page 20.

YOU MAY HEAR…

Παρακαλώ συμπληρώστε αυτήν την τελωνειακή δήλωση.
pah • rah • kah • <u>loh</u> seem • blee • <u>rohs</u> • teh ahf • <u>teen</u> teen teh • loh • nee • ah • kee <u>THee</u> • loh • see

Please fill out the customs declaration form.

Ποια είναι η αξία;
piah <u>ee</u> • neh ee ah • <u>ksee</u> • ah

What's the value?

Τι είναι μέσα;
tee <u>ee</u> • neh <u>meh</u> • sah

What's inside?

TELEPHONE ETIQUETTE

Hello. This is…	**Εμπρός. Είμαι ο** m **/ η** f **…** ehm • <u>brohs</u> <u>ee</u> • meh oh/ee…
I'd like to speak to…	**Θα ήθελα να μιλήσω με τον** m **/την** f**…** thah <u>ee</u> • theh • lah nah mee • <u>lee</u> • soh meh tohn/teen…
Extension…	**Εσωτερική γραμμή…** eh • soh • teh • ree • <u>kee</u> ghrah • <u>mee</u>…
Speak louder/more slowly.	**Μιλείστε πιο δυνατά/πιο αργά.** mee • <u>lees</u> • the pioh THee • nah • <u>tah</u>/ahr • <u>ghah</u>
Repeat that, please.	**Επαναλάβετέ το, παρακαλώ.** eh • pah • nah • <u>lah</u> • veh • teh toh pah • rah • kah • <u>loh</u>
I'll call back later.	**Θα έρθω σε επαφή μαζί σας αργότερα.** thah <u>ehr</u> • thoh seh eh • pah • <u>fee</u> mah • <u>zee</u> sahs ahr • <u>ghoh</u> • teh • rah
Bye.	**Αντίο.** ah • <u>dee</u> • oh

FAX

Can I send/receive a fax here?	**Μπορώ να στείλω/λάβω φαξ από εδώ;** boh • <u>roh</u> nah <u>stee</u> • loh/<u>lah</u> • voh fahks ah • <u>poh</u> eh • <u>THoh</u>
What's the fax number?	**Ποιος είναι ο αριθμός φαξ;** piohs <u>ee</u> • neh oh ah • <u>reeth</u> • <u>mohs</u> fahks
Please fax this to…	**Παρακαλώ στείλτε αυτό το φαξ σε…** pah • rah • kah • <u>loh</u> <u>steel</u> • teh ahf • <u>toh</u> toh fahks seh…

POST

Where's the post office/mailbox?	**Πού είναι το ταχυδρομείο/το γραμματοκιβώτιο;** *poo ee • neh toh tah • khee • roh • mee • oh/ toh ghrah • mah • toh kee voh • tee • oh*
A stamp for this postcard/letter.	**Ένα γραμματόσημο γι' αυτή την κάρτα/ αυτό το γράμμα.** *eh • nah ghrah • mah • toh • see • moh yah ahf • teen teen kahr • tah/ahf • toh toh ghrah • mah*
How much?	**Πόσο;** *poh • soh*
I want to send this package by airmail/express.	**Θέλω να στείλω αυτό τοπακέτο αεροπορικώς/ εξπρές.** *theh • lohnah stee • loh ahf • toh toh pah keh • toh • ah • eh • roh • poh • ree • kohs/ ehks • prehs*
Can I have a receipt?	**Μπορώ να έχω μια απόδειξη;** *boh • roh nah eh • khoh miah ah • poh • THee • ksee*

The post office is open from 8:00 a.m. to 8:00 p.m., except on Wednesday and Saturday when it closes at around 1:00 p.m. Main post offices are open Sunday morning. Mailboxes are yellow and bear the initials **ΕΛΤΑ** *(ehl • tah)*.

SIGHTSEEING

NEED TO KNOW

Where's the tourist information office?	**Πού είναι το γραφείο τουρισμού;** *poo ee • neh toh ghrah • fee • oh too • reez • moo*
What are the main points of interest?	**Ποια είναι τα κυριότερα αξιοθέατα;** *piah ee • neh tah kee • ree • oh • teh • rah ah • ksee • oh • theh • ah • tah*
Do you have tours in English?	**Γίνονται ξεναγήσεις στα αγγλικά;** *ghee • nohn • deh kseh • nah • ghee • sees stah ahng • lee • kah*
Could I have a map/guide?	**Μπορώ να έχω έναν χάρτη/οδηγό;** *boh • roh nah eh • khoh eh • nahn khahr • tee/oh • THee • ghoh*

TOURIST INFORMATION

Do you have any information on…?	**Έχετε πληροφορίες για…;** _eh_ • kheh • the plee • roh • foh • _ree_ • ehs yah…
Can you recommend…?	**Μπορείτε να συστήσετε έναν/μία/ένα…;** boh • _ree_ • teh nah sees • _tee_ • seh • teh _eh_ • nahn/mee • ah/eh • nah…
a bus tour	**περιήγηση με λεωφορείο** peh • ree • _ee_ • ghee • see meh leh • oh • foh • _ree_ • oh
a boat trip	**μια εκδρομή με βάρκα** _mee_ • ah ehk • THroh • _mee_ meh vahr • kah
an excursion	**μια εκδρομή** _mee_ • ah ehk • THroh • _mee_
a sightseeing tour	**μια ξενάγηση στα αξιοθέατα** _mee_ • ah kseh • _nah_ • yee • see stah ah • ksee • oh • _theh_ • ah • tah

For Asking Directions, see page 69.

The official, government-run tourist information offices are known as **EOT** (eh • oht), **Ελληνικός Οργανισμός Τουρισμού** (eh • lee • nee • _kohs_ ohr • ghah • nees • _mohs_ too • rees • _moo_), in Greece and **KOT** (koht), **Κυπριακός Οργανισμός Τουρισμού** (keep • ree • ah • _kohs_ ohr • ghah • nees • _mohs_ too • rees • _moo_) in Cyprus. They can be found in most tourist resorts and major towns.

ON TOUR

I'd like to go on the tour to…	**Θα ήθελα να πάω στην ξενάγηση στο…** _thah ee • theh • lah nah pah • oh steen kseh • nah • yee • see stoh…_
When's the next tour?	**Πότε είναι η επόμενη περιήγηση;** _poh • teh ee • neh ee eh • poh • meh • nee peh • ree • ee • ghee • see_
Are there tours in English?	**Γίνονται ξεναγήσεις στα αγγλικά;** _ghee • nohn • deh kseh • nah • yee • sees stah ahng • lee • kah_
What time do we leave/return?	**Τι ώρα αναχωρούμε/επιστρέφουμε;** _tee oh • rah ah • nah • khoh • roo • meh/ eh • pees • treh • foo • meh_
We'd like to have a look at the…	**Θα θέλαμε να ρίξουμε μια ματιά…** _thah theh • lah • meh nah ree • ksoo • meh miah mah • tiah…_
Can we stop here…?	**Μπορούμε να σταματήσουμε εδώ…;** _boh • roo • meh nah stah • mah • tee • soo • meh eh • THoh…_
to take photographs	**για να βγάλουμε φωτογραφίες** _yah nah vghah • loo • meh foh • toh • ghrah • fee • ehs_

to buy souvenirs	**για να αγοράσουμε σουβενίρ**
	yah nah ah • ghoh • <u>rah</u> • soo • meh
	soo • veh • <u>neer</u>
to use the	**για τουαλέτα**
restroom [toilet]	*yah too • ah • <u>leh</u> • tah*
Is there access for	**Υπάρχει πρόσβαση για άτομα με ειδικές**
the disabled?	**ανάγκες;**
	ee • <u>pahr</u> • khee <u>prohz</u> • vah • see yah
	<u>ah</u> • toh • mah meh ee • <u>THee</u> • <u>kehs</u>
	ah • <u>nahn</u> • gehs

For Tickets, see page 50.

SEEING THE SIGHTS

Where is…?	**Πού είναι…;**
	poo <u>ee</u> • neh…
the battleground	**το πεδίο μάχης**
	toh peh • <u>THee</u> • oh mah • khees
the botanical	**ο βοτανικός κήπος**
garden	*oh voh • tah • nee • <u>kohs</u> <u>kee</u> • pohs*
the castle	**το κάστρο**
	toh <u>kahs</u> • troh

Where is…?	**Πού είναι…;**
	poo ee • neh…
the downtown	**το κέντρο της πόλης**
area	*toh kehn • droh tees poh • lees*
the fountain	**το συντριβάνι**
	toh seen • dree • vah • nee
the library	**η βιβλιοθήκη**
	ee veev • lee • oh • thee • kee
the market	**η αγορά**
	ee ah • ghoh • rah
the museum	**το μουσείο**
	toh moo • see • oh
the old town	**η παλιά πόλη**
	ee pah • liah poh • lee
the opera house	**το μέγαρο μουσικής**
	toh meh • ghah • roh moo • see • kees
the palace	**τα ανάκτορα**
	tah ah • nahk • toh • rah
the park	**το πάρκο**
	toh pahr • koh
the ruins	**τα αρχαία**
	tah ahr • kheh • ah
the shopping area	**η εμπορική περιοχή**
	ee ehm • boh • ree • kee peh • ree • oh • khee

the town hall	**το Δημαρχείο**
	toh THee • mahr • khee • oh
Can you show me on the map?	**Μπορείτε να μου δείξετε στο χάρτη;**
	boh • ree • teh nah moo THee • kseh • teh stoh khahr • tee
It's…	**Είναι…**
	ee • neh…
amazing	**καταπληκτικό**
	kah • tah • plee • ktee • koh
beautiful	**όμορφο**
	oh • mohr • foh
boring	**βαρετός**
	vah • reh • toh
interesting	**ενδιαφέρον**
	ehn • THee • ah • feh • rohn
magnificent	**μεγαλοπρεπές**
	meh • ghah • lohp • reh • pehs
romantic	**ρομαντικό**
	roh • mahn • dee • koh
strange	**παράξενο**
	pah • rah • kseh • noh
terrible	**απαίσιο**
	ah • peh • see • oh
ugly	**άσχημο**
	ahs • khee • moh
I (don't) like it.	**(Δεν) Μου αρέσει.**
	(THen) moo ah • reh • see

RELIGIOUS SITES

Where is…?	**Πού είναι…;**
	poo ee • neh…
the cathedral	**ο καθεδρικός**
	oh kah • theh • THree • kohs

the Catholic/ Protestant church	**η καθολική/ προτεσταντική εκκλησία**
	ee kah•thoh• lee•kee/
	proh•teh•stahn•dee•kee
	ehk•lee•see•ah
the mosque	**το τζαμί**
	toh jah•mee
the shrine	**ο ιερός χώρος**
	oh ee•eh•rohs khoh•rohs
the synagogue	**η συναγωγή**
	ee see•nah•ghoh•yee
the temple	**ο ναός**
	oh nah•ohs
What time is mass/ the service?	**Τι ώρα είναι η λειτουργία;**
	tee oh•rah ee•neh
	ee lee•toor•yee•ah

LEISURE TIME

SHOPPING

NEED TO KNOW

Where is the market/mall?	**Πού είναι η αγορά/το εμπορικό κέντρο;** poo *ee* • neh ee ah • ghoh • *rah*/toh ehm • boh • ree • *koh* kehn • droh
I'm just looking.	**Απλώς κοιτάω.** ahp • *lohs* kee • *tah* • oh
Can you help me?	**Μπορείτε να με βοηθήσετε;** boh • *ree* • teh nah meh voh • ee • *thee* • seh • teh
I'm being helped.	**Με εξυπηρετούν.** meh eh • ksee • pee • reh • *toon*
How much?	**Πόσο;** *poh* • soh
This/That one, thanks.	**Αυτό/Εκείνο, παρακαλώ.** ahf • *toh*/eh • *kee* • noh pah • rah • kah • *loh*
That's all, thanks.	**Τίποτε άλλο, ευχαριστώ.** *tee* • poh • teh *ah* • loh ehf • khah • rees • *toh*
Where do I pay?	**Πού πληρώνω;** poo plee • *roh* • noh
I'll pay in cash/by credit card.	**Θα πληρώσω τοις μετρητοίς/με πιστωτική κάρτα.** thah plee • *roh* • soh tees meht • *ree* • *tees*/meh pees • toh • tee • *kee* *kahr* • tah
A receipt, please.	**Μια απόδειξη, παρακαλώ.** miah ah • *poh* • THee • ksee pah • rah • kah • *loh*

ℹ️

Shopping can be a great pleasure in Greece. Apart
from the standard department stores, you can wander
through flea markets and seek out the small handicraft stores
that line the narrow alleys of most islands and old towns.

AT THE SHOPS

Where is…?	**Πού είναι…;**
	poo ee • neh…
the antiques store	**το κατάστημα με αντίκες**
	toh kah • tahs • tee • mah meh
	ahn • tee • kehs
the bakery	**το αρτοποιείο**
	toh ahr • toh • pee • ee • oh
the bank	**η τράπεζα**
	ee • trah • peh • zah
the bookstore	**το βιβλιοπωλείο**
	toh veev • lee • oh • poh • lee • oh
the clothing store	**το κατάστημα ρούχων**
	toh kah • tahs • tee • mah roo • khohn
the delicatessen	**τα τυριά-αλλαντικά**
	tah teer • yah ah • lahn • dee • kah
the department store	**το πολυκατάστημα**
	toh poh • lee • kah • tahs • tee • mah
the gift shop	**το κατάστημα σουβενίρ**
	toh kah • tah • stee • mah soo • veh • neer
the health food store	**το κατάστημα με υγιεινές τροφές**
	toh kah • tahs • tee • mah meh
	ee • yee • ee • nehs troh • fehs
the jeweler	**το κοσμηματοπωλείο**
	toh kohz • mee • mah • toh • poh • lee • oh
the liquor store [off-licence]	**η κάβα**
	ee kah • vah

the market	**η αγορά**
	ee ah • ghoh • rah
the music store	**το κατάστημα μουσικής**
	toh kah • tah • stee • mah moo • see • kees
the pastry store	**το ζαχαροπλαστείο**
	toh zah • khah • rohp • lahs • tee • oh
Where is…?	**Πού είναι…;**
	poo ee • neh…
the pharmacy	**το φαρμακείο**
	toh fahr • mah • kee • oh
the produce [grocery] store	**το παντοπωλείο**
	toh pahn • doh • poh • lee • oh
the shoe store	**το κατάστημα υποδημάτων**
	toh kah • tahs • tee • mah ee • poh • THee • mah • tohn
the shopping mall	**το εμπορικό κέντρο**
	toh ehm • boh • ree • koh kehn • droh
the souvenir store	**το κατάστημα σουβενίρ**
	toh kah • tahs • tee • mah soo • veh • neer
the supermarket	**το σουπερμάρκετ**
	toh soo • pehr mahr • keht
the tobacconist	**το καπνοπωλείο**
	toh kahp • noh • poh • lee • oh
the toy store	**το κατάστημα παιχνιδιών**
	toh kah • tahs • tee • mah pehkh • neeTH • yohn

ASK AN ASSISTANT

When do you open/ close?	**Τι ώρα ανοίγετε/κλείνετε;**
	tee oh • rah ah • nee • gheh • teh/ klee • neh • teh
Where is…?	**Πού είναι…;**
	poo ee • neh…

the cashier	**το ταμείο**
	toh tah • mee • oh
the escalator	**οι κυλιόμενες σκάλες**
	ee kee • lee • oh • meh • nehs skah • lehs
the elevator [lift]	**το ασανσέρ**
	toh ah • sahn • sehr
the fitting room	**το δοκιμαστήριο**
	toh THoh • kee • mahs • tee • ree • oh
the store directory	**ο οδηγός καταστήματος**
	oh oh • THee • ghohs kah • tahs • tee • mah • tohs
Can you help me?	**Μπορείτε να με βοηθήσετε;**
	boh • ree • teh nah meh voh • ee • thee • seh • teh
I'm just looking.	**Απλώς κοιτάω.**
	ahp • lohs kee • tah • oh
I'm being helped.	**Εξυπηρετούμαι.**
	eh • ksee • pee • reh • too • meh
Do you have any…?	**Έχετε καθόλου…;**
	eh • kheh • teh kah • thoh • loo…
Could you show me…?	**Μπορείτε να μου δείξετε…;**
	boh • ree • teh nah moo THee • kseh • teh…
Can you ship/wrap it?	**Μπορείτε να το στείλετε/τυλίξετε;**
	boh • ree • teh nah toh stee • leh • teh/ tee • lee • kseh • teh
How much?	**Πόσο;**
	poh • soh
That's all, thanks.	**Τίποτε άλλο, ευχαριστώ.**
	tee • poh • teh ah • loh ehf • khahr • ees • toh

For Souvenirs, see page 127.

YOU MAY HEAR...

Μπορώ να σας βοηθήσω;
boh • <u>roh</u> nah sahs voh • ee • <u>thee</u> • soh

Can I help you?

Μισό λεπτό.
mee • <u>soh</u> lehp • <u>toh</u>

Just a moment.

Τί θα θέλατε;
tee thah <u>theh</u> • lah • teh

What would you like?

Τίποτε άλλο;
tee • poh • teh <u>ah</u> • loh

Anything else?

YOU MAY SEE...

ανοιχτό/κλειστό
ah • nee • <u>khtoh</u>/klee • <u>stoh</u>

open/closed

κλειστό για το μεσημέρι
klee • stoh yah toh meh • <u>see</u> • <u>meh</u> • ree

closed for lunch

δοκιμαστήριο
THoh • kee • mah • <u>stee</u> • ree • oh

fitting room

ταμείο
tah • <u>mee</u> • oh

cashier

μόνο μετρητά
<u>moh</u> • noh meh • tree • tah

cash only

δεκτές πιστωτικές κάρτες
THeh • <u>ktehs</u> pee • stoh • tee • <u>kehs</u>
<u>kahr</u> • tehs

credit cards accepted

εργάσιμες ώρες
ehr • <u>ghah</u> • see • mehs oh • rehs

business hours

έξοδος
<u>eh</u> • ksoh • THohs

exit

PERSONAL PREFERENCES

I want something…	**Θέλω κάτι…**
	theh • loh kah • tee…
cheap	**φτηνό**
	ftee • noh
expensive	**ακριβό**
	ahk • ree • voh
larger	**μεγαλύτερο**
	meh • ghah • lee • teh • roh
smaller	**μικρότερο**
	meek • roh • teh • roh
from this region	**από αυτό το μέρος**
	ah • poh ahf • toh toh meh • rohs
Around…euros.	**Γύρω στα…ευρώ.**
	yee • roh stah…ehv • roh
Is it real?	**Είναι αληθινό;**
	ee • neh ah • lee • thee • noh
Could you show me this/that?	**Μπορείτε να μου δείξετε αυτό/εκείνο;**
	boh • ree • teh nah moo THee • kseh • teh ahf • toh/eh • kee • noh
That's not quite what I want.	**Δεν είναι ακριβώς αυτό που θέλω.**
	THehn ee • neh ahk • ree • vohs ahf • toh poo theh • loh
I don't like it.	**Δεν μου αρέσει.**
	THehn moo ah • reh • see
That's too expensive.	**Είναι πολύ ακριβό.**
	ee • neh poh • lee ahk • ree • voh
I'd like to think about it.	**Θα ήθελα να το σκεφτώ.**
	thah ee • theh • lah nah toh skehf • toh
I'll take it.	**Θα το πάρω.**
	thah toh pah • roh

PAYING & BARGAINING

How much?	**Πόσο;**
	poh • soh
I'll pay…	**Θα πληρώσω…**
	thah plee • roh • soh…
by cash	**τοις μετρητοίς**
	tees meht • ree • tees
by credit card	**με πιστωτική κάρτα**
	meh pees • toh • tee • kee kahr • tah
by traveler's check	**με ταξιδιωτική επιταγή**
	meh tah • ksee • THyo • tee • kee
	eh • pee • tah • yee
A receipt, please.	**Μια απόδειξη, παρακαλώ.**
	miah ah • poh • THee • ksee
	pah • rah • kah • loh
That's too much.	**Είναι πολλά.**
	ee • neh poh • lah
I'll give you…	**Θα σας δώσω…**
	thah sahs THoh • soh…
I only have…euros.	**Έχω μόνο…ευρώ.**
	eh • khoh moh • noh…ehv • roh
Is that your best price?	**Αυτή είναι η καλύτερη τιμή σας;**
	ahf • tee ee • neh ee kah • lee • teh • ree
	tee • mee sahs
Can you give me a discount?	**Μπορείτε να μου κάνετε έκπτωση;**
	boh • ree • teh nah moo kah • neh • teh
	ehkp • toh • see

For Numbers, see page 20.

YOU MAY HEAR...

Πώς θα πληρώσετε;
pohs thah plee • roh • seh • teh
How are you paying?

Η πιστωτική σας κάρτα απορρίφθηκε.
ee pee • stoh • tee • kee sahs kahr • tah ah • poh • ree • fthee • keh
Your credit card has been declined.

Ταυτότητα, παρακαλώ.
tahf • toh • tee • tah, pah • rah • kah • loh
ID, please.

Δεν δεχόμαστε πιστωτικές κάρτες.
THehn THe • khoh • mah • steh pee • stoh • tee • kehs kahr • tehs
We don't accept credit cards.

Μόνο μετρητά, παρακαλώ.
moh • noh meht • ree • tah pah • rah • kah • loh
Cash only, please.

Εχετε ψιλά;
eh • kheh • teh psee • lah
Do you have any smaller change?

MAKING A COMPLAINT

I'd like...	**Θα ήθελα...** *thah ee • theh • lah...*
to exchange this	**να αλλάξω αυτό** *nah ah • lah • ksoh ahf • toh*
to return this	**να επιστρέψω αυτό** *nah eh • pees • treh • psoh ahf • toh*
a refund	**επιστροφή των χρημάτων μου** *eh • pees • troh • fee tohn khree • mah • tohn moo*
to see the manager	**να δω τον διευθυντή** *nah THoh tohn THee • ehf • theen • dee*

SERVICES

Can you recommend…?	**Μπορείτε να συστήσετε…;**
	boh • ree • teh nah
	sees • tee • seh • teh…
a barber	**έναν κουρέα**
	eh • nahn koo • reh • ah
a dry cleaner	**ένα καθαριστήριο**
	eh • nah kah • thah • rees • tee • ree • oh
a hairdresser	**ένα κομμωτήριο**
	eh • nah koh • moh • tee • ree • oh
a laundromat [launderette]	**πλυντήριο ρούχων**
	plee • dee • ree • oh roo • khohn
a nail salon	**ένα σαλόνι νυχιών**
	eh • nah sah • loh • nee nee • khiohn
a spa	**ένα σπα**
	eh • nah spah
a travel agency	**ένα ταξιδιωτικό γραφείο**
	eh • nah tah • ksee • THee • oh • tee • koh ghrah • fee • oh
Can you…this?	**Μπορείτε να…αυτό;**
	boh • ree • teh nah…ahf • toh
alter	**μεταποιήσετε**
	meh • tah • pee • ee • seh • teh
clean	**καθαρίσετε**
	kah • thah • ree • seh • teh
mend	**επιδιορθώσετε**
	eh • pee • THee • ohr • thoh • seh • teh
press	**σιδερώσετε**
	see • THeh • roh • seh • teh
When will it/they be ready?	**Πότε θα είναι έτοιμο/έτοιμα;**
	poh • teh thah ee • neh eh • tee • moh/ eh • tee • mah

HAIR & BEAUTY

I'd like...	**Θα ήθελα...**
	thah ee • theh • lah...
an appointment	**να κλείσω ένα ραντεβού για σήμερα/ αύριο**
for today/ tomorrow	*nah klee • soh eh • nah rahn • deh • voo yah see • meh • rah/ahv • ree • oh*
some colour/ highlights	**βαφή/ανταύγειες**
	vah • fee/ah • dahv • yehs
my hair styled/ blow-dried	**ένα χτένισμα/στέγνωμα με πιστολάκι**
	eh • nah khteh • nee • smah/ steh • ghnoh • mah meh pee • stoh • lah • kee
a haircut	**ένα κούρεμα**
	eh • nah koo • reh • mah
I'd like...	**Θα ήθελα...**
	thah ee • theh • lah...
an eyebrow/ bikini wax	**χαλάουα στα φρύδια/στο μπικίνι**
	khah • lah • oo • ah stah free • yah/ stoh bee • kee • nee
a facial	**έναν καθαρισμό προσώπου**
	eh • nahn kah • thah • reez • moh proh • soh • poo
a manicure/ pedicure	**ένα μανικιούρ/πεντικιούρ**
	eh • nahmah • nee • kee • oor/ pehn • dee • kee • oor
a (sports) massage	**ένα (αθλητικό) μασάζ**
	eh • nah (ahth • lee • tee • koh) mah • sahz
A trim, please.	**Κόψιμο, παρακαλώ.**
	koh • psee • moh, pah • rah • kah • loh
Don't cut it too short.	**Μην τα κόψετε πολύ κοντά.**
	meen tah koh • pseh • teh poh • lee kohn • dah

Shorter here.	**Πιο κοντά εδώ.**
	pioh kohn • <u>dah</u> eh • THoh
Do you do…?	**Κάνετε…;**
	<u>kah</u> • neh • teh…
acupuncture	**βελονισμό**
	veh • loh • neez • <u>moh</u>
aromatherapy	**αρωματοθεραπεία**
	ah • roh • mah • toh • theh • rah • <u>pee</u> • ah
oxygen treatment	**οξυγονοθεραπεία**
	oh • ksee • ghoh • noh • theh • rah • <u>pee</u> • ah
Is there a sauna?	**Υπάρχει σάουνα;**
	ee • <u>pahr</u> • kee <u>sah</u> • oo • nah

ℹ

You will find spas and wellness centers, particularly
at luxury hotels, in every major city and on most islands
in Greece. You can visit these spas for a full day or for
one treatment, without being a guest at the hotel. You will
usually have to make an appointment in advance. Tipping is
customary, particularly in hair salons, where customers may
choose to tip the assistants or trainees.

ANTIQUES

How old is this?	**Πόσο παλιό είναι αυτό;**
	<u>poh</u> • soh pah • <u>lioh</u> ee • neh ahf • <u>toh</u>
Do you have anything from the…period?	**Έχετε τίποτα από την…περίοδο;**
	eh • kheh • <u>teh</u> tee • <u>poh</u> • tah ah • poh
	teen….peh • <u>ree</u> • oh • THoh
Do I have to fill out any forms?	**Πρέπει να συμπληρώσω έντυπα;**
	<u>preh</u> • pee nah see • blee • <u>roh</u> • soh
	eh • ndee • pah

Will I have problems with customs?	**Θα έχω προβλήματα με το τελωνείο;** *thah eh • khoh prohv • lee • mah • tah meh toh teh • loh • nee • oh*
Is there a certificate of authenticity?	**Υπάρχει πιστοποιητικό γνησιότητας;** *ee • pahr • khee pees • toh • pee • ee • tee • koh ghnee • see • oh • tee • tahs*
Can you ship/ wrap it?	**Μπορείτε να το στείλετε/τυλίξετε;** *boh • ree • teh nah toh stee • leh • teh/ tee • lee • kseh • teh*

CLOTHING

I'd like...	**Θα ήθελα...** *thah ee • theh • lah...*
Can I try this on?	**Μπορώ να το δοκιμάσω;** *boh • roh nah toh THoh • kee • mah • soh*
It doesn't fit.	**Δεν μου κάνει.** *THehn moo kah • nee*
It's too...	**Είναι πολύ...** *ee • neh poh • lee...*
big	**μεγάλο** *meh • ghah • loh*
small	**μικρό** *meek • roh*
short	**κοντό** *kon • doh*
long	**μακρύ** *mak • ree*
tight	**στενό** *steh • noh*
loose	**φαρδύ** *fahr • THee*
Do you have this in size...?	**Το έχετε στο μέγεθος...;** *toh eh • kheh • teh stoh meh • yeh • thohs...*

Do you have this in a bigger/smaller size? | **Το έχετε σε μεγαλύτερο/μικρότερο μέγεθος;**
toh kheh • teh seh meh • ghah • lee • teh • roh/ meek • roh • teh • roh meh • gheh • thohs

For Numbers, see page 20.

YOU MAY SEE...

ΑΝΔΡΙΚΑ	men's clothing
ahn • THree • kah	
ΓΥΝΑΙΚΕΙΑ	women's clothing
yee • neh • kee • a	
ΠΑΙΔΙΚΑ	children's clothing
peh • THee • kah	

YOU MAY HEAR...

Σας πηγαίνει.	That looks
sahs pee • gheh • nee	great on you.
Πώς σας είναι;	How does it fit?
pohs sahs • ee • neh	
Δεν έχουμε το μέγεθός σας.	We don't have
THen eh • khoo • meh toh	your size.
meh • gheh • thohs sahs	

COLORS

I'm looking for something in... | **Ψάχνω κάτι σε...**
psahkh • noh kah • tee seh...

beige | **μπεζ**
behz

black	**μαύρο**	
	mahv • roh	
blue	**μπλε**	
	bleh	
brown	**καφέ**	
	kah • feh	
green	**πράσινο**	
	prah • see • noh	
gray	**γκρι**	
	gree	
orange	**πορτοκαλί**	
	pohr • toh • kah • lee	
pink	**ροζ**	
	rohz	
purple	**μωβ**	
	mohv	
red	**κόκκινο**	
	koh • kee • noh	
white	**άσπρο**	
	ahs • proh	
yellow	**κίτρινο**	
	keet • ree • noh	

CLOTHES & ACCESSORIES

a backpack	**το σακκίδιο**
	toh sah • kee • THee • oh
a belt	**η ζώνη**
	ee zoh • nee
a bikini	**το μπικίνι**
	toh bee • kee • nee
a blouse	**η μπλούζα**
	ee bloo • zah
a bra	**το σουτιέν**
	toh soo • tiehn

briefs [underpants] (women's)	**το κυλοτάκι** *toh kee • loh • tah • kee*
briefs [underpants] (men's and women's)	**το σλιπ** *toh sleep*
a coat	**το παλτό** *toh pahl • toh*
a dress	**το φόρεμα** *toh foh • reh • mah*
a hat	**το καπέλλο** *toh kah • peh • loh*
a jacket	**το σακάκι** *toh sah • kah • kee*
jeans	**το μπλου-τζην** *toh bloo • jeen*
pajamas	**πιτζάμες** *pee • tzah • mehs*
pants [trousers]	**το παντελόνι** *toh pahn • deh • loh • nee*
pantyhose [tights]	**το καλσόν** *toh kahl • sohn*
a purse [handbag]	**η τσάντα** *ee tsahn • dah*
a raincoat	**το αδιάβροχο** *toh ah • THee • ahv • roh • khoh sah • kah • kee*
a scarf	**το κασκώλ** *toh kahs • kohl*
a shirt	**το πουκάμισο** *toh poo • kah • mee • soh*
shorts	**το σόρτς** *toh sohrts*
a skirt	**η φούστα** *ee foos • tah*
socks	**οι κάλτσες** *ee kahl • tsehs*

a suit	**το κουστούμι/ταγιέρ**
(men's/women's)	*toh koos • too/ tah • yehr*
sunglasses	**τα γυαλιά ηλίου**
	tah yah • liah ee • lee • oo
a sweater	**το πουλόβερ**
	toh poo • loh • vehr
a sweatshirt	**το φούτερ**
	toh foo • ter
swimming trunks/	**το μαγιό**
a swimsuit	*toh mah • yoh*
a T-shirt	**το μπλουζάκι**
	toh bloo • zah • kee
a tie	**η γραβάτα**
	ee ghrah • vah • tah
underwear	**τα εσώρουχα**
	tah eh • soh • roo • khah

FABRIC

I'd like...	**Θα ήθελα...**
	thah ee • theh • lah...
cotton	**βαμβακερό**
	vahm • vah • keh • roh
denim	**τζιν**
	deh • neem jeen
lace	**δαντέλα**
	THahn • teh • lah
leather	**δερμάτινο**
	THehr • mah • tee • noh
linen	**λινό**
	lee • noh
silk	**μεταξωτό**
	meh • tah • ksoh • toh
wool	**μάλλινο**
	mah • lee • noh

Is it machine washable?	**Πλένεται στο πλυντήριο;**
	pleh • neh • teh stoh
	pleen • dee • ree • oh

SHOES

I'd like...	**Θα ήθελα...**
	thah ee • theh • lah...
high-heeled/ flat shoes	**τα ψηλοτάκουνα/επίπεδα παπούτσια**
	tah psee • loh • tah • koo • nah/ee • siah
	pah • poo • tsiah
boots	**οι μπότες**
	ee boh • tehs
loafers	**τα μοκασίνια**
	tah moh • kah • see • niah
sandals	**τα πέδιλα**
	tah peh • THee • lah
shoes	**τα παπούτσια**
	tah pah • poo • tsiah
slippers	**οι παντόφλες**
	ee pahn • dohf • lehs
sneakers	**τα αθλητικά παπούτσια**
	tah ahth • lee • tee • kah pah • poo • tsiah
In size...	**Στο νούμερο...**
	stoh noo • meh • roh...

For Numbers, see page 20.

SIZES

small (S)	**μικρό**
	meek • roh
medium (M)	**μεσαίο**
	meh • seh • oh
large (L)	**μεγάλο**
	meh • gha • loh

extra large (XL)	**extra large**
	eh • xtrah lahrj
petite	**μικρό νούμερο**
	mee • kroh noo • meh • roh
plus size	**μεγάλο νούμερο**
	meh • ghah • loh noo • meh • roh

NEWSSTAND & TOBACCONIST

Do you sell English-language books/newspapers?	**Πουλάτε αγγλικές εφημερίδες/περιοδικά;**
	poo • lah • teh ahng lee • kehs
	eh • fee • meh • ree • THes/
	peh • rioh • THee • kah
I'd like...	**Θα ήθελα...**
	thah ee • theh • lah...
candy [sweets]	**γλυκά**
	ghlee • kah
chewing gum	**τσίχλες**
	tseekh • lehs
a chocolate bar	**σοκολάτα**
	soh • koh • lah • tah
cigars	**πούρα**
	poo • rah
a pack/carton of cigarettes	**ένα πακέτο/μια κούτα τσιγάρα**
	eh • nah pah • keh • toh/miah koo • tah
	tsee • ghah • rah
a lighter	**έναν αναπτήρα**
	eh • nahn ah • nahp • tee • rah
a magazine	**ένα περιοδικό**
	eh • nah peh • ree • oh • THee • koh
matches	**σπίρτα**
	speer • tah
a newspaper	**μια εφημερίδα**
	miah eh • fee • meh • ree • THah

a pen	**ένα στυλό**
	eh • nah stee • loh
a postcard	**μια καρτ ποστάλ**
	miah kahrt poh • stahl
a road/town map of...	**έναν οδικό χάρτη/έναν χάρτη της πόλης για...**
	eh • nahn oh • THee • koh khahr • tee/ eh • nahn khahr • tee tees poh • lees yah...
stamps	**γραμματόσημα**
	ghrah • mah • toh • see • mah

PHOTOGRAPHY

I'm looking for...camera.	**Ψάχνω για...φωτογραφική μηχανή.**
	psahkh • noh yah... foh • tohgh • rah • fee • kee mee • khah • nee
an automatic	**μια αυτόματη**
	miah ahf • toh • mah • tee
a digital	**μια ψηφιακή**
	miah psee • fee • ah • kee
a disposable	**μια μιας χρήσεως**
	miah miahs khree • seh • ohs
I'd like...	**Θα ήθελα...**
	thah ee • theh • lah...
a battery	**μια μπαταρία**
	miah bah • tah • ree • ah
digital prints	**ψηφιακές εκτυπώσεις**
	psee • fee • ah • kehs ehk • tee • poh • sees
a memory card	**μια κάρτα μνήμης**
	miah kahr • tah mnee • mees
Can I print digital photos here?	**Μπορώ να εκτυπώσω ψηφιακές φωτογραφίες εδώ;**
	boh • roh nah ehk • tee • poh • soh psee • fee • ah • kehs foh • toh • ghrah • fee • ehs eh • THoh

SOUVENIRS

bottle of wine	**μπουκάλι κρασί**
	boo • kah • lee krah • see
box of pastries	**κουτί γλυκά**
	koo • tee ghlee • kah
dried Corinthian currants	**κορινθιακή σταφίδα**
	koh • reen • thee • ah • kee stah • fee • THah
ground Greek coffee	**ελληνικός καφές**
	eh • lee • nee • kohs kah • fehs
halva	**χαλβά**
	khahl • vahs
key ring	**μπρελόκ**
	breh • lohk
olives	**ελιές**
	eh • liehs
olive oil	**λάδι**
	lah • THee
pistachio nuts	**φυστίκια**
	fees • tee • kiah
postcard	**καρτποστάλ**
	kahrt • pohs • tahl
T-shirt	**μπλουζάκι**
	bloo • zah • kee

thyme honey	**θυμαρίσιο μέλι**
	thee•mah•<u>ree</u>•sioh <u>meh</u>•lee
Turkish delight	**λουκούμι**
	loo•<u>koo</u>•mee
Can I see this/ that?	**Μπορώ να δω αυτό/εκείνο;**
	boh•<u>roh</u> nah THoh
	ahf•<u>toh</u>/eh•<u>kee</u>•noh
The one in the window/display case.	**Αυτό στη βιτρίνα.**
	ahf•<u>toh</u> stee veet•<u>ree</u>•nah
I'd like…	**Θα ήθελα…**
	thah <u>ee</u>•theh•lah…
a battery	**μια μπαταρία**
	miah bah•tah•<u>ree</u>•ah
a bracelet	**ένα βραχιόλι**
	<u>eh</u>•nah vrah•<u>khioh</u>•lee
a brooch	**μια καρφίτσα**
	miah kahr•<u>fee</u>•tsah
earrings	**ένα ζευγάρι σκουλαρίκια**
	<u>eh</u>•nah zehv•<u>gah</u>•ree skoo•lah•<u>ree</u>•kiah
a necklace	**ένα κολλιέ**
	<u>eh</u>•nah koh•<u>lieh</u>

a ring	**ένα δαχτυλίδι**
	eh • nah THahkh • tee • lee • THee
a watch	**ένα ρολόι**
	eh • nah roh • loh • ee
copper	**χαλκό**
	khahl • koh
crystal	**κρύσταλλο**
	krees • tah • loh
diamond	**διαμάντι**
	THiah • mahn • dee
(white/yellow) gold	**λευκόχρυσο/χρυσό**
	lehf • koh • khree • soh/khree • soh
pearl	**μαργαριτάρι**
	mahr • ghah • ree • tah • ree
pewter	**κασσίτερο**
	kah • see • teh • roh
platinum	**πλατίνα**
	plah • tee • nah
sterling silver	**ασήμι**
	ah • see • mee
Is this real?	**Είναι αληθινό;**
	ee • neh ah • lee • thee • noh
Can you engrave it?	**Μπορείτε να το χαράξετε;**
	boh • ree • teh nah toh khah • rah • kseh • teh

There is a vast choice of souvenirs to buy in Greece. In all major tourist locations, you will find shops selling jewelry, handmade goods and other typical souvenirs. In Athens, there are some very nice jewelry shops in Monastiraki. You can find anything from ancient Greek-style jewelry to pieces made by contemporary designers. Handicrafts range from re-creations of ancient Greek pottery to textiles, and handmade backgammon sets.

SPORT & LEISURE

NEED TO KNOW

When's the game?	**Πότε είναι ο αγώνας;** _poh • teh ee • neh oh ah • ghoh • nahs_
Where's…?	**Πού είναι…;** _poo ee • neh…_
the beach	**η παραλία** _ee pah • rah • lee • ah_
the park	**το πάρκο** _toh pahr • koh_
the pool	**η πισίνα** _ee pee • see • nah_
Is it safe to swim/ dive here?	**Είναι ασφαλές εδώ για κολύμπι/ κατάδυση;** _ee • neh ahs • fah • lehs eh • THoh yah koh • leem bee/kah • tah • THee • see_
Can I hire golf clubs?	**Μπορώ να νοικιάσω μπαστούνια του γκόλφ;** _boh • roh nah nee • kiah • soh bahs • too • niah too gohlf_
How much per hour?	**Πόσο χρεώνεται η ώρα;** _poh • soh khreh • oh • neh • teh ee oh • rah_
How far is it to…?	**Πόσο μακριά είναι για…;** _poh • soh mahk • ree • ah ee • neh yah…_
Can you show me on the map?	**Μπορείτε να μου δείξετε στο χάρτη;** _boh • ree • teh nah moo THee • kseh • teh stoh khahr • tee_

WATCHING SPORT

When's...	**Πότε είναι...**
	poh • teh ee • neh...
the baseball	**ο αγώνας μπέιζμπολ**
game	_oh ah • ghoh • nahs beh • ee • zbohl_
the basketball	**ο αγώνας μπάσκετ**
game	_oh ah • ghoh • nahs bahs • keht_
the boxing match	**ο αγώνας μποξ**
	oh ah • ghoh • nahs bohks
the cricket game	**ο αγώνας κρίκετ**
	oh ah • ghoh • nahs kree • keht
the cycling race	**ο αγώνας ποδηλασίας**
	oh ah • ghoh • nahs
	poh • THee • lah • see • ahs
the golf	**το τουρνουά γκολφ**
tournament	_toh toor • noo • ah gohlf_
the soccer	**ο αγώνας ποδοσφαίρου**
[football] game	_oh ah • ghoh • nahs_
	poh • THohs • feh • roo
the tennis match	**ο αγώνας τέννις**
	oh ah • ghoh • nahs teh • nees
the volleyball	**ο αγώνας βόλεϊ**
game	_oh ah • ghoh • nahs voh • leh • ee_
Which teams are	**Ποιες ομάδες παίζουν;**
playing?	_pee • ehs oh • mah • THehs peh • zoon_
Where's...?	**Πού είναι...;**
	poo ee • neh...
the horse track	**το ιπποδρόμιο**
	toh ee • poh • THroh • mee • oh
the racetrack	**ο ιππόδρομος**
	oh ee • poh • THroh • mohs
the stadium	**το στάδιο**
	toh stah • THee • oh

Where can I place a bet?	**Πού μπορώ να βάλω στοίχημα;** *poo boh • roh nah vah • loh stee • khee • mah*

The most popular sport in Greece is **καλαθοσφαίρηση** *(kah • lah • thohs • feh • ree • see)*, basketball; even the smallest towns have their own basketball teams.
Ποδόσφαιρο *(poh • THohs • feh • roh)*, soccer, is also popular, and matches are usually played on Sunday.
Water sports are very popular on the islands and in coastal areas. However, you need a special permit to dive with oxygen tanks.
Winter skiing has gained popularity in the last few years – there are more than 15 ski resorts on the mainland. Contact the tourist information office for details on locations and snow conditions.

PLAYING SPORT

Where's…?	**Πού είναι…;** *poo ee • neh…*
the golf course	**το γήπεδο του γκόλφ** *toh yee • peh • THoh too gohlf*
the gym	**το γυμναστήριο** *toh gheem • nahs • tee • ree • oh*
the park	**το πάρκο** *toh pahr • koh*
Where are the tennis courts?	**Πού είναι τα γήπεδα του τέννις;** *poo ee • neh tah ghee • peh • THah too teh • nees*
How much per…?	**Ποιο είναι το κόστος για…;** *pioh ee • neh toh kohs • tohs yah…*

day	**την ημέρα**
	teen ee • _meh_ • rah
hour	**την ώρα**
	teen _oh_ • rah
game	**το παιχνίδι**
	toh peh • _khnee_ • THee
round	**το παιχνίδι**
	toh peh • _khnee_ • THee
Can I hire...?	**Μπορώ να νοικιάσω...;**
	boh • _roh_ nah nee • _kiah_ • soh...
golf clubs	**μπαστούνια του γκόλφ**
	bahs • _too_ • niah too gohlf
equipment	**εξοπλισμό**
	eh • ksohp • leez • _moh_
a racket	**μια ρακέτα**
	miah rah • _keh_ • tah

AT THE BEACH/POOL

Where's the beach/ pool?	**Πού είναι η παραλία/πισίνα;**
	poo ee • neh ee pah • rah • _lee_ • ah/
	pee • _see_ • nah
Is there...?	**Υπάρχει...;**
	ee • _pahr_ • khee...
a kiddie pool	**παιδική πισίνα**
	peh • THee • _kee_ pee • _see_ • nah
an indoor/ outdoor pool	**εσωτερική/εξωτερική πισίνα**
	eh • soh • teh • ree • _kee_/
	eh • ksoh • teh • ree • _kee_ pee • _see_ • nah
a lifeguard	**ναυαγοσώστης**
	nah • vah • ghoh • _sohs_ • tees
Is it safe...?	**Είναι ασφαλές...;**
	_ee_ • neh ahs • fah • _lehs_...
to swim	**εδώ για κολύμπι**
	eh • _THoh_ yah koh • _leem_ • bee

to dive	**εδώ για κατάδυση**
	eh • THoh yah kah • tah • THee • see
for children	**για παιδιά**
	yah peh • THyah
I want to hire…	**Θέλω να νοικιάσω…**
	theh • loh nah nee • kiah • soh…
a deck chair	**μια σεζ-λονγκ**
	miah sehz • lohng
diving equipment	**εξοπλισμό καταδύσεων**
	eh • ksoh • plee • smoh
	kah • tah • THee • seh • ohn
a jet-ski	**ένα τζετ-σκι**
	eh • nah jeht skee
a motorboat	**μια εξωλέμβιο**
	miah eh • ksoh • lehm • vee • oh
a rowboat	**βάρκα**
	vahr • kah
a sailing boat	**ένα ιστιοπλοϊκό**
	eh • nah ees • tee • oh • ploh • ee • koh
snorkeling equipment	**εξοπλισμό κατάδυσης με αναπνευστήρα**
	eh • ksoh • plee • smoh
	kah • tah • THee • sees meh
	ah • nah • pnehf • stee • rah
a surfboard	**μιασανίδα του σέρφινγκ**
	miah sah • nee • THah too sehrf
a towel	**μια πετσέτα**
	miah peh • tseh • tah
an umbrella	**μια ομπρέλλα θαλάσσης**
	miah ohm • breh • lah thah • lah • sees
water skis	**πέδιλα θαλάσσιου σκι**
	peh • THee • lah thah • lah • see • oo skee
For…hours.	**Για…ώρες.**
	yah… oh • rehs

Greek beaches, which are usually free of charge, often offer a range of water sports. Beaches that are run by **EOT** require an entrance fee, but they tend to have more facilities. The use of jet-skis is restricted to a few beaches only, at a certain distance from the land and at specific times. Topless and nude sunbathing is acceptable at many island and mainland resorts, though it might be worth checking with a local beforehand if you're the only one!

YOU MAY SEE...

ΤΕΛΕΣΚΙ	ski lift
teh • leh • <u>skee</u>	
ΤΕΛΕΣΕΖ	chair lift
teh • leh • <u>sehz</u>	
ΤΕΛΕΦΕΡΙΚ	cable car
teh • leh • feh • <u>reek</u>	
ΠΙΣΤΑ ΑΡΧΑΡΙΩΝ	baby slope
<u>pees</u> • tah ahr • khahr • <u>ee</u> • ohn	
ΜΕΣΑΙΑ ΠΙΣΤΑ	intermediate slope
meh • <u>seh</u> • ah pees • tah	
ΠΙΣΤΑ ΠΡΟΧΩΡΗΜΕΝΩΝ	advanced slope
<u>pees</u> • tah proh • khoh • ree • <u>meh</u> • nohn	
ΠΙΣΤΑ ΚΛΕΙΣΤΗ	trail closed
pees • tah klees • tee	

WINTER SPORTS

A lift pass for a day/ few days, please.

Μια άδεια για μια ημέρα/μερικές ημέρες, παρακαλώ.
miah <u>ah</u> • THee • ah yah miah
ee • <u>meh</u> • rah/meh • ree • <u>kehs</u>
ee • <u>meh</u> • rehs pah • rah • kah • <u>loh</u>

I'd like to hire…	**Θα ήθελα να νοικιάσω…**
	thah ee•theh•lah nah
	nee•<u>kiah</u>•soh…
boots	**μπότες του σκι**
	<u>boh</u>•tehs too skee
a helmet	**ένα κράνος**
	eh•nah <u>krah</u>•nohs
poles	**μπαστούνια του σκι**
	bahs•<u>too</u>•niah too skee
skis	**πέδιλα του σκι**
	<u>peh</u>•THee•lah too skee
a snowboard	**μια σανίδα snowboard**
	miah sah•<u>nee</u>•THah snoh•oo•<u>bohrd</u>
snowshoes	**παπούτσια χιονιού**
	pah•<u>poo</u>•tsiah khioh•<u>nioo</u>
These are too big/small.	**Αυτά είναι πολυ μεγάλα/μικρά.**
	ahf•<u>tah ee</u>•neh poh•<u>lee</u> meh•<u>ghah</u>•lah/meek•<u>rah</u>
Are there lessons?	**Γίνονται μαθήματα;**
	<u>yee</u>•nohn•deh mah•<u>thee</u>•mah•tah
I'm a beginner.	**Είμαι αρχάριος.**
	<u>ee</u>•meh ahr•<u>khah</u>•ree•ohs
I'm experienced.	**Είμαι έμπειρος** *m* /**έμπειρη** *f*.
	<u>ee</u>•meh <u>ehm</u>•bee•rohs/<u>ehm</u>•bee•ree

A trail [piste] map, please.	**Έναν χάρτη της πίστας.**
	_eh_ • nahn <u>khahr</u> • tee tees <u>pees</u> • tahs

OUT IN THE COUNTRY

I'd like a map of…	**Θα ήθελα ένα χάρτη…**
	thah <u>ee</u> • theh • lah <u>eh</u> • nah <u>khahr</u> • tee…
this region	**αυτής της περιοχής**
	ahf • <u>tees</u> tees peh • ree • oh • <u>khees</u>
walking routes	**των διαδρομών περιήγησης**
	tohn THee • ah • THroh • <u>mohn</u>
	peh • ree • <u>ee</u> • yee • sees
cycle routes	**των ποδηλατόδρομων**
	tohn poh • THee • lah • <u>toh</u> • THroh • mohn
the trails	**των μονοπατιών**
	tohn moh • noh • pah • <u>tiohn</u>
Is it easy/difficult?	**Είναι εύκολο/δύσκολο;**
	<u>ee</u> • neh <u>ehf</u> • koh • loh/<u>ees</u> • koh • loh
Is it far/steep?	**Είναι μακριά/απότομο;**
	<u>ee</u> • neh mahk • ree • <u>ah</u>/
	ah • <u>poh</u> • toh • moh
How far is it to…?	**Πόσο μακριά είναι για…;**
	<u>poh</u> • soh mahk • ree • <u>ah</u> ee • neh yah…
Can you show me on the map?	**Μπορείτε να μου δείξετε στο χάρτη;**
	boh • <u>ree</u> • teh nah moo <u>THee</u> • kseh • teh
	stoh <u>khahr</u> • tee
I'm lost.	**Έχω χαθεί.**
	<u>eh</u> • khoh khah • <u>thee</u>
Where's…?	**Πού είναι…;**
	poo <u>ee</u> • neh…
the ancient temple	**ο αρχαίος ναός**
	oh ahr • <u>kheh</u> • ohs nah • <u>ohs</u>
the ancient theater	**το αρχαίο θέατρο**
	toh ahr • <u>kheh</u> • oh <u>theh</u> • ah • troh

the bridge	**η γέφυρα**
	ee yeh • fee • rah
the cave	**το σπήλαιο**
	toh spee • leh • oh
the desert	**η έρημος**
	ee eh • ree • mohs
the cliff	**ο γκρεμός**
	oh greh • mohs
the farm	**η φάρμα**
	ee fahr • mah
the field	**το χωράφι**
	toh khoh • rah • fee
the forest	**το δάσος**
	toh THah • sohs
the gorge	**το φαράγγι**
	toh fah • rah • gee
the hill	**ο λόφος**
	oh loh • fohs
the lake	**η λίμνη**
	ee leem • nee
the mountain	**το βουνό**
	toh voo • noh
the nature reserve	**ο εθνικός δρυμός**
	oh ehth • nee • kohs THree • mohs

the viewpoint	**η πανοραμική θέση**
	ee pah • noh • rah • mee • kee theh • see
the park	**το πάρκο**
	toh pahr • koh
the path	**το μονοπάτι**
	toh moh • noh • pah • tee
the peak	**η κορυφή**
	ee koh • ree • fee
the picnic area	**η περιοχή για πικ-νικ**
	ee peh • ree • oh • khee yah peek • neek
the pond	**η λίμνη**
	ee lee • mnee
the river	**ο ποταμός**
	oh poh • tah • mohs
the sea	**η θάλασσα**
	ee thah • lah • sah
the thermal bath	**τα ιαματικά λουτρα**
	tah ee • ah • mah • tee • kah loot • rah
the hot spring	**τα ιαματικά λουτρα**
	tah ee • ah • mah • tee • kah loot • rah
the stream	**το ρέμα**
	toh reh • mah
the valley	**η κοιλάδα**
	ee kee • lah • THah
the vineyard	**ο αμπελώνας**
	oh ah • beh • loh • nahs
the volcano	**το ηφαίστειο**
	toh ee • feh • stee • oh
the waterfall	**ο καταρράκτης**
	oh kah • tah • rahk • tees

For Asking Directions, see page 69.

TRAVELING WITH CHILDREN

NEED TO KNOW

Is there a discount for children?	**Υπάρχει μειωμένο εισιτήριο για παιδιά;** *ee • <u>pahr</u> • khee mee • oh • <u>meh</u> • noh ee • see • <u>tee</u> • ree • oh yah peh • <u>THyah</u>*
Can you recommend a babysitter?	**Μπορείτε να συστήσετε μια υπεύθυνη μπέιμπυ-σίτερ;** *boh • <u>ree</u> • teh nah sees • <u>tee</u> • seh • teh miah ee • <u>pehf</u> • thee • nee beh • ee • bee <u>see</u> • tehr*
Could I have a child's seat/ highchair?	**Μπορούμε να έχουμε ένα παιδικό καθισματάκι/μια καρέκλα μωρού;** *boh • <u>roo</u> • meh nah eh • khoo • meh eh-nah peh • THee • <u>koh</u> kah • theez • mah • <u>tah</u> • kee/miah kah • <u>reh</u> • klah moh • <u>roo</u>*
Where can I change the baby?	**Πού μπορώ να αλλάξω το μωρό;** *poo boh • <u>roh</u> nah ah • <u>lah</u> • ksoh toh moh • <u>roh</u>*

OUT & ABOUT

Can you recommend something for the kids?	**Μπορείτε να μας συστήσετε κάτι για τα παιδιά;** *boh • ree • teh nah mahs* *sees • tee • seh • the kah • tee yah tah* *peh • THyah*
Where's…?	**Πού είναι…;** *poo ee • neh…*
the amusement park	**το πάρκο ψυχαγωγίας** *toh pahr • koh psee • khah • ghoh • yee • ahs*
the arcade	**η αίθουσα ψυχαγωγίας** *ee eh • thoo • sah* *psee • khah • ghoh • yee • ahs*
the kiddie pool	**η παιδική πισίνα** *ee peh • THee • kee pee • see • nah*
the park	**το πάρκο** *toh pahr • koh*
the playground	**η παιδική χαρά** *ee peh • THee • kee khah • rah*
the zoo	**ο ζωολογικός κήπος** *oh zoh • oh • loh • yee • kohs kee • pohs*
Are kids allowed?	**Επιτρέπονται τα παιδιά;** *eh • pee • treh • pohn • deh tah peh • THyah*
Is it safe for kids?	**Είναι ασφαλές για παιδιά;** *ee • neh ahs • fah • lehs yah tah* *peh • THyah*
Is it suitable for…year olds?	**Είναι κατάλληλο για παιδιά…ετών;** *ee • neh kah • tah • lee • loh yah* *peh • THyah…eh • tohn*

For Numbers, see page 20.

YOU MAY HEAR...

Τι όμορφο!
tee <u>oh</u> • mohr • foh

How cute!

Πως τον/την λένε;
pohs tohn/teen <u>leh</u> • neh

What's his/her name?

Πόσο χρονών είναι;
<u>poh</u> • soh khroh • <u>nohn</u> ee • neh

How old is he/she?

BABY ESSENTIALS

Do you have...?	**Έχετε...;**
	<u>eh</u> • kheh • teh...
a baby bottle	**ένα μπιμπερό**
	<u>eh</u> • nah bee • beh • <u>roh</u>
baby food	**παιδικές τροφές**
	peh • THee • <u>kehs</u> troh • <u>fehs</u>
baby wipes	**υγρά μαντηλάκια**
	eegh • <u>rah</u> mahn • dee • <u>lah</u> • kiah
a car seat	**ένα παιδικό κάθισμα**
	<u>eh</u> • nah peh • THee • <u>koh</u> kah • thee • smah
a children's menu	**έναν παιδικό κατάλογο**
	<u>eh</u> • nahn peh • THee • <u>koh</u> kah • <u>tah</u> • loh • ghoh
a child's portion	**μια παιδική μερίδα**
	miah peh • THee • <u>kee</u> meh • <u>ree</u> • THah
a child's seat/highchair	**ένα παιδικό κάθισμα/καρεκλάκι**
	<u>eh</u> • nah peh • ee • <u>koh</u> kah • theez • mah/kah • rehk • <u>lah</u> • kee moh • <u>roo</u>
a crib/cot	**μια κούνια/ένα παιδικό κρεβάτι**
	miah <u>koo</u> • niah/<u>eh</u> • nah peh • THee • <u>koh</u> kreh • <u>vah</u> • tee

diapers [nappies]	**πάνες μωρού**
	ee pah • nehs moh • roo
formula	**βρεφικό γάλα**
	vreh • fee • koh ghah • lah
a pacifier [dummy]	**μια πιπίλα**
	miah pee • pee • lah
a playpen	**ένα παιδικό παρκάκι**
	eh • nah peh • THee • koh pahr • kah • kee
a stroller [pushchair]	**ένα καροτσάκι**
	eh • nah kah • roh • tsah • kee
Can I breastfeed the baby here?	**Μπορώ να θηλάσω το μωρό εδώ;**
	boh • roh nah thee • lah • soh toh moh • roh eh • THoh
Where can I change the baby?	**Πού μπορώ να αλλάξω το μωρό;**
	poo boh • roh nah ah • lah • ksoh toh moh • roh

For Dining with Children, see page 178.

BABYSITTING

Can you recommend a reliable babysitter?	**Μπορείτε να συστήσετε μια υπεύθυνη μπέιμπυ-σίτερ;**
	boh • ree • teh nah sees • tee • seh • teh miah ee • pehf • thee • nee beh • ee • bee see • tehr
What's the charge?	**Ποιό είναι το κόστος;**
	pioh ee • neh toh kohs • tohs
I'll pick them up at...	**Θα τα πάρω στις...**
	thah tah pah • roh stees...
I can be reached at...	**Θα με βρείτε στο...**
	thah meh vree • teh stoh...

SAFE TRAVEL

EMERGENCIES

NEED TO KNOW

Help!	**Βοήθεια!**
	voh • ee • thee • ah
Go away!	**Φύγετε!**
	fee • yeh • teh
Stop, thief!	**Σταματήστε τον κλέφτη!**
	stah • mah • tees teh tohn klehf • tee
Get a doctor!	**Φωνάξτε ένα γιατρό!**
	foh • nahks • teh eh • nah yaht • roh
Fire!	**Φωτιά!**
	foh • tiah
I'm lost.	**Έχω χαθεί.**
	eh • khoh khah • thee
Can you help me?	**Μπορείτε να με βοηθήσετε;**
	boh • ree • teh nah meh
	voh • ee • thee • seh • the

YOU MAY HEAR...

Παρακαλώ συμπληρώστε αυτό το έντυπο.
pah • rah • kah • loh
sehm • blee • rohs • teh
ahf • toh toh ehn • tee • poh

Please fill
out this form.

Την ταυτότητά σας, παρακαλώ.
teen tahf • toh • tee • tah sahs
pah • rah • kah • loh

Your identification,
please.

Πότε/Πού έγινε;
poh • teh/poo eh • yee • neh

When/Where did it
happen?

Πώς είναι εμφανισιακά;
pohs ee • neh
ehm • fah • nee • see • ah • kah

What does he/she
look like?

In an emergency, dial: **100** for the police, **199** for the
fire brigade and **166** for the ambulance. Or you can
also dial the European SOS number: **112**

POLICE

NEED TO KNOW

Call the police!	**Φωνάξτε την αστυνομία!** _foh • <u>nahks</u> • teh teen_ _ahs • tee • noh • <u>mee</u> • ah_
Where's the nearest police station?	**Πού είναι το κοντινότερο αστυνομικό τμήμα;** _poo <u>ee</u> • neh toh_ _kohn • dee • <u>noh</u> • teh • roh_ _ahs • tee • noh • mee • <u>koh</u> <u>tmee</u> • mah_
There has been an accident.	**Έγινε ένα ατύχημα.** _<u>eh</u> • yee • neh eh • nah_ _ah • <u>tee</u> • khee • mah_
My child is missing.	**Λείπει το παιδί μου.** _<u>lee</u> • pee toh peh • <u>THee</u> moo_
I need…	**Χρειάζομαι…** _khree • <u>ah</u> • zoh • meh…_
an interpreter	**έναν διερμηνέα** _<u>eh</u> • nahn THee • ehr • mee • <u>neh</u> • ah_
I need…	**Χρειάζομαι…** _khree • <u>ah</u> • zoh • meh…_
to contact my lawyer	**να επικοινωνήσω με τον δικηγόρο μου** _nah eh • pee • kee • noh • <u>nee</u> • soh meh_ _tohn THee • kee • <u>ghoh</u> • roh moo_
to make a phone call	**να κάνω ένα τηλέφωνο** _nah <u>kah</u> • noh eh • nah_ _tee • <u>leh</u> • foh • noh_
I'm innocent.	**Είμαι αθώος** m /**αθώα** f. _ee • meh ah • <u>thoh</u> • ohs/ah • <u>thoh</u> • ah_

CRIME & LOST PROPERTY

I want to report…	**Θέλω να αναφέρω…**
	theh • loh nah ah nah • feh • roh…
a mugging	**μια ληστεία**
	miah lehs • tee • ah
a rape	**έναν βιασμό**
	eh • nahn vee • ahs • moh
a theft	**μια κλοπή**
	miah kloh • pee
I've been robbed/	**Με έκλεψαν/λήστεψαν.**
mugged.	*meh ehk • leh • psahn/lees • teh • psahn*
My…has/have	**Μου έκλεψαν…μου.**
been stolen.	*moo ehk • leh • psahn…moo*
I've lost my…	**Έχασα…**
	eh • khah • sah…
knapsack	**τον σάκκο**
	tohn sah • koh
bicycle	**το ποδήλατο**
	toh poh • THee • lah • toh
camera	**τη φωτογραφική μηχανή**
	tee foh • tohgh • rah • fee • kee
	mee • khah • nee
car	**το αυτοκίνητο**
	toh ahf • toh • kee • nee • toh
computer	**τον υπολογιστή**
	tohn ee • poh • loh • yees • tee
credit cards	**τις πιστωτικές κάρτες**
	tees pees • toh • tee • kehs kahr • tehs
jewelry	**τα κοσμήματα**
	tah kohs • mee • mah • tah
money	**τα χρήματα**
	tah khree • mah • tah
passport	**το διαβατήριο**
	toh THiah • vah • tee • ree • oh

purse	**την τσάντα**
	teen <u>tsahn</u> • dah
traveler's checks	**τις ταξιδιωτικές επιταγές**
	tees tah • ksee • THee • oh • tee • <u>kehs</u>
	eh • pee • tah • <u>yehs</u>
wallet	**το πορτοφόλι**
	toh pohr • toh • <u>foh</u> • lee
I need a police report.	**Θέλω να κάνω αναφορά στην αστυνομία.**
	<u>*theh*</u> • *loh nah <u>kah</u> • noh ah • nah • foh • <u>rah</u>*
	steen ah • stee • noh • <u>mee</u> • ah
Where is the British/ American/Irish embassy?	**Πού είναι η αγγλική/αμερικάνικη/ ιρλανδική πρεσβεία;**
	poo <u>ee</u> • neh ee ag • lee • <u>kee</u>
	ah • meh • ree • <u>kah</u> • nee • kee/
	eer • lahn • THee • <u>kee</u> preh • <u>svee</u> • ah

HEALTH

NEED TO KNOW

I'm sick [ill].	**Είμαι άρρωστος.**
	<u>ee</u> • meh <u>ah</u> • rohs • tohs
I need an English- speaking doctor.	**Χρειάζομαι έναν γιατρό που να μιλάει αγγλικά.**
	khree • <u>ah</u> • zoh • meh <u>eh</u> • nahn
	yaht • <u>roh</u> poo nah mee • <u>lah</u> • ee
	ang • lee • <u>kah</u>
It hurts here.	**Με πονάει εδώ.**
	meh poh • <u>nah</u> • ee eh • <u>THoh</u>
I have a stomachache.	**Έχω στομαχόπονο.**
	<u>eh</u> • khoh stoh • mah • <u>khoh</u> • poh • noh

FINDING A DOCTOR

Can you recommend a doctor/dentist?	**Μπορείτε να συστήσετε έναν γιατρό/ οδοντίατρο;**
	boh • <u>ree</u> • teh nah sees • <u>tee</u> • seh • the <u>eh</u> • nahn yaht • <u>roh</u>
	oh • THohn • <u>dee</u> • aht • roh
Could the doctor come to see me here?	**Μπορεί να έρθει να με δει εδώ ο γιατρός;**
	boh • <u>ree</u> nah ehr • thee nah meh THee eh • <u>THoh</u> oh yaht • <u>rohs</u>
I need an English-speaking doctor.	**Χρειάζομαι έναν γιατρό που να μιλάει αγγλικά.**
	khree • <u>ah</u> • zoh • meh eh • nahn yaht • <u>roh</u> poo nah mee • <u>lah</u> • ee ahng • lee • <u>kah</u>
What are the office hours?	**Ποιες ώρες δέχεται;**
	piehs <u>oh</u> • rehs THeh • kheh • teh
Can I make an appointment for...?	**Μπορώ να κλείσω ένα ραντεβού για...;**
	boh • <u>roh</u> nah klee • soh eh • nah rahn • deh • <u>voo</u> yah...
today	**σήμερα**
	<u>see</u> • meh • rah
tomorrow	**αύριο**
	<u>ahv</u> • ree • oh
as soon as possible	**όσο το δυνατό πιο σύντομα**
	<u>oh</u> • soh toh THee • nah • <u>toh</u> pioh seen • doh • mah
It's urgent.	**Είναι επείγον.**
	<u>ee</u> • neh eh • <u>pee</u> • ghohn

SYMPTOMS

I'm…	**Έχω…** _eh_ • khoh…
bleeding	**αιμορραγία** eh • moh • rah • _yee_ • ah
constipated	**δυσκοιλιότητα** THees • kee • lee • _oh_ • tee • tah
dizzy	**ζαλάδες** zah • _lah_ • THehs
nauseous	**ναυτία** nahf • _tee_ • ah
vomiting	**εμετούς** eh • meh • _toos_
It hurts here.	**Με πονάει εδώ.** meh poh • _nah_ • ee eh • _THoh_
I have…	**Έχω…** eh • khoh…
an allergic reaction	**αλλεργική αντίδραση** ah • lehr • yee • _kee_ ahn • _dee_ • THrah • see
a chest pain	**πόνο στο στήθος** _poh_ • noh stoh _stee_ • thohs
cramps	**κράμπες** _krah_ • behs
diarrhea	**διάρροια** THee • _ah_ • ree • ah
an earache	**πόνο στο αυτί** _poh_ • noh stoh ahf • _tee_
a fever	**πυρετό** pee • reh • _toh_
a pain	**πόνο** _poh_ • noh
a rash	**εξάνθημα** eh • _ksahn_ • thee • mah

a sprain	**διάστρεμμα**
	THee • <u>ahs</u> • treh • mah
some swelling	**πρήξιμο**
	<u>pree</u> • ksee • moh
a sore throat	**πονόλαιμο**
	poh • <u>noh</u> • leh • moh
a stomachache	**στομαχόπονο**
	stoh • mah • <u>khoh</u> • poh • noh
sunstroke	**ηλίαση**
	ee • <u>lee</u> • ah • see
I've been sick [ill] for...days.	**Αισθάνομαι άρρωστος εδώ και...ημέρες.**
	ehs • <u>thah</u> • noh • meh <u>ah</u> • rohs • tohs
	eh • <u>THoh</u> keh ee • <u>meh</u> • rehs

For Numbers, see page 20.

CONDITIONS

I'm...	**Έχω...**
	<u>eh</u> • khoh...
anemic	**αναιμία**
	ah • neh • <u>mee</u> • ah
asthmatic	**άσθμα**
	<u>ahs</u> • thmah
diabetic	**διαβήτη**
	THiah • <u>vee</u> • tee
epileptic	**επιληψία**
	eh • pee • lee • <u>psee</u> • ah
I'm allergic to antibiotics/ penicillin.	**Είμαι αλλεργικός στα αντιβιωτικά/στην πενικιλίνη.**
	<u>ee</u> • meh ah • lehr • yee • <u>kohs</u> stah
	ahn • dee • vee • oh • tee • <u>kah</u>/
	steen peh • nee • kee • <u>lee</u> • nee

YOU MAY HEAR...

Τι συμβαίνει;
tee seem • veh • nee

What's wrong?

Πού πονάει;
poo poh • nah • ee

Where does it hurt?

Πονάει εδώ;
poh • nah • ee eh • THoh

Does it hurt here?

Παίρνετε άλλα φάρμακα;
pehr • neh • teh ah • lah fahr • mah • kah

Are you taking any other medication?

Είστε αλλεργικός m **/αλλεργική** f **σε κάτι;**
ees • teh ah • lehr • yeek • ohs/ ah • lehr • yeek • ee seh kah • tee

Are you allergic to anything?

Ανοίξτε το στόμα σας.
ah • nee • ksteh toh stoh • mah sahs

Open your mouth.

Πάρτε μια βαθιά αναπνοή.
pahr • teh miah vah • thiah ah • nahp • noh • ee

Breathe deeply.

Βήξτε, παρακαλώ.
vee • ksteh, pah • rah • kah • loh

Cough, please.

Θέλω να πάτε στο νοσοκομείο.
theh • loh nah pah • teh stoh noh • soh • koh • mee • oh

I want you to go to the hospital.

I have arthritis/ (high/low) blood pressure.

Έχω αρθρίτιδα/(υψηλή/χαμηλή) πίεση.
eh • khoh ahr • three • tee • THah/ (ee • psee • lee/ khah • mee • lee) pee • eh • see

I have a heart condition.

Έχω πρόβλημα καρδιάς.
eh • khoh prohv • lee • mah kahrTH • yahs

I'm on...

Παίρνω...
pehr • noh...

TREATMENT

Do I need a prescription/medicine?	**Χρειάζομαι συνταγή/φάρμακο;** khree • _ah_ • zoh • meh see • ntah • _ghee_/ _fahr_ • mah • koh
Can you prescribe a generic drug [unbranded medication]?	**Μπορείτε να γράψετε ένα γένιο φάρμακο;** boh • _ree_ • teh nah _ghrah_ • pseh • teh _eh_ • nah _fahr_ • mah • koh
Where can I get it?	**Από πού μπορώ να το πάρω;** ah • _poh_ poo boh • _roh_ nah toh _pah_ • roh

For Dietary Requirements, see page 176.

HOSPITAL

Please notify my family.	**Παρακαλώ ειδοποιήστε την οικογένειά μου.** pah • rah • kah • _loh_ ee • THoh • pee • _ees_ • teh teen ee • koh • _yeh_ • nee • ah moo
I'm in pain.	**Πονάω.** poh • _nah_ • oh
I need a doctor/nurse.	**Χρειάζομαι έναν γιατρό/μια νοσοκόμα.** khree • _ah_ • zoh • meh eh • nahn yaht • _roh_/ miah noh • soh • _koh_ • mah
When are visiting hours?	**Ποιες είναι οι ώρες επισκεπτηρίου;** pee • _ehs ee_ • neh ee _oh_ • rehs eh • pees • kehp • tee • _ree_ • oo
I'm visiting…	**Επισκέπτομαι…** eh • pees • _kehp_ • toh • meh…

DENTIST

I've broken a tooth.	**Έσπασα ένα δόντι.** _ehs_ • _pah_ • sah eh • nah _THohn_ • dee
I'm lost a filling.	**Μου έφυγε ένα σφράγισμα.** moo _eh_ • fee • gheh _eh_ • nah _sfrah_ • yees • mah
This tooth hurts.	**Αυτό το δόντι με πονάει.** ahf • _toh_ toh _THohn_ • dee meh poh • _nah_ • ee
Can you fix this denture?	**Μπορείτε να φτιάξετε αυτή την τεχνητή οδοντοστοιχία;** boh • _ree_ • teh nah ftee • _ah_ • kseh • teh ahf • _tee_ teen tehkh • nee • _tee_ oh • THohn • dohs • tee • _khee_ • ah

GYNECOLOGIST

I have menstrual cramps/a vaginal infection.	**Έχω πόνους περιόδου/κολπική μόλυνση.** eh • khoh poh • noos peh • ree • _oh_ • THoo/ kohl • pee • _kee_ _moh_ • leen • see
I missed my period.	**Έχω καθυστέρηση.** eh • khoh kah • thees • _teh_ • ree • see
I'm on the Pill.	**Παίρνω αντισυλληπτικό χάπι.** _pehr_ • noh ahn • dee • see • leep • tee • _koh_ khah • pee
I'm (…months) pregnant.	**Είμαι (…μηνών) έγκυος.** _ee_ • meh (…mee • _nohn_) eh • gee • ohs
I'm (not) pregnant.	**(Δεν) Είμαι έγκυος.** (THehn) _ee_ • meh ehn • gee • ohs
I haven't had my period for…months.	**Δεν έχω περίοδο εδώ και…μήνες.** THehn eh • khoh peh • _ree_ • oh • THoh eh • _THoh_ keh…mee • nehs

For Numbers, see page 20.

OPTICIAN

I've lost…	**Έχασα…**
	eh • khah • sah…
a contact lens	**έναν φακό επαφής**
	eh • nahn fah • koh eh • pah • fees
my glasses	**τα γυαλιά μου**
	tah yah • lee • ah moo
a lens	**έναν φακό**
	eh • nahn fah • koh

PAYMENT & INSURANCE

How much?	**Πόσο;**
	poh • soh
Can I pay by credit card?	**Μπορώ να πληρώσω με αυτή την πιστωτική κάρτα;**
	boh • roh nah plee • roh • soh meh ahf • tee teen pees • toh • tee • kee kahr • tah
I have insurance.	**Έχω ασφάλεια.**
	eh • khoh ahs • fah • lee • ah
Can I have a receipt for my insurance?	**Μπορώ να έχω μια απόδειξη για την ασφάλεια υγείας μου;**
	boh • roh nah eh • khoh miah ah • poh • THee • ksee yah teen ahs • fah • lee • ah ee • yee • ahs moo

For Money, see page 33

PHARMACY

NEED TO KNOW

Where's the nearest pharmacy?	**Πού είναι το κοντινότερο φαρμακείο;**
	poo ee • neh toh kohn • dee • noh • teh • roh fahr • mah • kee • oh
What time does the pharmacy [chemist] open/close?	**Τι ώρα ανοίγει/κλείνει το φαρμακείο;**
	tee oh • rah ah • nee • yee/klee • nee toh fahr • mah • kee • oh
What would you recommend for...?	**Τι συνιστάτε για...;**
	tee see • nees • tah • teh yah...
How much should I take?	**Πόσο πρέπει να πάρω;**
	poh • soh preh • pee nah pah • roh
Can you fill [make up] this prescription for me?	**Μπορείτε να μου φτιάξετε αυτή τη συνταγή;**
	boh • ree • teh nah moo ftiah • kseh • teh ahf • tee tee seen • dah • yee
I'm allergic to...	**Είμαι αλλεργικός** *m/***αλλεργική** *f* **σε ...**
	ee • meh ah • lehr • yeek • ohs/ ah • lehr • yeek • ee seh...

Many medications that are prescription-only in other countries can be bought over the counter in Greece. Pharmacies are open during normal working hours and on a rotating basis at all other times, so that there will always be one open 24 hours a day in any given area. Read the list on display in all pharmacy windows to find the one nearest to you.

WHAT TO TAKE

How much should I take?	**Πόσο πρέπει να πάρω;**
	poh • soh _preh_ • pee nah _pah_ • roh
How many times a day should I take it?	**Πόσες φορές την ημέρα πρέπει να το παίρνω;**
	poh • sehs foh • _rehs_ teen ee • _meh_ • rah _preh_ • pee nah toh _pehr_ • noh
Is it suitable for children?	**Είναι κατάλληλο για παιδιά;**
	ee • neh kah • _tah_ • lee • loh yah peh • _THyah_
I'm taking…	**Παίρνω…**
	pehr • noh…
Are there side effects?	**Έχει παρενέργειες;**
	eh • khee pah • reh • _nehr_ • yee • ehs
I'd like some medicine for…	**Θα ήθελα ένα φάρμακο για…**
	thah _ee_ • theh • lah eh • nah _fahr_ • mah • koh yah…
a cold	**το κρυολόγημα**
	toh kree • oh • _loh_ • yee • mah
a cough	**το βήχα**
	toh _vee_ • khah
diarrhea	**τη διάρροια**
	tee THee • _ah_ • ree • ah
a headache	**πονοκέφαλο**
	poh • noh • _keh_ • fah • loh
hay fever	**την αλλεργία σε γύρη**
	teen ah • lehr • _yee_ • ah seh _yee_ • ree
insect bites	**το τσίμπημα από έντομο**
	toh _tseem_ • bee • mah ah • _poh_ ehn • doh • moh
motion sickness	**τη ναυτία**
	tee nahf • _tee_ • ah
a sore throat	**τον πονόλαιμο**
	tohn poh • _noh_ • leh • moh

sunburn	**τα εγκαύματα από τον ήλιο**
	tah eh • <u>gkahv</u> • mah • tah ahpoh tohn
	<u>ee</u> • lioh
a toothache	**πονόδοντο**
	poh • <u>noh</u> • THoh • doh
an upset stomach	**το στομαχόπονο**
	toh stoh • mah • <u>khoh</u> • poh • noh

YOU MAY SEE...

ΧΑΠΙ(Α)	tablet(s)
<u>khah</u> • pee(ah)	
ΣΤΑΓΟΝΕΣ	drops
stah • <u>ghoh</u> • nehs	
ΠΡΙΝ/ΜΕΤΑ/ΜΕ ΤΟ ΓΕΥΜΑ	before/after/with
preen/me • <u>tah</u>/meh toh <u>yehv</u> • mah	meals
ΜΕ ΑΔΕΙΟ ΣΤΟΜΑΧΙ	on an empty
meh <u>ah</u> • THioh stoh • <u>mah</u> • khee	stomach
ΜΟΝΟ ΓΙΑ ΕΞΩΤΕΡΙΚΗ ΧΡΗΣΗ	for external use
<u>moh</u> • noh ya eh • ksoh • teh • ree • <u>kee</u> <u>khree</u> • see	only
ΜΙΑ/ΔΥΟ/ΤΡΕΙΣ ΦΟΡΕΣ ΤΗΝ ΗΜΕΡΑ	once/twice/three times a day
miah/<u>ee</u> • oh/trees foh • <u>rehs</u> teen ee • <u>meh</u> • rah	

BASIC SUPPLIES

I'd like...	**Θα ήθελα...**
	thah <u>ee</u> • theh • lah...
acetaminophen	**παρακεταμόλη**
[paracetamol]	*pah • rah • keh • tah • <u>moh</u> • lee*

antiseptic cream	**μια αντισηπτική κρέμα**
	miah ahn • dee • seep • tee • kee kreh • mah
aspirin	**ασπιρίνη**
	ahs • pee • ree • nee
bandages	**επιδέσμους**
	eh • pee • THehz • moos
a comb	**μια χτένα**
	miah khteh • nah
condoms	**προφυλακτικά**
	proh • fee • lahk • tee • kah
contact lens	**ένα υγρό καθαρισμού φακών επαφής**
solution	*eegh • roh kah • thah • rees • moo*
	fah • kohn eh • pah • fees
deodorant	**ένα αποσμητικό**
	eh • nah ah • pohz • mee • tee • koh
a hairbrush	**μια βούρτσα**
	miah voor • tsah
hair spray	**μια λακ**
	miah lahk
ibuprofen	**ιμπουπροφέν**
	ee • boo • proh • fehn
insect repellent	**εντομοαπωθητικό**
	ehn • doh • moh • ah • poh • thee • tee • koh
a nail file	**μια λίμα για τα νύχια**
	miah lee • mah yah tah nee • khiah
a (disposable)	**ένα ξυραφάκι (μιας χρήσης)**
razor	*eh • nah ksee • rah • fah • kee (miahs*
	khree • sees)
razor blades	**ξυραφάκια**
	ksee • rah • fah • kiah
sanitary napkins	**σερβιέτες**
[towels]	*sehr • vee • eh • tehs*
shampoo/	**σαμπουάν/γαλάκτωμα για τα μαλλιά**
conditioner	*sahm • poo • ahn/ghah • lahk • toh • mah*
	yah tah mah • liah

soap	**ένα σαπούνι**
	eh • nah sah • poo • nee
I'd like…	**Θα ήθελα…**
	thah ee • theh • lah…
sunscreen	**αντιλιακό**
	ahn • dee • ee • lee • ah • koh
tampons	**ταμπόν**
	tahm • bohn
tissues	**χαρτομάντηλα**
	khahr • toh • mahn • dee • lah
toilet paper	**χαρτί υγείας**
	khahr • tee ee • yee • ahs
a toothbrush	**οδοντόβουρτσα**
	oh • THoh • ndoh • voor • tsah
toothpaste	**μια οδοντόπαστα**
	miah oh • THohn • doh • pah • stah

For Baby Essentials, see page 142.

CHILD HEALTH & EMERGENCY

Can you recommend a pediatrician?	**Μπορείτε να συστήσετε έναν παιδίατρο;**
	boh • ree • teh nah sees • tee • seh • teh eh • nahn peh • THee • aht • roh
My child is allergic to…	**Το παιδί μου είναι αλλεργικό σε…**
	toh peh • THee moo ee • neh ah • lehr • ghee • koh seh…
My child is missing.	**Λείπει το παιδί μου.**
	lee • pee toh peh • THee moo
Have you seen a boy/girl?	**Είδατε ένα αγόρι/κορίτσι;**
	ee • THah • the eh • nah ah • ghoh • ree/ koh • ree • tsee

For Police, see page 148.

DISABLED TRAVELERS

NEED TO KNOW

Is there…?	**Υπάρχει…;**
	ee • <u>pahr</u> • khee…
access for the disabled	**πρόσβαση για άτομα με ειδικές ανάγκες**
	<u>prohz</u> • vah • see yah <u>ah</u> • toh • mah meh ee • THee • <u>kehs</u> ah • <u>nahn</u> • gehs
a wheelchair ramp	**ράμπα για αναπηρικό καρότσι**
	<u>rahm</u> • bah yah ah • nah • pee • ree • <u>koh</u> kah • <u>roh</u> • tsee
a disabled-accessible toilet	**προσβάσιμη τουαλέτα για ανάπηρους**
	prohs • <u>vah</u> • see • mee too • ah • <u>leh</u> • tah yah ah • <u>nah</u> • pee • roos
I need…	**Χρειάζομαι…**
	khree • <u>ah</u> • zoh • meh…
assistance	**βοήθεια**
	voh • <u>ee</u> • thiah
an elevator [lift]	**ασανσέρ**
	ah • sahn • <u>sehr</u>
a ground-floor room	**ισόγειο**
	ee • <u>soh</u> • yee • oh

ASKING FOR ASSISTANCE

I'm disabled.	**Είμαι ανάπηρος.**
	ee • meh ah • <u>nah</u> • pee • rohs
I'm deaf.	**Είμαι κουφός.**
	<u>ee</u> • meh koo • <u>fohs</u>
I'm visually/ hearing impaired.	**Έχω προβλήματα όρασης/ακοής.**
	<u>eh</u> • khoh prohv • <u>lee</u> • mah • tah
	<u>oh</u> • rah • sees/ah • koh • <u>ees</u>
I'm unable to walk far/use the stairs.	**Δεν μπορώ να περπατήσω/χρησιμοποιήσω τις σκάλες.**
	thehn boh • <u>roh</u> nah pehr • pah • <u>tee</u> • soh/ khree • see • moh • pee <u>ee</u> • soh tees <u>skah</u> • lehs
Please speak louder.	**Μιλήστε πιο δυνατά.**
	mee • <u>lee</u> • steh pioh THee • nah • <u>tah</u>
Can I bring my wheelchair?	**Μπορώ να φέρω την αναπηρική μου καρέκλα;**
	boh • <u>roh</u> nah feh • roh teen ah • nah • pee • ree • <u>kee</u> moo kah • <u>rehk</u> • lah

Are guide dogs permitted?	**Επιτρέπονται οι σκύλοι οδηγοί;**
	eh • peet • reh • pohn • deh ee skee • lee oh • THee • ghee
Can you help me?	**Μπορείτε να με βοηθήσετε;**
	boh • ree • teh nah meh voh • ee • thee • seh • teh
Please open/hold the door.	**Παρακαλώ ανοίξτε/κρατείστε την πόρτα.**
	pah • rah • kah • loh ah • nee • ksteh/ krah • tee • steh teen pohr • tah

For Emergencies, see page 146.

FOOD

EATING OUT

NEED TO KNOW

Can you recommend a good restaurant/ bar?	**Μπορείτε να συστήσετε ένα καλό εστιατόριο/μπαρ;**
	boh • <u>ree</u> • teh nah sees • <u>tee</u> • seh • teh eh • nah kah • <u>loh</u> ehs • <u>tee</u> • ah • <u>toh</u> • ree • oh/bahr
Is there a traditional Greek/ an inexpensive restaurant near here?	**Υπάρχει κανένα ελληνικό/φθηνό εστιατόριο εδώ κοντά;**
	ee • <u>pahr</u> • khee kah • <u>neh</u> • nah eh • lee • nee • <u>koh</u>/fthee • <u>noh</u> ehs • <u>tee</u> • ah • <u>toh</u> • ree • oh eh • THoh kohn • <u>dah</u>
A table for..., please.	**Ένα τραπέζι για..., παρακαλώ.**
	<u>eh</u> • nah trah • <u>peh</u> • zee yah... pah • rah • kah • <u>loh</u>
Could we sit...?	**Μπορούμε να καθήσουμε...;**
	boh • <u>roo</u> • meh nah kah • <u>thee</u> • soo • meh...
here/there	**εδώ/εκεί**
	eh • <u>THoh</u>/eh • <u>kee</u>
outside	**έξω**
	<u>eh</u> • ksoh
in a non-smoking area	**σε έναν χώρο για μη καπνίζοντες**
	seh <u>eh</u> • nahn <u>khoh</u> • roh yah mee kahp • <u>nee</u> • zohn • dehs
I'm waiting for someone.	**Περιμένω κάποιον.**
	peh • ree • <u>meh</u> • noh <u>kah</u> • piohn
Where are the toilets?	**Πού είναι η τουαλέτα;**
	poo <u>ee</u> • neh ee too • ah • <u>leh</u> • tah

A menu, please.	**Έναν κατάλογο, παρακαλώ.**
	eh • nahn kah • tah • loh • ghoh
	pah • rah • kah • loh
What do you recommend?	**Τι προτείνετε;**
	tee proh • tee • neh • the
I'd like…	**Θα ήθελα…**
	thah ee • theh • lah…
Some more…, please.	**Λίγο ακόμη…, παρακαλώ.**
	lee • ghoh ah • koh • mee…
	pah • rah • kah • loh
Enjoy your meal!	**Καλή όρεξη!**
	kah • lee oh • reh • ksee
The check [bill], please.	**Τον λογαριασμό, παρακαλώ.**
	tohn loh • ghah • riahs • moh
	pah • rah • kah • loh
Is service included?	**Συμπεριλαμβάνεται και το φιλοδώρημα;**
	seem • beh • ree • lahm • vah • neh • teh
	keh toh fee • loh • THoh • ree • mah
Can I pay by credit card?	**Μπορώ να πληρώσω με πιστωτική κάρτα;**
	boh • roh nah plee • roh • soh meh
	pee • stoh • tee • kee kahr • tah
Can I have a receipt?	**Μπορώ να έχω απόδειξη;**
	boh • roh nah eh • khoh
	ah • poh • THee • ksee
Thank you.	**Ευχαριστώ.**
	ehf • hah • ree • stoh

WHERE TO EAT

Can you recommend...?	**Μπορείτε να συστήσετε...;** *boh • ree • teh nah sees • tee • seh • teh...*
a restaurant	**ένα εστιατόριο** *eh • nah ehs • tee • ah • toh • ree • oh*
a bar	**ένα μπαρ** *eh • nah bahr*
a cafe	**μια καφετέρια** *miah kah • feh • teh • ree • ah*
a fast-food place	**ένα φάστ φουντ** *eh • nah fahst food*
a cheap restaurant	**ένα φτηνό εστιατόριο** *eh • nah ftee • noh* *eh • stee • ah • toh • ree • oh*
an expensive restaurant	**ένα ακριβό εστιατόριο** *eh • nah ah • kree • voh* *eh • stee • ah • toh • ree • oh*
a restaurant with a good view	**ένα εστιατόριο με καλή θέα** *eh • nah eh • stee • ah • toh • ree • oh* *meh kah • lee theh • ah*
an authentic/a non-touristy restaurant	**ένα αυθεντικό/όχι τουριστικό εστιατόριο** *eh • nah ahf • theh • ntee • koh/oh • khee* *too • ree • stee • koh* *eh • stee • ah • toh • ree • oh*
a souvlaki/gyros stand	**ένα σουβλατζίδικο** *eh • nah soov • la • jee • THee • koh*

RESERVATIONS & PREFERENCES

I'd like to reserve a table...	**Θα ήθελα να κλείσω ένα τραπέζι...** *thah ee • theh • lah nah klee • soh eh • nah* *trah • peh • zee...*
for two	**για δύο** *yah THee • oh*

YOU MAY HEAR...

Έχετε κάνει κράτηση;
eh • kheh • teh kah • nee krah • tee • see

Do you have a reservation?

Πόσα άτομα;
poh • sah ah • toh • mah

How many?

Καπνίζοντες ή μη καπνίζοντες;
kah • pnee • zohn • dehs ee mee
kah • pnee • zohn • dehs

Smoking or non-smoking?

Είσαστε έτοιμοι να παραγγείλετε;
ee • sahs • teh eh • tee • mee nah
pah • rah • gee • leh • teh

Are you ready to order?

Τι θα πάρετε;
tee thah pah • reh • teh

What would you like?

Σας συστήνω...
sahs sees • tee • noh...

I recommend...

Καλή όρεξη.
kah • lee oh • reh • ksee

Enjoy your meal.

for this evening	**γι' απόψε** *yah ah • poh • pseh*
for tomorrow at...	**για αύριο στις...** *yah ahv • ree • oh stees...*
A table for two, please.	**Ένα τραπέζι για δύο, παρακαλώ.** *eh • nah trah • peh • zee yah THee • oh pah • rah • kah • loh*
We have a reservation.	**Έχουμε κλείσει τραπέζι.** *eh • khoo • meh klee • see trah • peh • zee*
My name is...	**Λέγομαι...** *leh • ghoh • meh...*
Can we sit...?	**Μπορούμε να καθίσουμε...;** *boh • roo • meh nah kah • thee • soo • meh*

here/there	**εδώ/εκεί**
	eh • THoh/eh • kee
outside	**έξω**
	eh • ksoh
in a non-smoking area	**στους μη καπνίζοντες**
	stoos mee kah • pnee • zoh • dehs
by the window	**δίπλα στο παράθυρο**
	THee • plah stoh pah • rah • thee • roh
in the shade	**στη σκιά**
	stee skee • ah
in the sun	**στον ήλιο**
	stohn ee • lioh
Where is the restroom [toilet]?	**Πού είναι η τουαλέτα;**
	poo ee • neh ee
	too • ah • leh • tah

HOW TO ORDER

Waiter!/Waitress!	**Γκαρσόν!/Δεσποινίς!**
	gahr • sohn/THehs • pee • nees
We're ready to order.	**Είμαστε έτοιμοι να παραγγείλουμε.**
	ee • mahs • teh eh • tee • mee nah
	pah • rah • gee • loo • meh

May I see the wine list?	**Μπορώ να δω τον κατάλογο κρασιών;**
	boh • roh nah THoh tohn kah • tah • loh • ghoh krah • siohn
I'd like…	**Θα ήθελα…**
	thah ee • theh • lah…
a bottle of…	**ένα μπουκάλι…**
	eh • nah boo • kah • lee…
carafe of…	**μια καράφα…**
	miah kah • rah • fah…
glass of…	**ένα ποτήρι…**
	eh • nah poh • tee • ree…
The menu, please.	**Τον κατάλογο, παρακαλώ.**
	tohn kah • tah • loh • ghoh pah • rah • kah • loh
Do you have…?	**Έχετε…;**
	eh • kheh • teh…
a menu in English	**έναν κατάλογο στα Αγγλικά**
	eh • nahn kah • tah • loh • ghoh stah ahng • lee • kah
a fixed-price menu	**έναν κατάλογο με σταθερές τιμές**
	eh • nahn kah • tah • loh • ghoh meh stah • theh • rehs tee • mehs
a children's menu	**παιδικό μενού**
	peh • THee • koh meh • noo
What do you recommend?	**Τι προτείνετε;**
	tee proh • tee • neh • the
What's this?	**Τι είναι αυτό;**
	tee ee • neh ahf • toh
What's in it?	**Τι περιέχει;**
	tee peh • ree • eh • khee
Is it spicy?	**Είναι πικάντικο;**
	ee • neh pee • kahn • dee • koh
I'd like…	**Θα ήθελα…**
	thah ee • theh • lah…

More…, please.	**Λίγο ακόμη…, παρακαλώ.** _lee_ • ghoh ah • _koh_ • mee… pah • rah • kah • _loh_
With/Without…	**Με/Χωρίς…** meh/khoh • _rees_…
I can't have…	**Δεν πρέπει να φάω φαγητό που περιέχει…** THehn _preh_ • pee nah _fah_ • oh fah • yee • _toh_ poo peh • ree • _eh_ • khee…
rare	**με το αίμα του, σενιάν** meh toh _eh_ • mah too seh • _nian_
medium	**μέτρια ψημένο** _meht_ • ree • ah psee • _meh_ • noh
well-done	**καλοψημένο** kah • loh • psee • _meh_ • noh
It's to go [take away].	**Είναι για το σπίτι.** _ee_ • neh yah toh _spee_ • tee

For Drinks, see page 200.

YOU MAY SEE…

ΚΟΥΒΕΡ koo • _vehr_	cover charge
ΣΤΑΘΕΡΗ ΤΙΜΗ stah • theh • _ree_ tee • _mee_	fixed-price
ΚΑΤΑΛΟΓΟΣ kah • _tah_ • loh • ghohs	menu
ΜΕΝΟΥ ΤΗΣ ΗΜΕΡΑΣ meh • _noo_ tees ee • _meh_ • rahs	menu of the day
Η ΕΞΥΠΗΡΕΤΗΣΗ (ΔΕΝ) **ΠΕΡΙΛΑΜΒΑΝΕΤΑΙ** ee eh • ksee • pee _reh_ • tee • see (THehn) peh • ree • lahm • _vahn_ • eh • the	service (not) included
ΠΙΑΤΑ ΤΗΣ ΗΜΕΡΑΣ pee • _ah_ • tah tees ee • _meh_ • rahs	specials

COOKING METHODS

baked	**του φούρνου**
	too <u>foor</u> • noo
barbecued, grilled	**της σχάρας**
	tees <u>skhah</u> • rahs
boiled	**βραστό**
	vrah • <u>stoh</u>
braised	**κατσαρόλας**
	kah • tsah • <u>roh</u> • lahs
breaded	**πανέ**
	pah • <u>neh</u>
cooked in olive oil	**λαδερό**
	lah • THeh • <u>roh</u>
creamed	**με κρέμα γάλακτος**
	meh <u>kreh</u> • mah <u>ghah</u> • lah • ktohs
diced	**σε κύβους**
	seh <u>kee</u> • voos
filleted	**φιλέτο**
	fee • <u>leh</u> • toh
fried	**τηγανητό**
	tee • ghah • nee • <u>toh</u>
marinated	**μαρινάτο**
	mah • ree • <u>nah</u> • toh

poached	**ποσέ**
	poh • seh
roasted	**ψητό**
	psee • toh
sautéed	**σωτέ**
	soh • teh
smoked	**καπνιστό**
	kah • pnee • stoh
steamed	**στον ατμό**
	stohn aht • moh
stewed	**μαγειρευτό**
	mah • yee • rehf • toh
stewed in tomato sauce	**γιαχνί**
	yahkh • nee
stewed in wine	**κρασάτο**
	krah • sah • toh
stuffed	**γεμιστό**
	yeh • mees • toh

DIETARY REQUIREMENTS

I'm...	**Είμαι...**
	ee • meh...
diabetic	**διαβητικός** m /**διαβητική** f
	THee • ah • vee • teek • ohs/
	THee • ah • vee • tee • kee
lactose intolerant	**έχω ευαισθησία στα γαλακτοκομικά**
	eh • khoh eh • vehs • thee • see • ah stah
	ghah • lahk • toh • koh • mee • kah
vegetarian	**χορτοφάγος**
	khohr • toh • fah • ghohs
vegan	**χορτοφάγος**
	khoh • rtoh • fah • ghos

I'm allergic to...	**είμαι αλλεργικός** m /**αλλεργική** f **σε...**
	ee • meh ah • lehr • yeek • ohs/
	ah • lehr • yeek • ee seh...
I can't eat...	**Δεν πρέπει να φάω φαγητό που περιέχει...**
	THehn preh • pee nah fah • oh fah • yee • toh
	poo peh • ree • eh • khee...
dairy	**γαλακτοκομικά**
	ghah • lahk • toh • koh • mee • kah
gluten	**γλουτένη**
	ghloo • teh • nee
nuts	**ξηρούς καρπούς**
	ksee • roos kahr • poos
pork	**χοιρινό**
	khee • ree • noh
shellfish	**οστρακοειδή**
	ohs • trah • koh • ee • THee
I can't eat...	**Δεν πρέπει να φάω φαγητό που περιέχει...**
	THehn preh • pee nah fah • oh fah • yee • toh
	poo peh • ree • eh • khee...
spicy foods	**πικάντικα τρόφιμα**
	pee • kahn • dee • kah troh • fee • mah
wheat	**σιτάρι**
	see • tah • ree

Is it halal/kosher?	**Αυτό είναι χαλάλ/κόσερ;**
	ahf toh ee • neh khah • lahl/koh • sehr
Do you have...?	**Έχετε...;**
	eh • kheh • teh
skimmed milk	**αποβουτυρωμένο γάλα**
	ah • poh • voo • tee • roh • meh • noh ghah • lah
whole milk	**πλήρες γάλα**
	plee • rehs ghah • lah
soya milk	**γάλα σόγιας**
	ghah • lah soh • yahs

DINING WITH CHILDREN

Do you have a children's menu?	**Έχετε παιδικό μενού;**
	eh • kheh • teh peh • THee • koh meh • noo
Can we have a child's seat?	**Μπορούμε να έχουμε ένα παιδικό κάθισμα;**
	boh • roo • meh nah eh • khoo • meh eh • nah peh • THee • koh kah • theez • mah
Where can I feed/ change the baby?	**Πού μπορώ να ταΐσω/αλλάξω το μωρό;**
	poo boh • roh nah tah • ee • soh/ ah • lah • ksoh toh moh • roh
Can you warm this?	**Μπορείτε να το ζεστάνετε;**
	boh • ree • teh nah toh zehs • tah • neh • teh

For Traveling with Children, see page 140.

HOW TO COMPLAIN

How much longer will our food be?	**Πόση ώρα ακόμη θα κάνει το φαγητό;**
	poh • see oh • rah ah • koh • mee thah kah • nee toh fah • yee • toh
We can't wait any longer.	**Δεν μπορούμε να περιμένουμε άλλο.**
	THehn boh • roo • meh nah peh • ree • meh • noo • meh ah • loh

We're leaving.	**Φεύγουμε.** _fehv_ • ghoo • meh
That's not what I ordered.	**Δεν παρήγγειλα αυτό.** THehn pah • _ree_ • ngee • lah ahf • _toh_
I asked for…	**Ζήτησα…** _zee_ • tee • sah…
I can't eat this.	**Δεν μπορώ να το φάω.** THehn boh • _roh_ nah toh _fah_ • oh
This is too…	**Αυτό είναι πολύ…** ahf • _toh_ ee • neh poh • _lee_…
cold/hot	**κρύο/ζεστό** _kree_ • oh/zehs • _toh_
salty/spicy	**αλμυρό/πικάντικο** ahl • mee • _roh_/pee • _kahn_ • dee • koh
tough/bland	**σκληρό/ανάλατο** sklee • _roh_/ahl • mee • _roh_
This isn't clean/fresh.	**Αυτό δεν είναι καθαρό/φρέσκο.** ahf • _toh_ THehn _ee_ • neh kah • thah • _roh_/ frehs • _koh_

PAYING

The check [bill], please.	**Τον λογαριασμό, παρακαλώ.** tohn loh • ghahr • yahs • _moh_ pah • rah • kah • _loh_
We'd like to pay separately.	**Θα πληρώσουμε ξεχωριστά.** thah plee • _roh_ • soo • meh kseh • khoh • rees • _tah_
It's all together.	**Όλοι μαζί.** _oh_ • lee mah • _zee_
Is service included?	**Συμπεριλαμβάνεται και το σέρβις;** seem • beh • ree • lahm • _vah_ • neh • teh keh toh _sehr_ • vees
What's this amount for?	**Τί είναι αυτό το ποσό;** tee _ee_ • neh ahf • _toh_ toh poh • _soh_

I didn't have that. I had…	**Δεν πήρα αυτό. Πήρα…** _THehn <u>pee</u> • rah ahf • <u>toh</u> <u>pee</u> • rah…_
Can I pay by credit card?	**Μπορώ να πληρώσω με αυτήν την πιστωτική κάρτα;** _boh • <u>roh</u> nah plee • <u>roh</u> • soh meh ahf • <u>teen</u> teen pees • toh • tee • <u>kee kahr</u> • tah_
Can I have an itemized bill/ a receipt?	**Μπορώ να έχω έναν αναλυτικό λογαριασμό/μια αναλυτική απόδειξη;** _boh • <u>roh</u> nah <u>eh</u> • khoh <u>eh</u> • nahn ah • nah • lee • tee • <u>koh</u> loh • ghahr • yahs • <u>moh</u>/ miah ah • nah • lee • tee • <u>kee</u> ah • <u>poh</u> • ee • ksee_
That was a delicious meal.	**Ήταν ένα πολύ νόστιμο γεύμα.** _ee • tahn <u>eh</u> • nah poh • <u>lee</u> <u>nohs</u> • tee • moh yehv • mah_
I've already paid.	**Πλήρωσα ήδη.** _plee • roh • sah ee • THee_

For Numbers, see page 20.

In Greek restaurants the service charge is included in
the price. However, it is still customary to leave a little
extra if you are satisfied with the service.

MEALS & COOKING

Greeks rarely eat breakfast (**πρωινό**/proh • ee • _noh_).
They usually have a strong coffee with sugar (**βαρύ
γλυκό**/vah • _ree_ ghlee • _koh_) in the morning, followed by
another one between 10:00 and 11:00 a.m., maybe with a
pastry.
Lunch (**μεσημεριανό**/meh • see • meh • riah • _noh_) is the
main meal, although because of the summer heat some
Greeks eat lighter at lunchtime and have their main meal in
the evening. It is usually eaten from 2:00 to 3:00 p.m., but
most restaurants will serve it until 4:00 p.m.
Dinner (**βραδυνό**/vrah • THee • _noh_) is often eaten
late — normally at 9:00 or 10:00 p.m. It is not unusual
to find restaurants serving food until midnight or later.
Snacks can be bought at souvlaki stalls (**σουβλατζήδικα**/
soov • lah • _jee_ • THee • kah) or snack bars (**σνακ μπαρ**/
snahk bahr) until the early hours of the morning. You can
also buy tasty snacks, such as cheese pie (**τυρόπιτα**/
tee • _rhoh_ • pee • tah), at bakeries, which are open from very
early in the morning until the afternoon.

BREAKFAST

bacon	**μπεϊκον**
	beh • ee • kohn
bread	**ψωμί**
	psoh • _mee_
butter	**βούτυρο**
	voo • tee • roh
cereal (cold/hot)	**δημητριακά με (ζεστό/κρύο) γάλα**
	THee • meet • ree • ah • _kah_ meh
	(zehs • _toh_/_kree_ • oh) _ghah_ • lah

cheese	**τυρί**
	tee • <u>ree</u>
coffee/tea	**καφέ/τσάι**
	kah • <u>feh</u>/<u>tsah</u> • ee
cold cuts	**αλλαντικά**
[charcuterie]	ah • lah • ndee • <u>kah</u>
scrambled eggs	**ομελέτα**
	oh • meh • <u>leh</u> • tah
juice	**χυμός**
	khee • <u>mohs</u>
granola [muesli]	**μούσλι**
	<u>moo</u> • slee
honey	**μέλι**
	<u>meh</u> • lee
muffin	**μάφιν**
	<u>mah</u> • feen
milk	**γάλα**
	<u>ghah</u> • lah
oatmeal	**κουάκερ**
	koo • <u>ah</u> • kehr
omelet	**ομελέτα**
	oh • meh • <u>leh</u> • tah
roll	**ψωμάκι**
	psoh • <u>mah</u> • kee
sausage	**λουκάνικο**
	loo • <u>kah</u> • nee • koh
toast	**ψωμί φρυγανιά**
	psoh • <u>mee</u> free • ghah • <u>niah</u>
yogurt (with honey)	**γιαούρτι (με μέλι)**
	yah • <u>oor</u> • tee (meh <u>meh</u> • lee)

APPETIZERS

cold meat	**κρύο κρέας**
	<u>kree</u> • oh <u>kreh</u> • ahs

...eggs	**αυγά...**
	ahv • ghah...
soft-boiled	**μελάτα**
	meh • lah • tah
hard-boiled	**σφικτά**
	sfeekh • tah
fried	**τηγανητά μάτια**
	tee • ghah • nee • tah mah • tiah
poached	**ποσέ**
	poh • seh
fish roe dip	**ταραμοσαλάτα**
	tah • rah • moh • sah • lah • tah
fried baby squid	**καλαμαράκια**
	kah • lah • mah • rah • kiah
fried meatballs	**κεφτεδάκια**
	kef • teh • THah • kiah
fried whitebait	**μαρίδα τηγανητή**
	mah • ree • THah tee • ghah • nee • tee
herring (smoked)	**ρέγγα (καπνιστή)**
	rehn • gah (kahp • nees • tee)
olive (stuffed)	**ελιά (γεμιστή)**
	eh • liah (yeh • mees • tee)
cheese omelet	**ομελέτα με τυρί**
	oh • meh • leh • tah meh tee • ree
ham omelet	**ομελέτα με ζαμπόν**
	oh • meh • leh • tah meh zahm • bohn
pâté	**πατέ**
	pah • teh

Μεζέδες *(meh • zeh • dehs)*, appetizers, can be a meal alone. Greeks will often go out for a glass of **ούζο** *(oo • zoh)*, an anise-flavored liqueur, accompanied by appetizers.

spinach and feta in pastry dough	**σπανακόπιτα**
	spah • nah • koh • pee • tah
stuffed grape leaves	**ντολμαδάκι**
	dohl • mah • THah • kee
yogurt, garlic and cucumber dip	**τζατζίκι**
	jah • jee • kee

A traditional and very tasty egg dish in Greece is **στραπατσάδα** *(strah • pah • tsah • THah),* scrambled eggs with fresh tomato, but sometimes with other ingredients depending on the region. Another traditional method of using egg is in **αυγολέμονο** *(ahv • ghoh • leh • moh • noh)*: egg yolk and lemon are added to a sauce or soup. This sauce usually accompanies warm stuffed grape leaves and other vegetable dishes or stews.

SOUP

| bean soup with tomatoes and parsley | **φασολάδα** |
| | *fah • soh • lah • THah* |

chicken soup	**κοτόσουπα**
	koh • toh • soo • pah
chickpea soup	**ρεβύθια σούπα**
	reh • vee • thiah soo • pah
cracked wheat soup	**τραχανάς**
	trah • khah • nahs
fish soup thickened with egg and lemon	**ψαρόσουπα αυγολέμονο**
	psah • roh • soo • pah
	ahv • ghoh • leh • moh • noh
fish stew with tomatoes	**κακαβιά**
	kah • kahv • yah
lentil soup	**φακές σούπα**
	fah • kehs soo • pah
meat soup	**κρεατόσουπα**
	kreh • ah • toh • soo • pah
soup with rice, eggs and lemon juice	**σούπα αυγολέμονο**
	soo • pah ahv • ghoh • leh • moh • noh
tripe soup	**πατσάς**
	pah • tsahs
tahini (sesame paste) soup	**ταχινόσουπα**
	tah • khee • noh • soo • pah
tomato soup	**τοματόσουπα**
	toh • mah • toh • soo • pah
vegetable soup	**χορτόσουπα**
	khohr • toh • soo • pah

FISH & SEAFOOD

anchovy	**αντσούγια**
	ahn • joo • yahs
crab	**καβούρι**
	kah • voo • ree
cuttlefish	**σουπιά**
	soo • piah

eel	**χέλι**
	kheh • lee
fresh cod	**μπακαλιάρος**
	bah • kah • _liah_ • rohs
grouper	**σφυρίδα**
	sfee • _ree_ • THah
mullet	**κέφαλος**
	keh • fah • lohs
lobster	**αστακός**
	ahs • tah • _kohs_
marinated mullet,	**ψάρι μαρινάτο**
sole or mackerel	_psah_ • ree mah • ree • _nah_ • toh
mussels	**μύδι**
	mee • THee
octopus	**χταπόδι**
	khtah • _poh_ • THee
oyster	**στρείδι**
	stree • THee
red mullet	**μπαρμπούνι**
	bahr • _boo_ • nee
salted cod	**μπακαλιάρος παστός**
	bah • kah • _liah_ • rohs pahs • _tohs_
sardine	**σαρδέλα**
	sahr • _THeh_ • lah
shrimp [prawn]	**γαρίδα**
	ghah • ree • THah
sole	**γλώσσα**
	ghloh • sah
squid	**καλαμάρι**
	kah • lah • _mah_ • ree
swordfish	**ξιφίας**
	ksee • _fee_ • ahs
tuna	**τόννος**
	toh • nohs

MEAT & POULTRY

beef	**βοδινό**
	voh • THee • noh
beef or veal stewed with tomatoes and eggplant [aubergine]	**μελιτζανάτο**
	meh • lee • jah • nah • toh
brains	**μυαλό**
	miah • loh
Greek burger	**μπιφτέκι**
	beef • teh • kee
chicken	**κοτόπουλο**
	koh • toh • poo • loh
cutlet	**κοτολέτα**
	koh • toh • leh • tah
duck	**πάπια**
	pah • piah
fillet	**φιλέτο**
	fee • leh • toh
goat	**κατσικάκι**
	kah • tsee • kah • kee
goose	**χήνα**
	khee • nah

ham	**ζαμπόν**
	zahm • bohn
kidney	**νεφρό**
	neh • froh
lamb	**αρνί**
	ahr • nee
liver	**συκώτι**
	see • koh • tee
layers of eggplant [aubergine], meat and white sauce	**μουσακάς**
	moo • sah • kahs
meat with orzo pasta baked with tomatoes	**γιουβέτσι**
	yoo • veh • tsee
pheasant	**φασιανός**
	fah • siah • nohs
pork	**χοιρινό**
	khee • ree • noh
rabbit	**κουνέλι**
	koo • neh • lee
sausage	**λουκάνικο**
	loo • kah • nee • koh
skewered pork or lamb, cooked over charcoal	**κοντοσούβλι**
	koh • ndoh • soov • lee dohs
spiced lamb and potatoes baked in parchment or in filo pastry	**αρνάκι εξοχικό**
	ahr • nah • kee eh • ksoh • khee • koh
turkey	**γαλοπούλα**
	ghah • loh • poo • lah
veal	**μοσχάρι**
	mohs • khah • ree
veal/pork steak	**μπριζόλα μοσχαρίσια/χοιρινή**
	bree • zoh • lah mohs • khah • ree • siah/ khee • ree • nee

VEGETABLES & STAPLES

artichokes	**αγκινάρες**
	ahn • gkee • nah • rehs
asparagus	**σπαράγγια**
	spah • rahn • giah
bay leaf	**δαφνόφυλλο**
	THah • fnoh • fee • loh
basil	**βασιλικός**
	vah • see • lee • kohs
bread	**ψωμί**
	psoh • mee
broad beans	**κουκί**
	koo • kee
butter bean	**φασόλι γίγαντας**
	fah • soh • lee yee • ghahn • dahs
cabbage	**λάχανο**
	lah • khah • noh
carrot	**καρότο**
	kah • roh • toh
cauliflower	**κουνουπίδι**
	koo • noo • pee • THee
celery	**σέλερι**
	seh • leh • ree
cinnamon	**κανέλλα**
	kah • neh • lah
cucumber	**αγγούρι**
	ahn • goo • ree
dill	**άνηθος**
	ah • nee • thohs
eggplant [aubergine]	**μελιτζάνα**
	meh • lee • jah • nah
garlic	**σκόρδο**
	skohr • THoh

green bean	**φασολάκι**
	fah • soh • <u>lah</u> • kee
green peppers	**πιπεριές πράσινες**
	pee • pehr • <u>yehs</u> <u>prah</u> • see • nehs
leek	**πράσο**
	<u>prah</u> • soh
mastic	**μαστίχα**
	mahs • <u>tee</u> • khah
mint	**δυόσμος**
	THee • <u>ohz</u> • mohs
mushroom	**μανιτάρι**
	mah • nee • <u>tah</u> • ree
okra	**μπάμια**
	<u>bah</u> • miah
onion	**κρεμμύδι**
	kreh • <u>mee</u> • THee
oregano	**ρίγανη**
	<u>ree</u> • ghah • nee
parsley	**μαϊντανός**
	mah • ee • dah • <u>nohs</u>
pasta	**ζυμαρικά**
	zee • mah • ree • <u>kah</u>
peas	**αρακάς**
	ah • rah • <u>kahs</u>

peppers	**πιπεριές**
	pee • pehr • yehs
potato	**πατάτα**
	pah • tah • tah
red cabbage	**κόκκινο λάχανο**
	koh • kee • noh lah • khah • noh
rosemary	**δεντρολίβανο**
	THehn • droh • lee • vah • noh
sage	**φασκόμηλο**
	fahs • koh • mee • loh
spinach	**σπανάκι**
	spah • nah • kee
sugar	**ζάχαρη**
	zah • khah • ree
thyme	**θυμάρι**
	thee • mah • ree
toast	**ψωμί φρυγανιά**
	psoh • mee free • ghah • niah
tomato	**ντομάτα**
	ndoh • mah • tah
unleavened bread	**λαγάνα**
	lah • ghah • nah
zucchini [courgette]	**κολοκυθάκι**
	koh • loh • kee • thah • kee

FRUIT

apple	**μήλο**
	mee • loh
apricot	**βερύκοκο**
	veh • ree • koh • koh
banana	**μπανάνα**
	bah • nah • nah
cherry	**κεράσι**
	keh • rah • see

date	**χουρμάς**
	khoor • mahs
fig	**σύκο**
	see • koh
grape	**σταφύλι**
	stah • fee • lee
grapefruit	**γκρέιπφρουτ**
	greh • eep • froot
lemon	**λεμόνι**
	leh • moh • nee
melon	**πεπόνι**
	peh • poh • nee
orange	**πορτοκάλι**
	pohr • toh • kah • lee
peach	**ροδάκινο**
	roh • THah • kee • noh
pear	**αχλάδι**
	akh • lah • THee
plum	**δαμάσκηνο**
	THah • mahs • kee • noh
pineapple	**ανανάς**
	ah • nah • nahs
tangerine	**μανταρίνι**
	mahn • dah • ree • nee

| watermelon | **καρπούζι** |
| | *kahr • poo • zee* |

CHEESE

feta cheese	**φέτα**
	feh • tah
Gruyere cheese	**γραβιέρα**
	ghrah • vieh • rah
Kaseri, yellow cheese	**κασέρι**
	kah • seh • ree
cottage cheese	**τυρί κότατζ**
	tee • ree koh • tahtz

DESSERT

apple pie	**μηλόπιτα**
	mee • loh • pee • tah
baklava, flaky pastry with nut filling	**μπακλαβάς**
	bah • klah • vahs
candy [sweets]	**καραμέλα**
	kah • rah • meh • lah
caramel custard	**κρέμα καραμελέ**
	kreh • mah kah • rah • meh • leh

filo pastry filled with almonds, orange juice and cinnamon	**κοπεγχάγη** *koh • pehn • khah • ghee*
flaky pastry filled with custard and steeped in syrup	**γαλακτομπούρεκο** *ghah • lah • ktoh • boo • reh • koh*
fruit salad	**φρουτοσαλάτα** *froo • toh • sah • lah • tah*
halva, sweet sesame seed paste	**χαλβάς** *khahl • vahs*
ice cream	**παγωτό** *pah • ghoh • toh*
rice pudding	**ρυζόγαλο** *ree • zoh • ghah • loh*
shredded pastry roll filled with nuts and steeped in syrup	**καταΐφι** *kah • tah • ee • fee*
Turkish delight	**λουκούμι** *loo • koo • mee*
walnut cake	**καρυδόπιτα** *kah • ree • THoh • pee • tah*

SAUCES & CONDIMENTS

salt	**Αλάτι** *ah • lah • tee*
pepper	**Πιπέρι** *pee • peh • ree*
mustard	**Μουστάρδα** *moo • stahr • THah*
ketchup	**Κέτσαπ** *keh • tsahp*

ℹ

Large-scale supermarkets can be found on the outskirts of most towns; smaller supermarkets are located near city centers. There are several large chains, including: **ΑΒ Βασιλόπουλος** (<u>ahl</u> • fah <u>vee</u> • tah vah • see • <u>loh</u> • poo • lohs), **Dia** (<u>dee</u> • ah), **Champion** (<u>chahm</u> • pee • ohn), **ΣΚΛΑΒΕΝΙΤΗΣ** (sklah • veh • <u>nee</u> • tees) and **Spar** (spahr).

AT THE MARKET

Where are the trolleys/baskets?	**Πού είναι τα καροτσάκια/καλάθια;** poo <u>ee</u> • neh tah kah • roh • <u>tsah</u> • kiah/ kah • <u>lah</u> • thiah
Where is/are…?	**Πού είναι…;** poo <u>ee</u> • neh…
I'd like some of that/those.	**Θα ήθελα μερικά από αυτά/εκείνα.** thah <u>ee</u> • theh • lah meh • ree • <u>kah</u> ah • <u>poh</u> ahf • <u>tah</u>/eh • <u>kee</u> • nah
Can I taste it?	**Μπορώ να το δοκιμάσω;** boh • <u>roh</u> nah toh THoh • kee • <u>mah</u> • soh

Measurements in Europe are metric — and that applies to the weight of food too. If you tend to think in pounds and ounces, it's worth brushing up on what the metric equivalent is before you go shopping for fruit and veg in markets and supermarkets. Five hundred grams, or half a kilo, is a common quantity to order, and that converts to just over a pound (17.65 ounces, to be precise).

YOU MAY HEAR...

Μπορώ να σας βοηθήσω;
boh • roh nah sahs voh • ee • thee • soh

Can I help you?

Τι θα πάρετε;
tee thah pah • reh • teh

What would you like?

Τίποτε άλλο;
tee • poh • teh ah • loh

Anything else?

Αυτά είναι…ευρώ.
ahf • tah ee • neh… ehv • roh

That's…euros.

YOU MAY SEE...

ΑΝΑΛΩΣΗ ΚΑΤΑ	best
ΠΡΟΤΙΜΗΣΗ ΠΡΙΝ ΑΠΟ...	before...
ah • nah • loh • see kah • tah	
proh • tee • mee • see preen ah • poh	
ΘΕΡΜΙΔΕΣ	calories
thehr • mee • THehs	
ΧΩΡΙΣ ΛΙΠΑΡΑ	fat free
khoh • rees lee • pah • rah	
ΔΙΑΤΗΡΕΙΤΑΙ ΣΤΟ ΨΥΓΕΙΟ	keep refrigerated
THee • ah • tee • ree • teh stoh	
psee • yee • oh	
ΜΠΟΡΕΙ ΝΑ ΠΕΡΙΕΧΕΙ	may contain
ΙΧΝΗ ΑΠΟ...	traces of...
boh • ree nah peh • ree • eh • khee	
eekh • nee ah • poh...	
για φούρνο μικροκυμάτων	microwaveable
yah foo • rnoh	
mee • kroh • kee • mah • tohn	
πώληση μέχρι...	sell by...
poh • lee • see meh • khree	
κατάλληλο για χορτοφάγους	suitable for
kah • tah • lee • loh yah	vegetarians
khoh • rtoh • fah • ghoos	

I'd like...	**Θα ήθελα...**
	thah ee • theh • lah...
a kilo/half-kilo of...	**ένα/μισό κιλό...**
	eh • nah/mee • soh kee • loh...
a liter/half-liter of...	**ένα/μισό λίτρο...**
	eh • nah/mee • soh leet • roh...

a piece of…	**ένα κομμάτι…**
	eh • nah koh • mah • tee…
a slice of…	**μια φέτα…**
	miah feh • tah…
More/Less.	**Περισσότερο/Λιγότερο.**
	peh • ree • soh • teh • roh/
	lee • ghoh • teh • roh
How much?	**Πόσο;**
	poh • soh
Where do I pay?	**Πού πληρώνω;**
	poo plee • roh • noh
A bag, please.	**Μια σακούλα, παρακαλώ.**
	miah sah • koo • lah pah • rah • kah • loh
I'm being helped.	**Εξυπηρετούμαι.**
	eh • ksee • pee • reh • too • meh

For Money, see page 33.

IN THE KITCHEN

bottle opener	**τιρμπουσόν**
	teer • mboo • sohn
bowls	**τα μπωλ**
	tah bohl
can opener	**ανοιχτήρι**
	ah • neekh • tee • ree
corkscrew	**τιρμπουσόν**
	teer • boo • sohn
cups	**τα φλυτζάνια**
	tah flee • jah • niah
forks	**τα πηρούνια**
	tah pee • roo • niah
frying pan	**τηγάνι**
	tee • ghah • nee

glasses	**τα ποτήρια**
	tah poh • teer • yah
knives	**τα μαχαίρια**
	tah mah • khehr • yah
measuring cup/	**μεζούρα φλυτζάνι/κουτάλι**
spoon	*meh • zoo • rah*
	flee • jah • nee/koo • tah • lee
napkin	**χαρτοπετσέτα**
	khahr • toh • peh • tseh • tah
plates	**τα πιάτα**
	tah piah • tah
pot	**κανάτα**
	kah • nah • tah
saucepan	**κατσαρόλα**
	kah • tsah • roh • lah
spatula	**σπάτουλα**
	spah • too • lah
spoons	**κουτάλια**
	koo • tah • liah

For Domestic Items, see page 85.

DRINKS

NEED TO KNOW

May I see the wine list/drinks menu?	**Μπορώ να δω τον κατάλογο με τα κρασιά/ποτά;**
	boh • roh nah THoh tohn kah • tah • loh • ghoh meh tah krah • siah/poh • tah
What do you recommend?	**Τι συστήνετε;**
	tee see • stee • neh • the
I'd like a bottle/ glass of red/white wine.	**Θα ήθελα ένα μπουκάλι/ποτήρι κόκκινο/λευκό κρασί.**
	thah ee • theh • lah eh • nah boo • kah lee/poh • tee • ree koh • kee • noh/lehf • koh krah • see
The house wine, please.	**Το κρασί του καταστήματος, παρακαλώ.**
	toh krah • see too kah • tah • stee • mah • tohs pah • rah • kah • loh
Another bottle/ glass, please.	**Άλλο ένα μπουκάλι/ποτήρι, παρακαλώ.**
	ah • loh eh • nah boo • kah lee/ poh • tee • ree pah • rah • kah • loh
I'd like a local beer.	**Θα ήθελα μια τοπική μπύρα.**
	thah ee • theh • lah miah toh • pee • kee bee • rah
Let me buy you a drink.	**Να σασκεράσω ένα ποτό.**
	nah sahs keh • rah • soh eh • nah poh • toh
Cheers!	**Στην υγειά σας!**
	steen ee • ghiah sahs

A sparkling water.	**Ενα ανθρακούχο νερό** _eh • nah ahn • thrah • koo • khoh neh • roh_
A still water.	**Ενα νερό χωρίς ανθρακικό** _eh • nah neh • roh khoh • rees ahn • thrah • kee • koh_
Is the tap water safe to drink?	**Είναι το νερό βρύσης πόσιμο;** _ee • neh toh neh • roh vree • sees poh • see • moh_

The most popular drinks in the summer are **φραπέ** _(frah • peh)_, iced instant coffee shaken to produce a thick coffee froth, with or without milk and sugar, and **φρέντο** _(frehd • doh)_, iced espresso with or without milk, found at most coffee shops and bars. Freshly squeezed juices are also widely consumed. Tap water is drinkable almost everywhere, but if you prefer you can get **εμφιαλωμένο νερό** _(ehm • fee • ah • loh • meh • noh neh • roh)_, bottled water.

NON-ALCOHOLIC DRINKS

...coffee	**έναν καφέ...** _eh • nahn kah • feh..._
instant	**ένα Νεσκαφέ** _eh • nah nehs • kah • feh_
Greek	**ελληνικό** _eh • lee • nee • koh_
with cream/milk	**με κρέμα/γάλα** _meh kreh • mah/ghah • lah_
...juice	**χυμός...** _khee • mohs..._

apple	**μήλο**
	mee • loh
grapefruit	**γκρέιπφρουτ**
	greh • eep • froot
orange	**πορτοκάλι**
	poh • rtoh • _kah_ • lee
iced tea	**παγωμένο τσάι**
	pah • ghoh • _meh_ • noh _tsah_ • ee
tea with milk/ lemon	**τσάι με γάλα/λεμόνι**
	tsah • ee meh _ghah_ • lah/ leh • _moh_ • nee
mineral water	**μεταλλικό νερό**
	meh • tah • lee • _koh_ neh • _roh_
hot chocolate	**ζεστή σοκολάτα**
	zeh • _stee_ soh • koh • _lah_ • tah

YOU MAY HEAR...

Θέλετε κάτι να πιείτε;
theh • leh • teh _kah_ • tee
nah pee • _ee_ • teh

Can I get you a drink?

Με γάλα/ζάχαρη;
meh _ghah_ • lah/_zah_ • khah • ree

With milk/ sugar?

Νερό ανθρακούχο/χωρίς ανθρακικό;
neh • _roh_ ahn • thrah • _koo_ • khoh/
khoh • _rees_ ahn • thrah • kee • _koh_

Sparkling/Still water?

APERITIFS, COCKTAILS & LIQUEURS

Greek brandy	**Μεταξά**
	meh • tah • _ksah_
kumquat liqueur (Corfu)	**κουμ-κουάτ**
	koom • koo • _aht_

straight [neat]	**σκέτο**
	skeh • toh
on the rocks	**με πάγο**
	meh _pah_ • ghoh
ouzo	**ούζο**
	_oo_ • zoh

BEER

beer	**μπύρα**
	bee • rah
bottled	**εμφιαλωμένη**
	ehm • fee • ah • loh • _meh_ • nee
draft	**βαρελίσια**
	vah • reh • _lee_ • siah
light/dark	**ξανθή/μαύρη**
	ksahn • _thee_/_mahv_ • ree
local/imported	**τοπικό/εισαγόμενο**
	toh • pee • _koh_/
	ee • sah • _ghoh_ • meh • noh

WINE

blush [rosé]	**ροζέ**
	roh • _zeh_
chilled	**παγωμένο**
	pah • ghoh • _meh_ • noh
dry	**ξηρό**
	ksee • _roh_
red	**μπουκάλι κόκκινο**
	boo • _kah_ • lee koh • kee • noh
sweet	**γλυκό**
	ghlee • _koh_
white	**λευκό**
	lehf • koh
wine	**κρασί**
	krah • _see_

A typical Greek wine that takes some getting used to is **ρετσίνα** (reh • _tsee_ • nah), a white wine containing pine resin. Wine is usually produced and consumed locally – a restaurant owner will often bring you a carafe of his or her very own wine if you ask for **κρασί βαρελίσιο** (krah • _see_ vah • reh • _lee_ • sioh), the house wine.

ON THE MENU

anchovy	**αντσούγια** _ahn • joo • yah_
apple	**μήλο** _mee • loh_
apple pie	**μηλόπιτα** _mee • loh • pee • tah_
apricot	**βερίκοκο** _veh • ree • koh • koh_
artichoke	**αγκινάρα** _ahn • gkee • nah • rah_
artificial sweetener	**ζαχαρίνη** _zah • khah • ree • nee_
asparagus	**σπαράγγι** _spah • rahn • gee_
bacon	**μπέικον** _beh • ee • kohn_
baklava, flaky pastry with nut filling	**μπακλαβάς** _bah • klah • vahs_
banana	**μπανάνα** _bah • nah • nah_
basil	**βασιλικός** _vah • see • lee • kohs_

bay leaf	**δαφνόφυλλο**
	THah • fnoh • fee • loh
bean soup with tomatoes and parsley	**φασολάδα**
	fah • soh • lah • THah
beef	**βοδινό**
	voh • THee • noh
beef or veal stewed with tomatoes and eggplant [aubergine]	**μελιτζανάτο**
	meh • lee • jah • nah • toh
beer	**μπίρα**
	bee • rah
brains	**μυαλό**
	miah • loh
bread	**ψωμί**
	psoh • mee
bread roll	**ψωμάκι**
	psoh • mah • kee
broad bean	**κουκί**
	koo • kee
butter	**βούτυρο**
	voo • tee • roh
butter bean	**φασόλι γίγαντας**
	fah • soh • lee yee • ghahn • dahs
cabbage	**λάχανο**
	lah • khah • noh
candy [sweets]	**καραμέλα**
	kah • rah • meh • lah
caramel custard	**κρέμα καραμελέ**
	kreh • mah kah • rah • meh • leh
carrot	**καρότο**
	kah • roh • toh
cauliflower	**κουνουπίδι**
	koo • noo • pee • THee

celery	**σέλερι**
	seh • leh • ree
cereal (cold/hot)	**δημητριακά με (ζεστό/κρύο) γάλα**
	THee • meet • ree • ah • _kah_ meh
	(zehs • _toh_/_kree_ • oh) _ghah_ • lah
cheese	**τυρί**
	tee • _ree_
cheese omelet	**ομελέττα με τυρί**
	oh • meh • _leh_ • tah meh tee • _ree_
cherry	**κεράσι**
	keh • _rah_ • see
chicken	**κοτόπουλο**
	koh • _toh_ • poo • loh
chicken soup	**κοτόσουπα**
	koh • _toh_ • soo • pah
chickpea soup	**ρεβύθια σούπα**
	reh • _vee_ • thiah soo • pah
chilled	**παγωμένο**
	pah • ghoh • _meh_ • noh
cinnamon	**κανέλλα**
	kah • _neh_ • lah
club soda	**σόδα**
	soh • THah

coffee	**καφέ**
	kah • fehs
cold cuts	**αλλαντικά**
[charcuterie]	*ah • lah • ndee • kah*
cold meat	**κρύο κρέας**
	kree • oh kreh • ahs
cottage cheese	**τυρί κότατζ**
	tee • ree koh • tahtz
crab	**καβούρι**
	kah • voo • ree
cracked wheat	**τραχανάς**
soup	*trah • khah • nahs*
cream	**κρέμα**
	kreh • mah
cucumber	**αγγούρι**
	ahn • goo • ree
cutlet	**κοτολέτα**
	koh • toh • leh • tah
cuttlefish	**σουπιά**
	soo • piah
date	**χουρμάς**
	khoor • mahs
dill	**άνηθος**
	ah • nee • thohs
draft	**βαρελίσια**
	vah • reh • lee • siah
duck	**πάπια**
	pah • piah
eel	**χέλι**
	kheh • lee
egg	**αυγό**
	ahv • ghoh
eggplant	**μελιτζάνα**
[aubergine]	*meh • lee • jah • nah*

fig	**σύκο** _see_ • koh
fillet	**φιλέτο** fee • _leh_ • toh
filo pastry filled with almonds, orange juice and cinnamon	**κοπεγχάγη** koh • pehn • _khah_ • ghee
filo pastry filled with custard and steeped in syrup	**γαλακτομπούρεκο** ghah • lah • ktoh • _boo_ • reh • koh
fish	**ψάρι** _psah_ • ree
fish soup thickened with egg and lemon	**ψαρόσουπα αυγολέμονο** psah • _roh_ • soo • pah ahv • ghoh • _leh_ • moh • noh
fish stew with tomatoes	**κακαβιά** kah • kahv • _yah_
fresh cod	**μπακαλιάρος** bah • kah • _liah_ • rohs
fried baby squid	**καλαμαράκια** kah • lah • mah • _rah_ • kiah
fried meatballs	**κεφτεδάκια** kef • teh • _THah_ • kiah
fried whitebait	**μαρίδα τηγανητή** mah • _ree_ • THah tee • ghah • nee • _tee_
fruit	**φρούτο** _froo_ • toh
fruit juice	**χυμός φρούτων** khee • _mohs_ _froo_ • tohn
fruit salad	**φρουτοσαλάτα** froo • toh • sah • _lah_ • tah
garlic	**σκόρδο** _skohr_ • THoh
goat	**κατσικάκι** kah • tsee • _kah_ • kee

goose	**χήνα**
	khee • nah
granola [muesli]	**μούσλι**
	moos • lee
grape	**σταφύλι**
	stah • _fee_ • lee
grapefruit	**γκρέιπφρουτ**
	greh • eep • froot
Greek brandy	**Μεταξά**
	meh • tah • _ksah_
green bean	**φασολάκι**
	fah • soh • _lah_ • kee
green peppers	**πιπεριές πράσινες**
	pee • pehr • _yehs prah_ • see • nehs
grouper	**σφυρίδα**
	sfee • _ree_ • THah
halva, sweet	**χαλβάς**
sesame seed paste	khahl • _vahs_
ham	**ζαμπόν**
	zahm • _bohn_
ham omelet	**ομελέττα με ζαμπόν**
	oh • meh • _leh_ • tah meh zahm • _bohn_
herring (smoked)	**ρέγγα (καπνιστή)**
	rehn • gah (kahp • nees • _tee_)

honey	**μέλι**
	meh • lee
ice cream	**παγωτό**
	pah • ghoh • toh
iced tea	**παγωμένο τσάι**
	pah • ghoh • meh • noh tsah • ee
instant coffee	**Νεσκαφέ**
	nehs • kah • feh
juice	**χυμός**
	khee • mohs
kidney	**νεφρό**
	neh • froh
kumquat liqueur (Corfu)	**κουμ-κουάτ**
	koom • koo • aht
lamb	**αρνί**
	ahr • nee
layers of eggplant [aubergine], meat and white sauce	**μουσακάς**
	moo • sah • kahs
leek	**πράσο**
	prah • soh
lemon	**λεμόνι**
	leh • moh • nee

lentil soup	**φακές σούπα**	
	fah • kehs soo • pah	
liqueur	**λικέρ**	
	lee • kehr	
liver	**συκώτι**	
	see • koh • tee	
lobster	**αστακός**	
	ahs • tah • kohs	
mackerel	**σκουμπρί**	
	skoo • mbree	
marinated mullet,	**ψάρι μαρινάτο**	
sole or mackerel	*psah • ree mah • ree • nah • toh*	
mastic	**μαστίχα**	
	mahs • tee • khah	
mayonnaise	**μαγιονέζα**	
	mah • yoh • neh • zah	
meat	**κρέας**	
	kreh • ahs	
meat soup	**κρεατόσουπα**	
	kreh • ah • toh • soo • pah	
meat with orzo pasta	**γιουβέτσι**	
baked with tomatoes	*yoo • veh • tsee*	
melon	**πεπόνι**	
	peh • poh • nee	
milk	**γάλα**	
	ghah • lah	
mint	**δυόσμος**	
	THee • ohz • mohs	
muffin	**μάφιν**	
	mah • feen	
mullet	**κέφαλος**	
	keh • fah • lohs	
mushroom	**μανιτάρι**	
	mah • nee • tah • ree	

mussels	**μύδι**
	mee • THee
nuts	**ξηροί καρποί**
	ksee • _ree_ kah • _rpee_
oatmeal	**κουάκερ**
	koo • _ah_ • kehr
octopus	**χταπόδι**
	khtah • _poh_ • THee
okra	**μπάμια**
	bah • miah
olive (stuffed)	**ελιά (γεμιστή)**
	eh • _liah_ (yeh • mees • _tee_)
olive oil	**ελαιόλαδο**
	eh • leh • _oh_ • lah • THoh
omelet	**ομελέτα**
	oh • meh • _leh_ • tah
on the rocks	**με πάγο**
	meh _pah_ • ghoh
onion	**κρεμμύδι**
	kreh • _mee_ • THee
orange	**πορτοκάλι**
	poh • rtoh • _kah_ • lee
oregano	**ρίγανη**
	ree • ghah • nee
ouzo	**ούζο**
	_oo_ • zoh
oyster	**στρείδι**
	stree • THee
parsley	**μαϊντανός**
	mah • ee • dah • _nohs_
pasta	**ζυμαρικά**
	zee • mah • ree • _kah_
paté	**πατέ**
	pah • _teh_

peach	**ροδάκινο**
	roh • <u>THah</u> • kee • noh
pear	**αχλάδι**
	akh • lah • <u>lah</u> • THee
peas	**αρακάς**
	ah • rah • <u>kahs</u>
pheasant	**φασιανός**
	fah • siah • <u>nohs</u>
pineapple	**ανανάς**
	ah • nah • <u>nahs</u>
plum	**δαμάσκηνο**
	THah • <u>mahs</u> • kee • noh
poached	**ποσέ**
	poh • <u>seh</u>
pork	**χοιρινό**
	khee • ree • <u>noh</u>
porksteak	**μπριζόλα χοιρινή**
	bree • <u>zoh</u> • lah khee • ree • <u>nee</u>
potato	**πατάτα**
	pah • <u>tah</u> • tah
rabbit	**κουνέλι**
	koo • <u>neh</u> • lee
red cabbage	**κόκκινο λάχανο**
	<u>koh</u> • kee • noh <u>lah</u> • khah • noh

red mullet	**μπαρμπούνι** *bahr • <u>boo</u> • nee*
red wine	**κόκκινο κρασί** *<u>koh</u> • kee • noh <u>krah</u> • see*
rice	**ρύζι** *<u>ree</u> • zee*
rice pudding	**ρυζόγαλο** *ree • <u>zoh</u> • ghah • loh*
roast	**ψητό** *psee • <u>toh</u>*
roll	**ψωμάκι** *psoh • <u>mah</u> • kee*
rosemary	**δεντρολίβανο** *THehn • droh • <u>lee</u> • vah • noh*
sage	**φασκόμηλο** *fahs • <u>koh</u> • mee • loh*
salad	**σαλάτα** *sah • <u>lah</u> • tah*
salted cod	**μπακαλιάρος παστός** *bah • kah • <u>liah</u> • rohs pahs • <u>tohs</u>*
sardine	**σαρδέλα** *sahr • <u>THeh</u> • lah*
sauce	**σάλτσα** *<u>sah</u> • ltsah*
sausage	**λουκάνικο** *loo • <u>kah</u> • nee • koh*
scrambled eggs	**ομελέτα** *oh • meh • <u>leh</u> • tah*
shellfish	**όστρακα** *<u>oh</u> • strah • kah*
shredded pastry roll filled with nuts and steeped in syrup	**καταΐφι** *kah • tah • <u>ee</u> • fee*
shrimp [prawn]	**γαρίδα** *<u>ghah</u> • ree • THah*

skewered pork or lamb cooked over charcoal	**κοντοσούβλι** *koh • ndoh • <u>soov</u> • lee*
snack	**σνακ** *snahk*
soda	**αναψυκτικό** *ah • nah • psee • ktee • <u>koh</u>*
soft-boiled eggs	**μελάτα αυγά** *meh • <u>lah</u> • tah ahv • <u>gah</u>*
sole (fish)	**γλώσσα** *ghloh • sah*
soup	**σούπα** *<u>soo</u> • pah*
soup with rice, eggs and lemon juice	**σούπα αυγολέμονο** *<u>soo</u> • pah ahv • ghoh • <u>leh</u> • moh • noh*
spiced lamb and potatoes baked in parchment or in filo pastry	**αρνάκι εξοχικό** *ahr • <u>nah</u> • kee eh • ksoh • khee • <u>koh</u>*
spices	**μπαχαρικά** *bah • khah • ree • <u>kah</u>*
spinach	**σπανάκι** *spah • <u>nah</u> • kee*
spinach and feta in pastry dough	**σπανακόπιτα** *spah • nah • <u>koh</u> • pee • tah*
stuffed grape leaves	**ντολμαδάκι** *dohl • mah • <u>THah</u> • kee*
squid	**καλαμάρι** *kah • lah • <u>mah</u> • ree*
steak	**μπριζόλα** *bree • <u>zoh</u> • lah*
sugar	**ζάχαρη** *<u>zah</u> • khah • ree*
swordfish	**ξιφίας** *ksee • <u>fee</u> • ahs*

syrup	**σιρόπι**
	see • roh • pee
tahini (sesame paste) soup	**ταχινόσουπα**
	tah • khee • noh • soo • pah
tangerine	**μανταρίνι**
	mahn • dah • ree • nee
taramosalata, fish roe dip	**ταραμοσαλάτα**
	tah • rah • moh • sah • lah • tah
tea	**τσάι**
	tsah • ee
thyme	**θυμάρι**
	thee • mah • ree
toast	**ψωμί φρυγανιά**
	psoh • mee free • ghah • niah
tomato	**ντομάτα**
	ndoh • mah • tah
tomato soup	**τοματόσουπα**
	toh • mah • toh • soo • pah
tongue (meat)	**γλώσσα**
	ghloh • sah
tonic water	**τόνικ**
	toh • neek
tripe soup	**πατσάς**
	pah • tsahs

tuna	**τόννος**
	toh • nohs
turkey	**γαλοπούλα**
	ghah • loh • _poo_ • lah
Turkish delight	**λουκούμι**
	loo • _koo_ • mee
unleavened bread	**λαγάνα**
	lah • _ghah_ • nah
veal	**μοσχάρι**
	mohs • _khah_ • ree
veal steak	**μπριζόλα μοσχαρίσια**
	bree • _zoh_ • lah mohs • khah • _ree_ • siah
vegetable	**λαχανικό**
	lah • khah • nee • _koh_
vegetable soup	**χορτόσουπα**
	khohr • _toh_ • soo • pah
walnut cake	**καρυδόπιτα**
	kah • ree • _THoh_ • pee • tah
water	**νερό**
	neh • _roh_
watermelon	**καρπούζι**
	kahr • _poo_ • zee
wheat	**σιτάρι**
	see • _tah_ • ree
wine	**κρασί**
	krah • _see_
yogurt (with honey)	**γιαούρτι (με μέλι)**
	yah • _oor_ • tee (meh _meh_ • lee)
yogurt, garlic and	**τζατζίκι**
cucumber dip	jah • _jee_ • kee
zucchini [courgette]	**κολοκυθάκι**
	koh • loh • kee • _thah_ • kee

PEOPLE

GOING OUT

NEED TO KNOW

What's there to do in the evenings?	**Τι μπορώ να κάνω τα βράδια;** _tee boh • roh nah kah • noh tah vrahTH • yah_
Do you have a program of events?	**Έχετε ένα πρόγραμμα εκδηλώσεων;** _eh • kheh • teh eh • nah prohgh • rah • mah ehk • THee • loh • seh • ohn_
What's playing at the movies [cinema] tonight?	**Τι παίζει ο κινηματογράφος απόψε;** _tee peh • zee oh kee • nee • mah • tohgh • rah • fohs ah • poh • pseh_
Where's…?	**Πού είναι…;** _poo ee • neh…_
the downtown area	**το κέντρο της πόλης** _toh kehn • droh tees poh • lees_
the bar	**το μπαρ** _toh bahr_

the dance club	**η ντισκοτέκ**
	ee dees • koh • tehk
Is there a cover charge?	**Υπάρχει κουβέρ;**
	ee • pahr • hee koo • vehr

Nightlife in Greece is excellent. There are a great number of cafes, bars and dance and music clubs throughout cities and on the islands. Greeks will often start the evening around 10:00 p.m.; the evening will most likely go on well into the early hours at a nightclub or at **μπουζούκια** (*boo • zoo • kee • ah*), live music clubs. **Bouzoukia** are a big part of Greek nightlife, where Greeks often reserve a table and spend the evening listening, throwing flowers at their favorite singers and sometimes dancing on the tables. These clubs offer a range of musical genres: from traditional Greek music to contemporary pop. A typical evening there would end at around 5:00 a.m., when you will often encounter traffic jams along the main club strips. Clubbing is also very popular, with open-air summer clubs operating from about April to October.

ENTERTAINMENT

Can you recommend...?	**Μπορείτε να συστήσετε...;**
	boh • ree • teh nah sees • tee • seh • teh...
a concert	**μια συναυλία**
	miah see • nahv • lee • ah
a movie	**μια ταινία**
	miah teh • nee • ah
an opera	**μια όπερα**
	miah oh • peh • rah

a play	**μια θεατρική παράσταση**
	miah theh • aht • ree • kee
	pah • rahs • tah • see
When does it start/end?	**Πότε αρχίζει/τελειώνει;**
	poh • the ahr • khee • zee/teh • lioh • nee
What's the dress code?	**Πώς πρέπει να ντυθώ;**
	pohs preh • pee nah dee • thoh
I like…	**Μου αρέσει…**
	moo ah • reh • see…
classical music	**η κλασική μουσική**
	ee klah • see • kee moo • see • kee
folk music	**η δημοτική μουσική**
	ee THee • moh • tee • kee moo • see • kee
jazz	**η τζαζ**
	ee jahz
pop music	**η ποπ μουσική**
	ee pohp moo • see • kee
rap	**η ραπ**
	ee rahp

For Tickets, see page 50.

NIGHTLIFE

YOU MAY HEAR…

Παρακαλώ απενεργοποιήστε τα κινητά σας τηλέφωνα.	Turn off your mobile phones, please.
pah • rah • kah • loh	
ah • peh • nehr • ghoh • pee • ees • teh	
tah kee • nee • tah sahs tee • leh • foh • nah	

What's there to do in the evenings/ at night?	**Τι μπορώ να κάνω τα βράδια;/τη νύχτα;**
	tee boh • roh nah kah • noh tah vrahTH • yah/tee nee • khtah
Can you recommend…?	**Μπορείτε να συστήσετε…;**
	boh • ree • teh nah sees • tee • seh • teh…
a bar	**ένα μπαρ**
	eh • nah bahr
a cabaret	**ένα καμπαρέ**
	eh • nah kah • bah • reh
a casino	**ένα καζίνο**
	eh • nah kah • zee • noh
a dance club	**μια ντισκοτέκ**
	miah dees • koh • tehk
a gay club	**ένα κλαμπ για γκέι**
	eh • nah geh • ee klahb
a jazz club	**ένα κλαμπ με τζαζ μουσική**
	eh • nah klahb meh jahz moo • see • kee
a club with local music	**ένα κλαμπ με τοπική μουσική**
	eh • nah klahb meh toh • pee • kee moo • see • kee
Is there live music?	**Παίζει live μουσική;**
	peh • zee lah • eev moo • see • kee
How do I get there?	**Πώς πάω εκεί;**
	pohs pah • oh eh • kee

Is there a cover charge?	**Το κουβέρ χρεώνεται;**
	toh koo • <u>vehr</u> khreh • <u>oh</u> • neh • teh
Let's go dancing.	**Πάμε για χορό.**
	pah • meh yah khoh • <u>roh</u>
Is this area safe at night?	**Η περιοχή είναι ασφαλής τη νύχτα;**
	ee peh • ree • oh • <u>khee</u> ee • neh
	ah • sfah • <u>lees</u> tee nee • khtah

For The Dating Game, see page 225.

For The Dating Game, see page 225.

The Athens Festival takes place every summer and includes various concerts and theatrical performances particularly in the Odeion of Herod Atticus and the Epidaurus Ancient Theater, among other venues. Look out for feast days, especially on the islands. Some smaller villages or towns will often hold an amazing party with food, drink and music to celebrate the feast day of the patron saint of the local church or of the town.

Very useful information in English can be found in the Athens News, a newspaper which includes TV, movie, theater and other cultural listings. *Athens News* also includes information on where to buy tickets for various events.

ROMANCE

NEED TO KNOW

Would you like to go out for a drink/dinner?	**Θέλετε να βγούμε για ποτό/φαγητό;** _theh_ • leh • teh nah _vghoo_ • meh yah poh • _toh_/fah • yee • _toh_
What are your plans for tonight/tomorrow?	**Ποια είναι τα σχέδιά σας για απόψε/αύριο;** piah _ee_ • neh tah _skheh_ • THee • _ah_ sahs yah ah • _poh_ • pseh/_ahv_ • ree • oh
Can I have your number?	**Μπορώ να έχω τον αριθμό τηλεφώνου σας;** boh • _roh_ nah eh • khoh tohn ah • reeth • _moh_ tee • leh • _foh_ • noo sahs
May we join you?	**Να έρθουμε μαζί σας;** nah _ehr_ • thoo • meh mah • _zee_ sahs
Let me buy you a drink.	**Να σε κεράσω ένα ποτό.** nah seh keh • _rah_ • soh eh • nah poh • _toh_
I like you.	**Μου αρέσεις.** moo ah • _reh_ • sees
I love you.	**Σ' αγαπώ.** sah • ghah • _poh_

THE DATING GAME

Would you like to go out for coffee?	**Θα θέλατε να βγούμε για καφέ;** thah _theh_ • lah • teh nah _vghoo_ • meh yah kah • _feh_
Would you like to go out for a drink/dinner?	**Θέλεις να βγεις για ποτό/φαγητό;** _theh_ • lees nah vghees yah poh • _toh_/fah • ghee • _toh_

What are your plans for…?	**Ποια είναι τα σχέδιά σας για…;**
	piah ee • neh tah skheh • THee • ah sahs yah…
tonight	**απόψε**
	ah • poh • pseh
tomorrow	**αύριο**
	ahv • ree • oh
this weekend	**αυτό το Σαββατοκύριακο**
	ahf • toh toh sah • vah • toh • kee • riah • koh
Where would you like to go?	**Πού θα θέλατε να πάμε;**
	poo thah theh • lah • the nah pah • meh
I'd like to go to…	**Θα ήθελα να πάω…**
	thah ee • theh • lah nah pah • oh…
Do you like…?	**Σου αρέσει…;**
	soo ah • reh • see…
Can I have your number/e-mail?	**Μου δίνετε το τηλέφωνο/e-mail σας;**
	moo THee • neh • teh toh tee • leh • foh • noh/ee • meh • eel sahs
Are you on Facebook/Twitter?	**Είσαι στο Facebook/Twitter;**
	ee • seh stoh Facebook/Twitter
Can I join you?	**Να έρθω κι εγώ στην παρέα σας;**
	nah ehr • thoh kee eh • ghoh steen pah • reh • ah sahs
You look great!	**Είστε πολύ όμορφος** m **/όμορφη** f **!**
	ee • steh poh • lee oh • mohr • fohs/ oh • mohr • fee
Shall we go somewhere quieter?	**Πάμε κάπου πιο ήσυχα;**
	pah • meh kah • poo pioh ee • see • khah

For Communications, see page 89.

ACCEPTING & REJECTING

Thank you. I'd love to.	**Ευχαριστώ. Θα το ήθελα πολύ.** *ehf • khah • rees • toh thah toh* *ee • theh • lah poh • lee*
Where should we meet?	**Πού θα συναντηθούμε;** *poo thah see • nahn • dee • thoo • meh*
I'll meet you at the bar/your hotel.	**Θα σε συναντήσω στο μπαρ/στο ξενοδοχείο σου.** *thah seh see • nahn • dee • soh stoh bahr/ stoh kseh • noh • THoh • khee • oh soo*
I'll come by at…	**Θα περάσω στις…** *thah peh • rah • soh stees…*
Thank you, but I'm busy.	**Σας ευχαριστώ, αλλά είμαι πολύ απασχολημένος** m /**απασχολημένη** f . *sahs ehf • khah • rees • toh ah • lah ee • meh poh • lee ah • pahs • khoh • lee • meh • nohs/ ah • pahs • khoh • lee • meh • nee*
I'm not interested.	**Δεν ενδιαφέρομαι.** *THehn ehn • THee • ah • feh • roh • meh*
Leave me alone, please!	**Σας παρακαλώ, αφήστε με ήσυχο** m /**ήσυχη** f ! *sahs pah • rah • kah • loh ah • fees • the meh ee • see • khoh/ee • see • khee*
Stop bothering me!	**Σταματείστε να με ενοχλείτε!** *stah • mah • tee • steh nah meh eh • noh • khlee • the*

For Time, see page 24.

GETTING INTIMATE

Can I hug/kiss you?	**Μπορώ να σε αγκαλιάσω/φιλήσω;**	
	boh • roh nah seh ahn • gah • liah • soh/	
	fee • lee • soh	
Yes.	**Ναι.**	
	neh	
No.	**Όχι.**	
	oh • khee	
Stop!	**Σταμάτα!**	
	stah • mah • tah	
I love you.	**Σ' αγαπώ.**	
	sah • ghah • poh	

SEXUAL PREFERENCES

Are you gay?	**Είσαι γκέι;**	
	ee • seh geh • ee	
I'm…	**Είμαι…**	
	ee • meh…	
heterosexual	**ετεροφυλόφιλος** *m* /**ετεροφυλόφιλη** *f*	
	eh • teh • roh • fee • loh • fee • lohs/	
	eh • teh • roh • fee • loh • fee • lee	

homosexual	**ομοφυλόφιλος** m /**ομοφυλόφιλη** f
	oh•moh•fee•<u>loh</u>•fee•lohs/
	oh•moh•fee•<u>loh</u>•fee•lee
bisexual	**αμφιφυλόφιλος** m /**αμφιφυλόφιλη** f
	ahm•fee•fee•<u>loh</u>•fee•lohs/
	ahm•fee•fee•<u>loh</u>•fee•lee
Do you like men/women?	**Σου αρέσουν οι άνδρες/γυναίκες;**
	soo ah•<u>reh</u>•soon ee <u>ahn</u>•THrehs/
	ghee•<u>neh</u>•kehs

DICTIONARY

ENGLISH–GREEK

A

access n **πρόσβαση** prohz-vah-see

accessory αξεσουάρ ah-kseh-soo-ahr

accident ατύχημα ah-tee-khee-mah

accompany συνοδεύω see-noh-THeh-voh

account n **λογαριασμός**
loh-ghahr-yahz-mohs

adaptor προσαρμοστής
proh-sahr-moh-stees

address n **διεύθυνση** THee-ehf-theen-see

admission είσοδος ee-soh-Thohs

adult ενήλικας eh-nee-lee-kahs

advance προκαταβολή
proh-kah-tah-voh-lee

after μετά meh-tah

afternoon απόγευμα ah-poh-yehv-mah

**after-sun lotion λοσιόν μετά την
ηλιοθεραπεία** loh-siohn meh-tah teen
ee-lioh-theh-rah-pee-ah

age n **ηλικία** ee-lee-kee-ah

agree συμφωνώ seem-foh-noh

air conditioning κλιματισμός
klee-mah-teez-mohs

air pump n **αντλία αέρος** ahn-dlee-ah
ah-eh-rohs

airline αεροπορική εταιρία
ah-eh-roh-poh-ree-kee eh-the-ree-ah

airmail αεροπορικώς
ah-eh-roh-poh-ree-kohs

airport αεροδρόμιο
ah-eh-roh-THroh-mee-oh

aisle seat διάδρομος
THee-ah-Throh-mohs

allergic αλλεργικός ahl-ehr-yee-kohs

allergy αλλεργία ah-lehr-yee-ah

alone μόνος moh-nohs

aluminum foil αλουμινόχαρτο
ah-loo-mee-noh-khah-rtoh

amazing καταπληκτικός
kah-tahp-leek-tee-kohs

ambassador πρεσβευτής prehz-vehf-tees

amber κεχριμπάρι kehkh-reem-bah-ree

ambulance ασθενοφόρο
ahs-theh-noh-foh-roh

American adj **αμερικάνικος**
ah-meh-ree-kah-nee-kohs; (nationality)
Αμερικανός ah-meh-ree-kah-nohs

amount n **ποσό** poh-soh

amusement park πάρκο ψυχαγωγίας
pahr-koh psee-khah-ghoh-yee-ahs

animal ζώο zoh-oh

another άλλος ah-lohs

antibiotic αντιβιοτικό
ahn-dee-vee-oh-tee-koh

antiques store κατάστημα με αντίκες
kah-tah-stee-mah meh ahn-tee-kehs

antiseptic cream αντισηπτική κρέμα
ahn-dee-seep-tee-kee kreh-mah

adj adjective	**BE** British English	**prep** preposition
adv adverb	**n** noun	**v** verb

anything οτιδήποτε
oh-tee-THee-poh-teh

apartment διαμέρισμα
THee-ah-meh-reez-mah

apologize ζητώ συγγνώμη zee-toh
seegh-noh-mee

appendix σκωληκοειδίτιδα
skoh-lee-koh-ee-THee-tee-THah

appointment ραντεβού rahn-deh-voo

architecture αρχιτεκτονική
ahr-khee-teh-ktoh-nee-kee

area code κωδικός περιοχής
koh-THee-kohs peh-ree-oh-khees

arm n **χέρι** kheh-ree

arrange κανονίζω kah-noh-nee-zoh

arrest v **συλλαμβάνω** see-lahm-vah-noh

arrive φτάνω ftah-noh

art τέχνη tekh-nee

art gallery γκαλερί τέχνης gah-leh-ree
tekh-nees

ashtray σταχτοδοχείο
stakh-toh-THoh-khee-oh

ask ζητώ zee-toh

aspirin ασπιρίνη ahs-pee-ree-nee

asthmatic ασθματικός
ahsth-mah-tee-kohs

ATM ATM ehee-tee-ehm

attack n **επίθεση** eh-pee-theh-see; v
επιτίθεμαι eh-pee-tee-theh-meh

attractive ελκυστικός ehl-kees-tee-kohs

authenticity αυθεντικότητα
ahf-thehn-dee-koh-tee-tah

B

baby μωρό moh-roh

baby food βρεφική τροφή vreh-fee-kee
troh-fee

baby seat καρέκλα μωρού kah-reh-klah
moh-roo

babysitter μπέιμπι σίτερ beh-ee-bee
see-tehr

back n **πλάτη** plah-tee

back ache πόνος στην πλάτη poh-nohs
steen plah-tee

backgammon τάβλι tah-vlee

bad κακός kah-kohs

baggage αποσκευές ah-pohs-keh-vehs

baggage check φύλαξη αποσκευών
fee-lah-ksee ah-poh-skeh-vohn

baggage reclaim παραλαβή
αποσκευών pah-rah-lah-vee
ah-poh-skeh-vohn

bakery αρτοποιείο ah-rtoh-pee-ee-oh

balcony μπαλκόνι bahl-koh-nee

ballet μπαλέτο bah-leh-toh

bandage γάζα ghah-zah

bank τράπεζα trah-peh-zah

bank account λογαριασμός τραπέζης
loh-ghahr-yahz-mohs trah-peh-zees

bank loan τραπεζικό δάνειο
trah-peh-zee-koh THah-nee-oh

bar μπαρ bahr

barber κουρείο koo-ree-oh

basket καλάθι kah-lah-THee

basketball μπάσκετ bah-skeht

bathing suit μαγιό mah-yoh

bathroom μπάνιο bah-nioh

battery μπαταρία bah-tah-ree-ah

beach παραλία pah-rah-lee-ah

beautiful όμορφος oh-mohr-fohs

bed κρεβάτι kreh-vah-tee

bed and breakfast διαμονή με
πρωινό THiah-moh-nee meh
proh-ee-noh

bedding σεντόνια sehn-doh-niah

bedroom υπνοδωμάτιο
eep·noh·_THoh_·_mah_·tee·oh

before πριν preen

beginner αρχάριος ahr·_khah_·ree·ohs

belong ανήκω ah·_nee_·koh

belt ζώνη _zoh_·nee

bicycle ποδήλατο poh·_THee_·lah·toh

big μεγάλος meh·_ghah_·lohs

bikini μπικίνι bee·_kee_·nee

bird πουλί poo·_lee_

bite *n* (insect) **τσίμπημα** _tsee_·bee·mah

bladder ουροδόχος κύστη
oo·roh·_THoh_·khohs _kee_·stee

blanket κουβέρτα koo·_veh_·rtah

bleed *n* **αιμορραγία** eh·moh·rah·_yee_·ah;
v **αιμορραγώ** eh·moh·rah·_yoh_

blinds περσίδες peh·_rsee_·THehs

blister φουσκάλα foo·_skah_·lah

blood αίμα _eh_·mah

blood group ομάδα αίματος
oh·_mah_·THah _eh_·mah·tohs

blood pressure πίεση _pee_·eh·see

blouse μπλούζα _bloo_·zah

boarding card κάρτα επιβίβασης
kah·rtah eh·pee·_vee_·vah·sees

boat βάρκα _vahr_·kah

boat trip ταξίδι με πλοίο tah·_ksee_·THee
meh _plee_·oh

body σώμα _soh_·mah

bone οστό oh·_stoh_

book *n* **βιβλίο** veev·_lee_·oh; *v* **κάνω
κράτηση** _kah_·noh krah·tee·see

bookstore βιβλιοπωλείο
veev·lee·oh·poh·_lee_·oh

boot μπότα _boh_·tah

border (country) **σύνορο** _see_·noh·roh

boring βαρετός vah·reh·_tohs_

borrow δανείζομαι THah·_nee_·zoh·meh

botanical garden βοτανικός κήπος
voh·tah·nee·_kohs_ kee·pohs

bottle μπουκάλι boo·_kah_·lee

bottle opener τιρμπουσόν
teer·boo·_sohn_

bowel έντερο _ehn_·deh·roh

box office ταχυδρομική θυρίδα
tah·khee·THroh·mee·_kee_ THee·_ree_·THah

boxing *n* **μποξ** bohks

boy αγόρι ah·_ghoh_·ree

boyfriend φίλος _fee_·lohs

bra σουτιέν soo·_tiehn_

break *n* **διάλειμμα** THee·_ah_·lee·mah; *v*
σπάω _spah_·oh

breakdown *n* (car) **βλάβη** _vlah_·vee

breakfast πρωινό proh·ee·_noh_

break-in *n* **διάρρηξη** THee·_ah_·ree·ksee

breast στήθος _stee_·THohs

breathe αναπνέω ah·nahp·_neh_·oh

breathtaking φαντασμαγορικός
fahn·dahz·mah·ghoh·ree·_kohs_

bridge *n* (over water) **γέφυρα** _yeh_·fee·rah;
(card game) **μπριτζ** breetz

briefcase χαρτοφύλακας
khah·rtoh·_fee_·lah·kahs

briefs (men's, women's) **σλιπ** sleep
(women's); **κυλοτάκι** kee·loh·_tah_·kee

bring φέρνω _fehr_·noh

Britain Βρετανία vreh·tah·_nee_·ah

British *adj* **βρετανικός** vreh·tah·nee·_kohs_;
(nationality) **Βρετανός** vreh·tah·_nohs_

brochure φυλλάδιο fee·_lah_·THee·oh

broken σπασμένος spahz·_meh_·nohs

broom *n* **σκούπα** _skoo_·pah

browse ξεφυλλίζω kseh·fee·_lee_·zoh

bruise *n* **μελανιά** meh·lah·_niah_

brush *n* **βούρτσα** _voor_·tsah; *v* **βουρτσίζω**
voor·_tsee_·zoh

build **κτίζω** <u>ktee</u>·zoh

building **κτίριο** <u>ktee</u>·ree·oh

burn n **έγκαυμα** <u>eh</u>·gahv·mah

bus **λεωφορείο** leh·oh·foh·<u>ree</u>·oh

bus route **διαδρομή λεωφορείων** THee·ah·THroh·<u>mee</u> leh·oh·foh·<u>ree</u>·ohn

bus station **σταθμός λεωφορείων** stahTH·<u>mohs</u> leh·oh·foh·<u>ree</u>·ohn

bus stop **στάση λεωφορείου** <u>stah</u>·see leh·oh·foh·<u>ree</u>·oo

business class **μπίζνες θέση** <u>bee</u>·znehs <u>theh</u>·see

business trip **επαγγελματικό ταξίδι** eh·pah·gehl·mah·tee·<u>koh</u> tah·<u>ksee</u>·THee

busy (occupied) **απασχολημένος** ah·pahs·khoh·lee·<u>meh</u>·nohs

but **αλλά** ah·<u>lah</u>

butane gas **υγραέριο** eegh·rah·<u>eh</u>·ree·oh

butcher shop **κρεοπωλείο** kreh·oh·poh·<u>lee</u>·oh

button **κουμπί** koo·<u>bee</u>

buy **αγοράζω** ah·ghoh·<u>rah</u>·zoh

C

cabaret **καμπαρέ** kah·bah·<u>reh</u>

cabin **καμπίνα** kah·<u>bee</u>·nah

cable car **τελεφερίκ** teh·leh·feh·<u>reek</u>

cafe **καφετέρια** kah·feh·<u>teh</u>·ree·ah

calendar **ημερολόγιο** ee·meh·roh·<u>loh</u>·yee·oh

call collect **με χρέωση του καλούμενου** meh <u>khreh</u>·oh·see too kah·<u>loo</u>·meh·noo

call n **κλήση** <u>klee</u>·see; v **καλώ** kah·<u>loh</u>

camcorder **φορητή βιντεοκάμερα** foh·ree·<u>tee</u> vee·deh·oh·<u>kah</u>·meh·rah

camera **φωτογραφική μηχανή** foh·tohgh·rah·fee·<u>kee</u> mee·khah·<u>nee</u>

camera case **θήκη μηχανής** <u>thee</u>·kee mee·khah·<u>nees</u>

camera store **κατάστημα με φωτογραφικά είδη** kah·<u>tah</u>·stee·mah meh foh·tohgh·rah·fee·<u>kah</u> ee·THee

camp bed **κρεβάτι εκστρατείας** kreh·<u>vah</u>·tee ehk·strah·<u>tee</u>·ahs

camping **κάμπινγκ** <u>kah</u>·mpeeng

camping equipment **εξοπλισμός κάμπιγκ** eh·ksohp·leez·<u>mohs</u> <u>kah</u>·mpeeng

campsite **χώρος κάμπινγκ** <u>khoh</u>·rohs <u>kah</u>·mpeeng

can opener **ανοιχτήρι** ah·neekh·<u>tee</u>·ree

Canada **Καναδάς** kah·nah·<u>THahs</u>

canal **κανάλι** kah·<u>nah</u>·lee

cancel v **ακυρώνω** ah·kee·<u>roh</u>·noh

cancer (disease) **καρκίνος** kahr·<u>kee</u>·nohs

candle **κερί** keh·<u>ree</u>

canoe **κανό** kah·<u>noh</u>

car **αυτοκίνητο** ahf·toh·<u>kee</u>·nee·toh

car park [BE] **χώρος στάθμευσης** <u>khoh</u>·rohs stahth·mehf·sees

car rental **ενοικίαση αυτοκινήτων** eh·nee·<u>kee</u>·ah·see ahf·toh·kee·<u>nee</u>·tohn

car wash **πλύσιμο αυτοκινήτου** <u>plee</u>·see·moh ahf·toh·kee·<u>nee</u>·too

carafe **καράφα** kah·<u>rah</u>·fah

caravan **τροχόσπιτο** troh·<u>khohs</u>·pee·toh

cards **χαρτιά** khahr·<u>tiah</u>

carpet (fitted) **μοκέτα** moh·<u>keh</u>·tah

carton **κουτί** koo·<u>tee</u>

cash desk [BE] **ταμείο** tah·<u>mee</u>·oh

cash n **μετρητά** meht·ree·<u>tah</u>; v **εξαργυρώνω** eh·ksahr·ghee·<u>roh</u>·noh

casino **καζίνο** kah·<u>see</u>·noh

castle **κάστρο** <u>kahs</u>·troh

catch v (bus) **παίρνω** <u>pehr</u>·noh

cathedral καθεδρικός ναός
kah·theh·THree·<u>kohs</u> nah·<u>ohs</u>

cave n **σπήλαιο** <u>spee</u>·leh·oh

CD σι ντι see dee

cell phone κινητό kee·nee·<u>toh</u>

change n **αλλαγή** ah·lah·<u>yee</u>; v **αλλάζω**
ah·<u>lah</u>·zoh

cheap φτηνός ftee·<u>nohs</u>

check n (bank) **επιταγή**
eh·pee·tah·<u>yee</u>; (bill) **λογαριασμός**
loh·ghahr·yahz·<u>mohs</u>

choose διαλέγω THiah·<u>leh</u>·ghoh

clean καθαρός kah·thah·<u>rohs</u>

cling film [BE] διαφανή μεμβράνη
THee·ah·fah·<u>nee</u> mehm·<u>vrah</u>·nee

clothing store κατάστημα ρούχων
kah·<u>tahs</u>·tee·mah <u>roo</u>·khohn

cold adj (temperature) **κρύος**
<u>kree</u>·ohs; n (chill) **κρυολόγημα**
kree·oh·<u>loh</u>·yee·mah

collapse v **καταρρέω** kah·tah·<u>reh</u>·oh

collect v **παίρνω** <u>peh</u>·rnoh

color n **χρώμα** <u>khroh</u>·mah

comb n **χτένα** <u>khteh</u>·nah; v **χτενίζω**
khteh·<u>nee</u>·zoh

come έρχομαι <u>ehr</u>·khoh·meh

come back v (return) **επιστρέφω**
eh·pees·<u>treh</u>·foh

commission n (agent fee) **προμήθεια**
proh·<u>mee</u>·thee·ah

company n (business) **εταιρία**
eh·teh·<u>ree</u>·ah; (companionship) **παρέα**
pah·<u>reh</u>·ah

complain παραπονιέμαι
pah·rah·poh·<u>nieh</u>·meh

computer υπολογιστής
ee·poh·loh·yee·<u>stees</u>

concert συναυλία see·nahv·<u>lee</u>·ah

concert hall αίθουσα συναυλιών
<u>eh</u>·thoo·sah see·nahv·lee·<u>ohn</u>

conditioner (hair) **γαλάκτωμα για τα
μαλλιά** ghah·<u>lah</u>·ktoh·mah yah tah
mah·<u>liah</u>

condom προφυλακτικό
proh·fee·lah·ktee·<u>koh</u>

conference συνέδριο see·<u>neh</u>·THree·oh

confirm επιβεβαιώνω
eh·pee·veh·veh·<u>oh</u>·noh

constipation δυσκοιλιότητα
thees·kee·lee·<u>oh</u>·tee·tah

Consulate Προξενείο proh·kseh·<u>nee</u>·oh

consult v **συμβουλεύομαι**
seem·voo·<u>leh</u>·voh·meh

contact v **επικοινωνώ**
eh·pee·kee·noh·<u>noh</u>

contact fluid υγρό για φακούς επαφής
eegh·<u>roh</u> yah fah·<u>koos</u> eh·pah·<u>fees</u>

contact lens φακός επαφής fah·<u>kohs</u>
eh·pah·<u>fees</u>

contagious μεταδοτικός
meh·tah·THoh·tee·<u>kohs</u>

contain περιέχω peh·ree·<u>eh</u>·khoh

contraceptive pill αντισυλληπτικό χάπι
ahn·dee·see·leep·tee·<u>koh</u> <u>khah</u>·pee

cook n (chef) **μάγειρας** <u>mah</u>·yee·rahs; v
μαγειρεύω mah·yee·<u>reh</u>·voh

copper χαλκός khahl·<u>kohs</u>

corkscrew τιρμπουσόν teer·boo·<u>sohn</u>

corner γωνία ghoh·<u>nee</u>·ah

correct v **διορθώνω** THee·ohr·<u>thoh</u>·noh

cosmetics καλλυντικά kah·leen·dee·<u>kah</u>

cot [BE] παιδικό κρεβάτι peh·THee·<u>koh</u>
kreh·<u>vah</u>·tee

cotton βαμβάκι vahm·<u>vah</u>·kee

cough n **βήχας** <u>vee</u>·khahs; v **βήχω** vee·khoh

counter ταμείο tah·<u>mee</u>·oh

country (nation) **χώρα** khoh·rah

countryside εξοχή eh·ksoh·khee

couple n (pair) **ζευγάρι** zehv·ghah·ree

courier n (messenger) **κούριερ** koo·ree·ehr

court house δικαστήριο THee·kahs·tee·ree·oh

cramp n **κράμπα** krahm·bah

credit card πιστωτική κάρτα pees·toh·tee·kee kahr·tah

crib [cot BE] **παιδικό κρεβάτι** peh·THee·koh kreh·vah·tee

crown n (dental, royal) **κορώνα** koh·roh·nah

cruise n **κρουαζιέρα** kroo·ahz·yeh·rah

crutch n (walking support) **δεκανίκι** THeh·kah·nee·kee

crystal n **κρύσταλλο** kree·stah·loh

cup φλυτζάνι flee·jah·nee

cupboard ντουλάπα doo·lah·pah

currency νόμισμα noh·meez·mah

currency exchange office γραφείο ανταλλαγής συναλλάγματος ghrah·fee·oh ahn·dah·lah·yees see·nah·lahgh·mah·tohs

customs (tolls) **τελωνείο** teh·loh·nee·oh

customs declaration (tolls) **τελωνειακή δήλωση** teh·loh·nee·ah·kee THee·loh·see

cut n (wound) **κόψιμο** koh·psee·moh

cut glass n **σκαλιστό γυαλί** skah·lees·toh yah·lee

cycle helmet κράνος ποδηλάτη krah·nohs poh·THee·lah·tee

cyclist ποδηλάτης poh·THee·lah·tees

Cypriot adj **κυπριακός** keep·ree·ah·kohs; (nationality) **Κύπριος** kee·pree·ohs

Cyprus Κύπρος kee·prohs

D

damage n **ζημιά** zee·miah; v **καταστρέφω** kah·tah·streh·foh

dance v **χορεύω** khoh·reh·voh

dangerous επικίνδυνος eh·pee·keen·THee·nohs

dark adj (color) **σκούρος** skoo·rohs

dawn n **ξημερώματα** ksee·meh·roh·mah·tah

day trip ημερήσια εκδρομή ee·meh·ree·see·ah ehk·THroh·mee

deaf κουφός koo·fohs

decide αποφασίζω ah·poh·fah·see·zoh

deck n **κατάστρωμα** kah·tah·stroh·mah

deck chair σεζ-λονγκ sehz lohng

declare δηλώνω THee·loh·noh

deduct (money) **αφαιρώ** ah·feh·roh

defrost ξεπαγώνω kseh·pah·ghoh·noh

degrees (temperature) **βαθμοί** vahth·mee

delay n **καθυστέρηση** kah·thee·steh·ree·see; v **καθυστερώ** kah·thee·steh·roh

delicious νόστιμος nohs·tee·mohs

deliver παραδίδω pah·rah·THee·THoh

dental floss οδοντικό νήμα oh·THohn·dee·koh nee·mah

dentist οδοντίατρος oh·THohn·dee·ah·trohs

deodorant αποσμητικό ah·pohz·mee·tee·koh

department store πολυκατάστημα poh·lee·kah·tahs·tee·mah

departure (travel) **αναχώρηση** ah·nah·khoh·ree·see

departure lounge αίθουσα αναχωρήσεων eh·thoo·sah ah·nah·khoh·ree·seh·ohn

depend **εξαρτώμαι** eh·ksahr·<u>toh</u>·meh
deposit *n* (down payment) **προκαταβολή**
  proh·kah·tah·voh·<u>lee</u>
describe **περιγράφω** peh·reegh·<u>rah</u>·foh
designer **σχεδιαστής**
  skheh·THee·ahs·<u>tees</u>
detergent **απορρυπαντικό**
  ah·poh·ree·pahn·dee·<u>koh</u>
develop (photos) **εμφανίζω**
  ehm·fah·<u>nee</u>·zoh
diabetes **διαβήτης** THee·ah·<u>vee</u>·tees
diabetic **διαβητικός**
  THee·ah·vee·tee·<u>kohs</u>
diagnosis **διάγνωση** THee·<u>ahgh</u>·noh·see
dialing code **κωδικός** koh·THee·<u>kohs</u>
diamond *n* **διαμάντι** THiah·<u>mahn</u>·dee
diaper **πάνα μωρού** <u>pah</u>·nah moh·<u>roo</u>
diarrhea **διάρροια** THee·<u>ah</u>·ree·ah
dice *n* **ζάρια** <u>zah</u>·riah
dictionary **λεξικό** leh·ksee·<u>koh</u>
diesel **ντήζελ** <u>dee</u>·zehl
diet *n* **δίαιτα** <u>THee</u>·eh·tah
difficult **δύσκολος** <u>THee</u>·skoh·lohs
dining room **τραπεζαρία**
  trah·peh·zah·<u>ree</u>·ah
dinner **βραδινό** vrah·THee·<u>noh</u>
direct *v* **κατευθύνω** kah·tehf·<u>thee</u>·noh
direction *n* (instruction) **οδηγία**
  oh·THee·<u>yee</u>·ah
dirty *adj* **βρώμικος** <u>vroh</u>·mee·kohs
disabled **άτομο με ειδικές ανάγκες**
  <u>ah</u>·toh·moh meh eh·• ·<u>nahn</u> THee·<u>kehs</u>
  ah·gehs
discounted ticket **μειωμένο εισιτήριο**
  mee·oh·<u>meh</u>·noh ee·see·<u>tee</u>·ree·oh
dishwashing liquid **λίγο υγρό πιάτων**
  <u>lee</u>·ghoh ee·<u>ghroh</u> piah·tohn
district **περιφέρεια** peh·ree·<u>feh</u>·ree·ah

disturb **ενοχλώ** eh·noh·<u>khloh</u>
diving equipment **καταδυτικός**
  εξοπλισμός kah·tah·THee·tee·<u>kohs</u>
  eh·ksoh·pleez·<u>mohs</u>
divorced **διαζευγμένος**
  THee·ah·zehv·<u>ghmeh</u>·nohs
dock **προκυμαία** proh·kee·<u>meh</u>·ah
doctor **γιατρός** yah·<u>trohs</u>
doll **κούκλα** <u>kook</u>·lah
dollar **δολάριο** THoh·<u>lah</u>·ree·oh
door **πόρτα** <u>pohr</u>·tah
dosage **δοσολογία** THoh·soh·loh·<u>yee</u>·ah
double *adj* **διπλός** THeep·<u>lohs</u>
double bed **διπλό κρεβάτι** THeep·<u>loh</u>
  kreh·<u>vah</u>·tee
double room **δίκλινο δωμάτιο**
  <u>THeek</u>·lee·noh THoh·<u>mah</u>·tee·oh
downtown area **κέντρο της πόλης**
  <u>kehn</u>·droh tees <u>poh</u>·lees
dozen **ντουζίνα** doo·<u>zee</u>·nah
dress *n* **φόρεμα** <u>foh</u>·reh·mah
drink *n* **ποτό** poh·<u>toh</u>; *v* **πίνω** <u>pee</u>·noh
drive *v* **οδηγώ** oh·THee·<u>ghoh</u>
drugstore **φαρμακείο** fahr·mah·<u>kee</u>·oh
dry cleaner **καθαριστήριο**
  kah·thah·rees·<u>tee</u>·ree·oh
dubbed **μεταγλωττισμένος**
  meh·tahgh·loh·teez·<u>meh</u>·nohs
dusty **σκονισμένος** skoh·neez·<u>meh</u>·nohs
duty (customs) **φόρος** <u>foh</u>·rohs;
  (obligation) **καθήκον** kah·<u>thee</u>·kohn
duty-free goods **αφορολόγητα είδη**
  ah·foh·roh·<u>loh</u>·yee·tah ee·<u>THee</u>
duty-free shop **κατάστημα**
  αφορολόγητων kah·<u>tahs</u>·tee·mah
  ah·foh·roh·<u>loh</u>·yee·tohn

E

each κάθε ένα kah·theh <u>eh</u>·nah

ear αυτί ahf·<u>tee</u>

earache πόνος στο αυτί <u>poh</u>·nohs stoh ahf·<u>tee</u>

early νωρίς noh·<u>rees</u>

east ανατολικά ah·nah·toh·lee·<u>kah</u>

easy adj **εύκολος** <u>ehf</u>·koh·lohs

eat τρώω <u>troh</u>·oh

economical οικονομικός ee·koh·noh·mee·<u>kohs</u>

economy class τουριστική θέση too·ree·stee·<u>kee</u> <u>theh</u>·see

elastic ελαστικός eh·lahs·tee·<u>kohs</u>

electrical outlet πρίζα <u>pree</u>·zah

e-mail ηλεκτρονικό ταχυδρομείο (e-mail) ee·lehk·troh·nee·<u>koh</u> tah·hee·dro·<u>mee</u>·oh (ee·<u>meh</u>·eel)

embassy πρεσβεία prehz·<u>vee</u>·ah

emerald σμαράγδι zmah·<u>rahgh</u>·THee

emergency έκτακτη ανάγκη <u>ehk</u>·tahk·tee ah·<u>nah</u>·gee

emergency exit έξοδος κινδύνου <u>eh</u>·ksoh·THohs keen·<u>THee</u>·noo

empty adj **άδειος** <u>ahTH</u>·yohs

end n **τέλος** <u>teh</u>·lohs; v **τελειώνω** teh·lee·<u>oh</u>·noh

engine μηχανή mee·khah·<u>nee</u>

England Αγγλία ahng·<u>lee</u>·ah

English adj **αγγλικός** ahng·lee·<u>kohs</u>; (nationality) **Άγγλος** <u>ahng</u>·lohs; (language) **αγγλικά** ahng·lee·<u>kah</u>

enjoy ευχαριστιέμαι ehf·khah·rees·<u>tieh</u>·meh

enough αρκετά ahr·keh·<u>tah</u>

entertainment guide οδηγός ψυχαγωγίας oh·THee·<u>ghohs</u> psee·khah·ghoh·<u>yee</u>·ahs

entrance fee τιμή εισόδου tee·<u>mee</u> ee·<u>soh</u>·THoo

epileptic επιληπτικός eh·pee·leep·tee·<u>kohs</u>

error λάθος <u>lah</u>·thohs

escalator κυλιόμενες σκάλες kee·lee·<u>oh</u>·meh·nehs <u>skah</u>·lehs

essential απαραίτητος ah·pah·<u>reh</u>·tee·tohs

e-ticket ηλεκτρονικό εισιτήριο ee·lehk·troh·nee·<u>koh</u> ee·see·<u>tee</u>·ree·oh

European Union Ευρωπαϊκή Ένωση ehv·roh·pah·ee·<u>kee</u> <u>eh</u>·noh·see

euro ευρώ ehv·<u>roh</u>

evening βράδυ <u>vrah</u>·THee

examination (medical) **ιατρική εξέταση** ee·ah·tree·<u>kee</u> eh·<u>kseh</u>·tah·see

example παράδειγμα pah·<u>rah</u>·THeegh·mah

excess baggage υπέρβαρο ee·<u>pehr</u>·vah·roh

exchange v (money) **αλλάζω** ah·<u>lah</u>·zoh

exchange rate τιμή συναλλάγματος tee·<u>mee</u> see·nah·<u>lahgh</u>·mah·tohs

excursion εκδρομή ehk·THroh·<u>mee</u>

exhibition έκθεση <u>ehk</u>·theh·see

exit n **έξοδος** <u>eh</u>·ksoh·THohs

expensive ακριβός ahk·ree·<u>vohs</u>

expiration date ημερομηνία λήξεως ee·meh·roh·mee·<u>nee</u>·ah <u>lee</u>·kseh·ohs

exposure (photos) **στάση** <u>stah</u>·see

express (mail) **εξπρές** ehk·<u>sprehs</u>

extension (number) **εσωτερική γραμμή** eh·soh·theh·ree·<u>kee</u> ghrah·<u>mee</u>

extra (additional) **άλλο ένα** <u>ah</u>·loh <u>eh</u>·nah

eye n **μάτι** <u>mah</u>·tee

F

fabric ύφασμα ee·fahs·mah

face n **πρόσωπο** proh·soh·poh

facial καθαρισμός προσώπου kah·thah·reez·mohs proh·soh·poo

facility εξυπηρέτηση eh·ksee·pee·reh·tee·see

faint λιποθυμώ lee·poh·thee·moh

fall v **πέφτω** pehf·toh

family οικογένεια ee·koh·yeh·nee·ah

famous διάσημος THee·ah·see·mohs

fan n (air) **ανεμιστήρας** ah·neh·mees·tee·rahs

far adv **μακριά** mahk·ree·ah

fare εισιτήριο ee·see·tee·ree·oh

farm n **φάρμα** fahr·mah

fast adv **γρήγορα** ghree·ghoh·rah

fat adj (person) **παχύς** pah·khees

faucet βρύση vree·see

fault λάθος lah·thohs

favorite αγαπημένος ah·ghah·pee·meh·nohs

fax facility υπηρεσία φαξ ee·pee·reh·see·ah fahks

feed v **ταΐζω** tah·ee·zoh

female θηλυκός thee·lee·kohs

fence n **φράχτης** frahkh·tees

ferry φέρυ-μπωτ feh·ree·boht

festival φεστιβάλ fehs·tee·vahl

fever πυρετός pee·reh·tohs

fiancé αρραβωνιαστικός ah·rah·voh·niahs·tee·kohs

fiancée αρραβωνιαστικιά ah·rah·voh·niahs·tee·kiah

filling (dental) **σφράγισμα** sfrah·yeez·mah

film n (camera) **φιλμ** feelm

filter n **φίλτρο** feel·troh

fine adv **καλά** kah·lah; n **πρόστιμο** prohs·tee·moh

finger n **δάχτυλο** THakh·tee·loh

fire n **φωτιά** foh·tiah

fire brigade [BE] πυροσβεστική pee·rohz·vehs·tee·kee

fire escape έξοδος κινδύνου eh·ksoh·THohs keen·THee·noo

fire extinguisher πυροσβεστήρας pee·rohz·vehs·tee·rahs

first class πρώτη θέση proh·tee theh·see

first-aid kit κουτί πρώτων βοηθειών koo·tee proh·tohn voh·ee·thee·ohn

fishing ψάρεμα psah·reh·mah

flag n **σημαία** see·meh·ah

flashlight φακός fah·kohs

flat adj **επίπεδος** eh·pee·peh·Thohs; n **διαμέρισμα** THee·ah·mehr·ees·mah

flea ψύλλος psee·lohs

flight πτήση ptee·see

flight number αριθμός πτήσεως ah·reeth·mohs ptee·seh·ohs

flip-flops σαγιονάρες sah·yoh·nah·rehs

flood n **πλημμύρα** plee·mee·rah

florist ανθοπωλείο ahn·thoh·poh·lee·oh

flower n **λουλούδι** loo·loo·THee

flu γρίππη ghree·pee

flush τραβώ το καζανάκι trah·voh toh kah·zah·nah·kee

fly n **μύγα** mee·ghah; v **πετάω** peh·tah·oh

follow v **ακολουθώ** ah·koh·loo·thoh

foot πόδι poh·THee

football [BE] ποδόσφαιρο poh·THohs·feh·roh

footpath μονοπάτι moh·noh·pah·tee

forecast n **πρόβλεψη** prohv·leh·psee

foreign ξένος kseh·nohs

foreign currency ξένο συνάλλαγμα
kseh-noh see-<u>nah</u>-lahgh-mah
forest n **δάσος** THah-sohs
forget ξεχνώ ksehkh-<u>noh</u>
form n **έντυπο** <u>ehn</u>-dee-poh
fortunately ευτυχώς ehf-tee-<u>khohs</u>
forward προωθώ proh-oh-<u>thoh</u>
fountain συντριβάνι seen-dree-<u>vah</u>-nee
free adj (available) **ελεύθερος**
eh-<u>lehf</u>-theh-rohs
freezer κατάψυξη kah-<u>tah</u>-psee-ksee
frequent adj **συχνός** seekh-<u>nohs</u>
fresh adj **φρέσκος** <u>frehs</u>-kohs
friend n **φίλος** <u>fee</u>-lohs
frightened φοβισμένος
foh-veez-<u>meh</u>-nohs
from από ah-<u>poh</u>
front n **προκυμαία** proh-kee-<u>meh</u>-ah
full adj **γεμάτος** yeh-<u>mah</u>-tohs
furniture έπιπλα <u>eh</u>-peep-lah
fuse n **ασφάλεια** ahs-<u>fah</u>-lee-ah

G

gambling τζόγος <u>joh</u>-ghohs
game (toy) **παιχνίδι** pehkh-<u>nee</u>-THee
garage γκαράζ gah-<u>rahz</u>
garden n **κήπος** <u>kee</u>-pohs
gas βενζίνη vehn-<u>zee</u>-nee
gas station βενζινάδικο
vehn-zee-<u>nah</u>-THee-koh
gastritis γαστρίτιδα ghahs-<u>tree</u>-tee-THah
gate (airport) **έξοδος** <u>eh</u>-ksoh-THohs
genuine αυθεντικός ahf-thehn-dee-<u>kohs</u>
get off (transport) **κατεβαίνω**
kah-teh-<u>veh</u>-noh
get out (of vehicle) **βγαίνω** <u>vyeh</u>-noh
gift δώρο <u>THoh</u>-roh

gift store κατάστημα με είδη δώρων
kah-<u>tahs</u>-tee-mah meh ee-<u>THee</u> <u>THoh</u>-rohn
girl κορίτσι koh-<u>ree</u>-tsee
girlfriend φίλη <u>fee</u>-lee
give δίνω <u>THee</u>-noh
glass (container) **ποτήρι** poh-<u>tee</u>-ree
glasses (optical) **γυαλιά** yah-<u>liah</u>
glove n **γάντι** <u>ghahn</u>-dee
go πηγαίνω pee-<u>yeh</u>-noh
gold n **χρυσός** khree-<u>sohs</u>
golf γκόλφ gohlf
golf course γήπεδο γκολφ <u>yee</u>-peh-THoh
gohlf
good καλός kah-<u>lohs</u>
grass γρασίδι ghrah-<u>see</u>-THee
gratuity φιλοδώρημα
fee-loh-<u>THoh</u>-ree-mah
greasy (hair, skin) **λιπαρός** lee-pah-<u>rohs</u>
Greece Ελλάδα eh-<u>lah</u>-THah
Greek adj **ελληνικός** eh-lee-nee-<u>kohs</u>;
(nationality) **Έλληνας** <u>eh</u>-lee-nahs
greengrocer [BE] οπωροπωλείο
oh-poh-roh-poh-<u>lee</u>-oh
ground (earth) **έδαφος** <u>eh</u>-THah-fohs
group n **γκρουπ** groop
guarantee n **εγγύηση** eh-<u>gee</u>-ee-see; v
εγγυώμαι eh-gee-<u>oh</u>-meh
guide book τουριστικός οδηγός
too-ree-stee-<u>kohs</u> oh-THee-<u>ghohs</u>
guided tour ξενάγηση kseh-<u>nah</u>-yee-see
guitar κιθάρα kee-<u>thah</u>-rah
gynecologist γυναικολόγος
yee-neh-koh-<u>loh</u>-ghohs

H

hair μαλλιά mah-<u>liah</u>
hairbrush βούρτσα <u>voor</u>-tsah

hair dresser κομμωτήριο
koh·moh·<u>tee</u>·ree·oh

hair dryer σεσουάρ seh·soo·<u>ahr</u>

half μισός mee·<u>sohs</u>

hammer σφυρί sfee·<u>ree</u>

hand n **χέρι** <u>kheh</u>·ree

hand luggage αποσκευές χειρός
ah·pohs·keh·<u>vehs</u> khee·<u>rohs</u>

handbag τσάντα <u>tsahn</u>·dah

handicraft λαϊκή τέχνη lah·ee·<u>kee</u>
tehkh·nee

**handicapped-accessible toilet
προσβάσιμη τουαλέτα για
ανάπηρους** prohs·<u>vah</u>·see·mee
too·ah·<u>leh</u>·tah yah ah·<u>nah</u>·pee·roos

handkerchief χαρτομάντηλο
khah·rtoh·<u>mahn</u>·dee·loh

handle n **πόμολο** <u>poh</u>·moh·loh

hanger κρεμάστρα kreh·<u>mahs</u>·trah

harbor n **λιμάνι** lee·<u>mah</u>·nee

hat καπέλο kah·<u>peh</u>·loh

have (possession) **έχω** <u>eh</u>·khoh

have to (obligation) **οφείλω**
oh·<u>fee</u>·loh

head n **κεφάλι** keh·<u>fah</u>·lee

headache πονοκέφαλος
poh·noh·<u>keh</u>·fah·lohs

**health food store κατάστημα με
υγιεινές τροφές** kah·<u>tahs</u>·tee·mah meh
ee·yee·ee·<u>nehs</u> troh·<u>fehs</u>

health insurance ασφάλεια υγείας
ahs·<u>fah</u>·lee·ah ee·<u>yee</u>·ahs

hearing aid ακουστικό βαρυκοΐας
ah·koo·stee·<u>koh</u> vah·ree·koh·<u>ee</u>·ahs

heart v **καρδιά** kahr·<u>THee</u>·ah

heart attack καρδιακό έμφραγμα
kahr·THee·ah·<u>koh</u> ehm·frahgh·mah

heat wave καύσωνας <u>kahf</u>·soh·nahs

heater (water) **θερμοσίφωνας**
thehr·moh·<u>see</u>·foh·nahs

heating θέρμανση <u>thehr</u>·mahn·see

heavy βαρύς vah·<u>rees</u>

height ύψος <u>ee</u>·psohs

helicopter ελικόπτερο
eh·lee·<u>kohp</u>·teh·roh

help n **βοήθεια** voh·<u>ee</u>·thee·ah; v **βοηθώ**
voh·ee·<u>thoh</u>

here εδώ eh·<u>THoh</u>

highway εθνική οδός ehth·nee·<u>kee</u>
oh·<u>THohs</u>

hike v **κάνω πεζοπορία** <u>kah</u>·noh
peh·zoh·poh·<u>ree</u>·ah

hill λόφος <u>loh</u>·fohs

hire [BE] v **νοικιάζω** nee·<u>kiah</u>·zoh

history ιστορία ee·stoh·<u>ree</u>·ah

hitchhiking οτοστόπ oh·toh·<u>stohp</u>

hobby (pastime) **χόμπυ** <u>khoh</u>·bee

hold on περιμένω peh·ree·<u>meh</u>·noh

hole (in clothes) **τρύπα** <u>tree</u>·pah

holiday [BE] διακοπές THee·ah·koh·<u>pehs</u>

honeymoon μήνας του μέλιτος
<u>mee</u>·nahs too <u>meh</u>·lee·tohs

horse track ιπποδρόμιο
ee·poh·<u>THroh</u>·mee·oh

hospital νοσοκομείο
noh·soh·koh·<u>mee</u>·oh

hot (weather) **ζεστός** zehs·<u>tohs</u>

hot spring θερμή πηγή thehr·<u>mee</u>
pee·<u>yee</u>

hotel ξενοδοχείο kseh·noh·THoh·<u>khee</u>·oh

household articles **είδη οικιακής χρήσεως**
<u>ee</u>·THee ee·kee·ah·<u>kees</u> <u>khree</u>·seh·ohs

husband σύζυγος <u>see</u>·zee·ghohs

I

ice *n* **πάγος** pah·ghohs

identification ταυτότητα
tahf·<u>toh</u>·tee·tah

illegal παράνομος pah·<u>rah</u>·noh·mohs

illness αρρώστεια ahr·<u>ohs</u>·tee·ah

imitation απομίμηση
ah·poh·<u>mee</u>·mee·see

immediately αμέσως ah·<u>meh</u>·sohs

impressive εντυπωσιακός
ehn·dee·poh·see·ah·<u>kohs</u>

included συμπεριλαμβάνεται
seem·beh·ree·lahm·<u>vah</u>·neh·teh

indigestion δυσπεψία
THehs·peh·<u>psee</u>·ah

indoor εσωτερικός eh·soh·teh·ree·<u>kohs</u>

indoor pool εσωτερική πισίνα
eh·soh·teh·ree·<u>kee</u> pee·<u>see</u>·nah

inexpensive φτηνός ftee·<u>nohs</u>

infected μολυσμένος
moh·leez·<u>meh</u>·nohs

inflammation φλεγμονή
flegh·moh·<u>nee</u>

information πληροφορίες
plee·roh·foh·<u>ree</u>·ehs

**information office γραφείο
πληροφοριών** ghrah·<u>fee</u>·oh
plee·roh·foh·ree·<u>ohn</u>

injection ένεση <u>eh</u>·neh·see

injured τραυματισμένος
trahv·mah·teez·<u>meh</u>·nohs

innocent αθώος ah·<u>thoh</u>·ohs

insect bite τσίμπημα από έντομο
<u>tseem</u>·bee·mah ah·<u>poh</u> <u>ehn</u>·toh·moh

insect repellent εντομοαπωθητικό
ehn·toh·moh·ah·poh·thee·tee·<u>koh</u>

inside μέσα <u>meh</u>·sah

insist επιμένω eh·pee·<u>meh</u>·noh

insomnia αϋπνία ah·eep·<u>nee</u>·ah

instruction οδηγία oh·THee·<u>yee</u>·ah

insulin ινσουλίνη een·soo·<u>lee</u>·nee

insurance ασφάλεια ahs·<u>fah</u>·lee·ah

**insurance certificate πιστοποιητικό
ασφάλειας** pees·toh·pee·ee·tee·<u>koh</u>
ahs·<u>fah</u>·lee·ahs

**insurance claim ασφάλεια
αποζημίωσης** ahs·<u>fah</u>·lee·ah
ah·poh·zee·<u>mee</u>·oh·sees

**insurance company ασφαλιστική
εταιρία** ahs·fah·lees·tee·<u>kee</u>
eh·teh·<u>ree</u>·ah

interest rate επιτόκιο
eh·pee·<u>toh</u>·kee·oh

interesting ενδιαφέρων
ehn·THee·ah·<u>feh</u>·rohn

international διεθνής THee·eth·<u>nees</u>

**International Student Card διεθνής
φοιτητική κάρτα** THee·eth·<u>nees</u>
fee·tee·tee·<u>kee</u> <u>kahr</u>·tah

internet ίντερνετ <u>ee</u>·nteh·rnet

internet cafe ίντερνετ καφέ
<u>ee</u>·nteh·rnet kah·<u>feh</u>

interpreter διερμηνέας
THee·ehr·mee·<u>neh</u>·ahs

interval διάλειμμα THee·<u>ah</u>·lee·mah

introduce συστήνω see·<u>stee</u>·noh

introductions συστάσεις see·<u>stah</u>·sees

invitation πρόσκληση <u>prohs</u>·klee·see

invite *v* **προσκαλώ** prohs·kah·<u>loh</u>

iodine ιώδειο ee·<u>oh</u>·THee·oh

iron *n* **σίδερο** <u>see</u>·THee·roh; *v* **σιδερώνω**
see·THee·<u>roh</u>·noh

**itemized bill αναλυτικός
λογαριασμός** ah·nah·lee·tee·<u>kohs</u>
loh·ghahr·yahz·<u>mohs</u>

J

jacket σακάκι sah-<u>kah</u>-kee
jammed σφηνωμένος sfee-noh-<u>meh</u>-nohs
jar *n* βάζο <u>vah</u>-zoh
jaw σαγόνι sah-<u>ghoh</u>-nee
jeans μπλου-τζην bloo-<u>jeen</u>
jellyfish μέδουσα meh-THoo-sah
jet-ski τζετ-σκι jeht-skee
jeweler κοσμηματοπωλείο
    kohz-mee-mah-toh-poh-<u>lee</u>-oh
job δουλειά THoo-<u>liah</u>
jogging τζόγκιγκ joh-geeng
joke *n* ανέκδοτο ah-<u>nehk</u>-THoh-toh
journey ταξίδι tah-<u>ksee</u>-THee
junction (intersection*)* **κόμβος** <u>kohm</u>-vohs

K

keep *v* **κρατώ** krah-<u>toh</u>
key *n* **κλειδί** klee-<u>THee</u>
key card **κάρτα-κλειδί** <u>kahr</u>-tah-klee-<u>dee</u>
key ring **μπρελόκ** breh-<u>lohk</u>
kidney **νεφρό** nehf-<u>roh</u>
kind **είδος** <u>ee</u>-THohs
king **βασιλιάς** vah-see-<u>liahs</u>
kiosk **περίπτερο** peh-<u>ree</u>-pteh-roh
kiss **φιλί** fee-<u>lee</u>; *v* φιλώ fee-<u>loh</u>
kitchen **χαρτί κουζίνας** khah-<u>rtee</u>
    koo-<u>zee</u>-nahs
knapsack **σάκκος** <u>sah</u>-kohs
knee **γόνατο** <u>ghoh</u>-nah-toh
knife **μαχαίρι** mah-<u>kheh</u>-ree
know **γνωρίζω** ghnoh-<u>ree</u>-zoh

L

label *n* **ετικέτα** eh-tee-<u>keh</u>-tah
ladder **σκάλα** <u>skah</u>-lah

lake **λίμνη** <u>leem</u>-nee
lamp **λάμπα** <u>lahm</u>-bah
land *n* **γη** ghee; *v* **προσγειώνομαι**
    prohz-yee-<u>oh</u>-noh-meh
language course **μάθημα ξένης**
    γλώσσας <u>mah</u>-thee-mah <u>kseh</u>-nees
    <u>ghloh</u>-sahs
large *adj* **μεγάλος** meh-<u>ghah</u>-lohs
last **τελευταίος** teh-lehf-<u>teh</u>-ohs
late *adv* **αργά** ahr-<u>ghah</u>
laugh *v* **γελώ** yeh-<u>loh</u>
laundry facility **πλυντήριο**
    pleen-<u>dee</u>-ree-oh
lavatory **μπάνιο** <u>bah</u>-nioh
lawyer **δικηγόρος** THee-kee-<u>ghoh</u>-rohs
laxative **καθαρτικό** kah-thahr-tee-<u>koh</u>
learn **μαθαίνω** mah-<u>theh</u>-noh
leave (*v* (depart) **φεύγω** <u>fehv</u>-ghoh; (let
    go) **αφήνω** ah-<u>fee</u>-noh
left *adj* **αριστερός** ah-rees-teh-<u>rohs</u>; *adv*
    αριστερά ah-rees-teh-<u>rah</u>
leg **πόδι** poh-<u>THee</u>
legal **νόμιμος** <u>noh</u>-mee-mohs
lend **δανείζω** THah-<u>nee</u>-zoh
length **μήκος** <u>mee</u>-kohs
lens **φακός** fah-<u>kohs</u>
lens cap **κάλυμμα φακού** <u>kah</u>-lee-mah
    fah-<u>koo</u>
less **λιγότερο** lee-<u>ghoh</u>-teh-roh
letter **γράμμα** <u>ghrah</u>-mah
level (even) **επίπεδο** eh-<u>pee</u>-peh-THoh
library **βιβλιοθήκη** veev-lee-oh-<u>thee</u>-kee
lie down **ξαπλώνω** ksah-<u>ploh</u>-noh
life boat **ναυαγοσωστική λέμβος**
    nah-vah-ghoh-sohs-tee-<u>kee</u> <u>lehm</u>-vohs
lifeguard **ναυαγοσώστης**
    nah-vah-ghoh-<u>sohs</u>-tees
life jacket **σωσίβιο** soh-<u>see</u>-vee-oh

lift [BE] *n* (elevator) **ασανσέρ** ah‑sahn‑<u>sehr</u>

lift pass άδεια σκι <u>ah</u>‑THee‑ah skee

light *adj* (color) **ανοιχτός** ah‑neekh‑<u>tohs</u>; *n* (electric) **φως** fohs

light bulb λάμπα <u>lahm</u>‑bah

lighter *adj* **ανοιχτότερος** ah‑neekh‑<u>toh</u>‑teh‑rohs; *n* **αναπτήρας** ah‑nahp‑<u>tee</u>‑rahs

lighthouse φάρος <u>fah</u>‑rohs

lights (car) **φώτα** <u>foh</u>‑tah

line *n* (subway) **γραμμή** ghrah‑<u>mee</u>

lips χείλη <u>khee</u>‑lee

lipstick κραγιόν krah‑<u>yohn</u>

liter λίτρο <u>lee</u>‑troh

little μικρός meek‑<u>rohs</u>

liver συκώτι see‑<u>koh</u>‑tee

living room σαλόνι sah‑<u>loh</u>‑nee

local τοπικός toh‑pee‑<u>kohs</u>

location (space) **θέση** <u>theh</u>‑see

lock *n* (door) **κλειδαριά** klee‑THah‑<u>ryah</u>; (river, canal) **φράγμα** <u>frahgh</u>‑mah; *v* **κλειδώνω** klee‑<u>THoh</u>‑noh

long *adj* **μακρύς** mak‑<u>rees</u>

long‑distance bus υπεραστικό λεωφορείο ee‑peh‑rahs‑tee‑<u>koh</u> leh‑oh‑foh‑<u>ree</u>‑oh

long‑distance call υπεραστικό τηλεφώνημα ee‑pehr‑ahs‑tee‑<u>koh</u> tee‑leh‑<u>foh</u>‑nee‑mah

long‑sighted [BE] **πρεσβύωπας** prehz‑<u>vee</u>‑oh‑pahs

look *v* **κοιτάω** kee‑<u>tah</u>‑oh

look for ψάχνω <u>psahkh</u>‑noh

loose (fitting) **φαρδύς** fahr‑<u>THees</u>

loss *n* **απώλεια** ah‑<u>poh</u>‑lee‑ah

lotion λοσιόν loh‑<u>siohn</u>

loud *adj* **δυνατός** THee‑nah‑<u>tohs</u>

love *v* **αγαπώ** ah‑ghah‑<u>poh</u>

lower *adj* (berth) **κάτω** kah‑toh

lubricant λιπαντικό lee‑pahn‑dee‑<u>koh</u>

luck τύχη <u>tee</u>‑khee

luggage αποσκευές ah‑pohs‑keh‑<u>vehs</u>

luggage cart καροτσάκι αποσκευών kah‑roh‑<u>tsah</u>‑kee ah‑pohs‑keh‑<u>vohn</u>

luggage locker θυρίδα thee‑<u>ree</u>‑THah

lukewarm χλιαρός khlee‑ah‑<u>rohs</u>

lump *n* **σβώλος** <u>svoh</u>‑lohs; (medical) **εξόγκωμα** eh‑<u>kso</u>‑goh‑mah

lunch *n* **μεσημεριανό** meh‑see‑mehr‑yah‑<u>noh</u>

lung πνεύμονας <u>pnehv</u>‑moh‑nahs

luxury πολυτέλεια poh‑lee‑<u>teh</u>‑lee‑ah

M

magazine περιοδικό peh‑ree‑oh‑THee‑<u>koh</u>

magnificent μεγαλοπρεπής meh‑ghah‑lohp‑reh‑<u>pees</u>

mailbox ταχυδρομικό κουτί tah‑kheeTH‑roh‑mee‑<u>koh</u> koo‑tee

mail *n* **αλληλογραφία** ah‑lee‑lohgh‑rah‑<u>fee</u>‑ah

main κύριος <u>kee</u>‑ree‑ohs

make‑up μακιγιάζ mah‑kee‑<u>yahz</u>

man (male) **άνδρας** <u>ahn</u>‑THrahs

manager διευθυντής THee‑ehf‑theen‑<u>dees</u>

manicure μανικιούρ mah‑nee‑<u>kioor</u>

manual (car) **χειροκίνητος** khee‑roh‑<u>kee</u>‑nee‑tohs

map *n* **χάρτης** <u>khahr</u>‑tees

market *n* **αγορά** ah‑ghoh‑<u>rah</u>

married παντρεμένος pahn‑dreh‑<u>meh</u>‑nohs

mask n (diving) **μάσκα** <u>mahs</u>·kah

mass n (church) **λειτουργία**
lee·toor·<u>yee</u>·ah

massage n **μασάζ** mah·<u>sahz</u>

match n (sport) **αγώνας** ah·<u>ghoh</u>·nahs;
(fire starter) **σπίρτο** <u>speer</u>·toh

maybe **ίσως** <u>ee</u>·sohs

meal **γεύμα** <u>yehv</u>·mah

mean v **σημαίνω** see·<u>meh</u>·noh

measure v **μετρώ** meht·<u>roh</u>

measurement **μέτρηση** <u>meh</u>·tree·see

medication **φάρμακα** <u>fahr</u>·mah·kah

meet **συναντώ** see·nahn·<u>doh</u>

memorial **μνημείο** mnee·<u>mee</u>·oh

mend **διορθώνω** THee·ohr·<u>thoh</u>·noh

menstrual cramp **πόνος περιόδου**
<u>poh</u>·nohs peh·ree·<u>oh</u>·THoo

mention **αναφέρω** ah·nah·<u>feh</u>·roh

message n **μήνυμα** <u>mee</u>·nee·mah

metal n **μέταλλο** <u>meh</u>·tah·loh

microwave (oven) **φούρνος**
μικροκυμάτων <u>foor</u>·nohs
mee·kroh·kee·<u>mah</u>·tohn

migraine **ημικρανία** ee·mee·krah·<u>nee</u>·ah

mileage **χιλιόμετρα** khee·<u>lioh</u>·meh·trah

mini-bar **μίνι-μπαρ** <u>mee</u>·nee·bahr

minimart **παντοπωλείο**
pahn·doh·poh·<u>lee</u>·oh

minimum **ελάχιστος** eh·<u>lah</u>·khees·tohs

minute n (time) **λεπτό** lehp·<u>toh</u>

mirror n **καθρέφτης** kah·<u>threhf</u>·tees

mistake **λάθος** <u>lah</u>·thohs

misunderstanding **παρεξήγηση**
pah·reh·<u>ksee</u>·yee·see

mobile phone [BE] **κινητό** kee·nee·<u>toh</u>

modern **μοντέρνος** moh·<u>deh</u>·rnohs

moisturizer (cream) **ενυδατική κρέμα**
eh·nee·THah·tee·<u>kee</u> <u>kreh</u>·mah

money **χρήματα** <u>khree</u>·mah·tah

money order **ταχυδρομική επιταγή**
tah·kheeTH·roh·mee·<u>kee</u> eh·pee·tah·<u>yee</u>

money-belt **ζώνη για χρήματα** <u>zoh</u>·nee
yah <u>khree</u>·mah·tah

monument **μνημείο** mnee·<u>mee</u>·oh

moped **μοτοποδήλατο**
moh·toh·poh·<u>THee</u>·lah·toh

more **παραπάνω** pah·rah·<u>pah</u>·noh

morning **πρωί** proh·<u>ee</u>

mosquito **κουνούπι** koo·<u>noo</u>·pee

mosquito bite **τσίμπημα κουνουπιού**
<u>tseem</u>·bee·mah koo·noo·<u>piooh</u>

motorboat **εξωλέμβιο**
eh·ksoh·<u>lehm</u>·vee·oh

motorway [BE] **εθνική οδός**
ehth·nee·<u>kee</u> oh·<u>THohs</u>

mountain **βουνό** voo·<u>noh</u>

moustache **μουστάκι** moos·<u>tah</u>·kee

mouth n **στόμα** <u>stoh</u>·mah

move v (room) **μετακομίζω**
meh·tah·koh·<u>mee</u>·zoh

movie **ταινία** teh·<u>nee</u>·ah

movie theater **κινηματογράφος**
kee·nee·mah·tohgh·<u>rah</u>·fohs

much **πολύ** poh·<u>lee</u>

muscle n **μυς** mees

museum **μουσείο** moo·<u>see</u>·oh

music **μουσική** moo·see·<u>kee</u>

musician **μουσικός** moo·see·<u>kohs</u>

must v **πρέπει** <u>preh</u>·pee

N

nail salon **σαλόνι νυχιών** sah·<u>loh</u>·nee
nee·<u>khiohn</u>

name n **όνομα** <u>oh</u>·noh·mah

napkin **πετσέτα** peh·<u>tseh</u>·tah

nappy [BE] **πάνα μωρού** pah·nah moh·**roo**

narrow **στενός** steh·**nohs**

national **εθνικός** eth·nee·**kohs**

nationality **υπηκοότητα** ee·pee·koh·**oh**·tee·tah

nature **φύση** **fee**·see

nature reserve **εθνικός δρυμός** eth·nee·**kohs** THree·**mohs**

nature trail **μονοπάτι** moh·noh·**pah**·tee

nausea **ναυτία** nahf·**tee**·ah

near adv **κοντά** kohn·**dah**

nearby **εδώ κοντά** eh·**THoh** kohn·**dah**

necessary **απαραίτητος** ah·pah·**reh**·tee·tohs

necklace **κολλιέ** koh·**lieh**

need v **χρειάζομαι** khree·**ah**·zoh·meh

neighbor n **γείτονας** **yee**·toh·nahs

nerve **νεύρο** **nehv**·roh

never **ποτέ** poh·**teh**

new **καινούργιος** keh·**noor**·yohs

newspaper **εφημερίδα** eh·fee·meh·**ree**·THah

newsstand **περίπτερο** peh·**ree**·pteh·roh

next **επόμενος** eh·**poh**·meh·nohs

next to **δίπλα** **THeep**·lah

night **νύχτα** **neekh**·tah

night club **νυχτερινό κέντρο** neekh·teh·ree·**noh** **kehn**·droh

noisy **θορυβώδης** thoh·ree·**voh**·THees

none adj **κανένας** kah·**neh**·nahs

non-smoking **μη καπνίζοντες** mee kap·**nee**·zohn·dehs

north **βόρεια** **voh**·ree·ah

nose n **μύτη** **mee**·tee

nudist beach **παραλία γυμνιστών** pah·rah·**lee**·ah yeem·nees·**tohn**

nurse n **νοσοκόμα** noh·soh·**koh**·mah

O

occupied **κατειλημένος** kah·tee·lee·**meh**·nohs

office **γραφείο** ghrah·**fee**·oh

old adj (thing) **παλιός** pah·**liohs**; (person) **γέρικος** **yeh**·ree·kohs

old town **παλιά πόλη** pah·**liah** poh·lee

old-fashioned **ντεμοντέ** deh·mohn·**deh**

once **μια φορά** miah foh·**rah**

one-way ticket **απλό εισιτήριο** ahp·**loh** ee·see·**tee**·ree·oh

open adj **ανοιχτός** ah·neekh·**tohs**; v **ανοίγω** ah·**nee**·ghoh

opening hours **ώρες λειτουργίας** **oh**·rehs lee·toor·**yee**·ahs

opera **όπερα** **oh**·peh·rah

opposite **απέναντι** ah·**peh**·nahn·dee

optician **οφθαλμίατρος** ohf·thahl·**mee**·aht·rohs

orchestra **ορχήστρα** ohr·**khees**·trah

order v **παραγγέλνω** pah·rah·**gehl**·noh

organized **οργανωμένος** ohr·ghah·noh·**meh**·nohs

others **άλλα** **ah**·lah

out adv **έξω** **eh**·ksoh

outdoor **εξωτερικός** eh·ksoh·teh·ree·**kohs**

outside adj **έξω** **eh**·ksoh

oval **οβάλ** oh·**vahl**

oven **φούρνος** **foor**·nohs

over there **εκεί** eh·**kee**

overnight (package) **ένα βράδυ** <u>eh</u>·nah <u>vrah</u>·THee

owe **χρωστώ** khroh·<u>stoh</u>

owner **κάτοχος** <u>kah</u>·toh·khohs

P

pacifier **πιπίλα** pee·<u>pee</u>·lah

pack v (baggage) **φτιάχνω τις βαλίτσες** ftee·<u>ahkh</u>·noh tees vah·<u>lee</u>·tsehs

paddling pool [BE] **ρηχή πισίνα** ree·<u>khee</u> pee·<u>see</u>·nah

padlock **λουκέτο** loo·<u>keh</u>·toh

pain n **πόνος** <u>poh</u>·nohs

painkiller **παυσίπονο** pahf·<u>see</u>·poh·noh

paint v **ζωγραφίζω** zohgh·rah·<u>fee</u>·zoh

pair **ζευγάρι** zehv·<u>ghah</u>·ree

pajamas **πυτζάμες** pee·<u>jah</u>·mehs

palace **ανάκτορα** ah·<u>nahk</u>·toh·rah

panorama **πανόραμα** pah·<u>noh</u>·rah·mah

pants **παντελόνι** pahn·deh·<u>loh</u>·nee

paper **χαρτί** khar·<u>tee</u>

paralysis **παραλυσία** pah·rah·lee·<u>see</u>·ah

parcel **πακέτο** pah·<u>keh</u>·toh

parents **γονείς** ghoh·<u>nees</u>

park n **πάρκο** <u>pahr</u>·koh

parking lot **χώρος στάθμευσης** <u>khoh</u>·rohs <u>stahth</u>·mehf·sees

parking meter **παρκόμετρο** pahr·<u>koh</u>·meht·roh

party n (social gathering) **πάρτυ** <u>pah</u>·rtee

pass v **περνώ** pehr·<u>noh</u>

passenger **επιβάτης** eh·pee·<u>vah</u>·tees

passport **διαβατήριο** THiah·vah·<u>tee</u>·ree·oh

pastry store **ζαχαροπλαστείο** zah·khah·rohp·lahs·<u>tee</u>·oh

path **μονοπάτι** moh·noh·<u>pah</u>·tee

pay v **πληρώνω** plee·<u>roh</u>·noh

payment **πληρωμή** plee·roh·<u>mee</u>

peak n **κορυφή** koh·ree·<u>fee</u>

pearl **μαργαριτάρι** mahr·ghah·ree·<u>tah</u>·ree

pebbly (beach) **με χαλίκια** meh khah·<u>lee</u>·kiah

pedestrian crossing **διάβαση πεζών** THee·<u>ah</u>·vah·see peh·<u>zohn</u>

pedestrian zone **πεζόδρομος** peh·<u>zohTH</u>·roh·mohs

pen n **στυλό** stee·<u>loh</u>

per **την** teen

perhaps **ίσως** <u>ee</u>·sohs

period (menstrual) **περίοδος** peh·<u>ree</u>·oh·THohs; (time) **χρονική περίοδος** khroh·nee·<u>kee</u> peh·<u>ree</u>·oh·Thohs

permit n **άδεια** <u>ah</u>·THee·ah

petrol [BE] **βενζίνη** vehn·<u>zee</u>·nee

pewter **κασσίτερος** kah·<u>see</u>·teh·rohs

phone n **τηλέφωνο** tee·<u>leh</u>·foh·noh

phone call **τηλεφώνημα** tee·leh·<u>foh</u>·nee·mah

phone card **τηλεκάρτα** tee·leh·<u>kahr</u>·tah

photo v **φωτογραφία** foh·tohgh·rah·<u>fee</u>·ah

photocopier **φωτοτυπικό** foh·toh·tee·pee·<u>koh</u>

phrase n **φράση** <u>frah</u>·see

pick up **παίρνω** <u>pehr</u>·noh

picnic area **περιοχή για πικνίκ** peh·ree·oh·<u>khee</u> yah peek·neek

piece **τεμάχιο** teh·<u>mah</u>·khee·oh

pillow **μαξιλάρι** mah·ksee·<u>lah</u>·ree

pillow case **μαξιλαροθήκη** mah·ksee·lah·roh·<u>thee</u>·kee

pipe (smoking) **πίπα** pee·pah

piste [BE] **μονοπάτι** moh·noh·<u>pah</u>·tee

pizzeria **πιτσαρία** pee·tsah·<u>ree</u>·ah

plan n **σχέδιο** skheh·<u>THee</u>·oh

plane n **αεροπλάνο** ah·eh·rohp·<u>lah</u>·noh

plant n **φυτό** fee·<u>toh</u>

plastic wrap **διαφανή μεμβράνη**
THee·ah·fah·<u>nee</u> mehm·<u>vrah</u>·nee

platform **αποβάθρα** ah·poh·<u>vahth</u>·rah

platinum **πλατίνα** plah·<u>tee</u>·nah

play v (games) **παίζω** peh·zoh; (music)
παίζω peh·zoh

playground **παιδική χαρά** peh·THee·<u>kee</u>
khah·<u>rah</u>

pleasant **ευχάριστος** ehf·<u>khah</u>·rees·tohs

plug n **πρίζα** <u>pree</u>·zah

point n **σημείο** see·<u>mee</u>·oh; v **δείχνω**
<u>THeekh</u>·noh

poison n **δηλητήριο** THee·lee·<u>tee</u>·ree·oh

poisonous **δηλητηριώδης**
THee·lee·tee·ree·<u>oh</u>·THees

police n **αστυνομία** ah·stee·noh·<u>mee</u>·ah

police station **αστυνομικό τμήμα**
ah·stee·noh·mee·<u>koh</u> <u>tmee</u>·mah

pond n **λιμνούλα** leem·<u>noo</u>·lah

popular **δημοφιλής** THee·moh·fee·<u>lees</u>

porter **αχθοφόρος** ahkh·thoh·<u>foh</u>·rohs

portion n **μερίδα** meh·<u>ree</u>·THah

possible **πιθανός** pee·thah·<u>nohs</u>

postbox [BE] **ταχυδρομικό κουτί**
tah·kheeTH·roh·mee·<u>koh</u> koo·<u>tee</u>

post card **καρτποστάλ** kahrt·poh·<u>stahl</u>

post office **ταχυδρομείο**
tah·kheeTH·roh·<u>mee</u>·oh

pottery **αγγειοπλαστική**
ahn·gee·ohp·lahs·tee·<u>kee</u>

pound (sterling) **λίρα** <u>lee</u>·rah

pregnant **έγκυος** <u>eh</u>·gee·ohs

prescribe **συνταγογραφώ**
seen·dah·ghoh·ghrah·<u>foh</u>

prescription **συνταγή γιατρού**
seen·dah·<u>yee</u> yaht·<u>roo</u>

present **δώρο** <u>THoh</u>·roh

press v **σιδερώνω** see·THeh·<u>roh</u>·noh

pretty adj **όμορφος** <u>oh</u>·mohr·fohs

prison n **φυλακή** fee·lah·<u>kee</u>

private bathroom **ιδιωτικό μπάνιο**
ee·THee·oh·tee·<u>koh</u> bah·nioh

problem **πρόβλημα** <u>prohv</u>·lee·mah

program n **πρόγραμμα** <u>prohgh</u>·rah·mah

program of events **πρόγραμμα**
θεαμάτων <u>proh</u>·ghrah·mah
theh·ah·<u>mah</u>·tohn

prohibited **απαγορευμένος**
ah·pah·ghoh·rehv·<u>meh</u>·nohs

pronounce **προφέρω** proh·<u>feh</u>·roh

public **δημόσιος** THee·<u>moh</u>·see·ohs

public holiday **αργία** ahr·<u>yee</u>·ah

pump n **τρόμπα** <u>troh</u>·mbah

purpose **σκοπός** skoh·<u>pohs</u>

put v **βάζω** <u>vah</u>·zoh

Q

quality **ποιότητα** pee·<u>oh</u>·tee·tah

quantity **ποσότητα** poh·<u>soh</u>·tee·tah

quarantine n **καραντίνα**
kah·rahn·<u>dee</u>·nah

quarter (quantity) **ένα τέταρτο** <u>eh</u>·nah
<u>teh</u>·tah·rtoh

quay **αποβάθρα** ah·poh·<u>vath</u>·rah

question n **ερώτηση** eh·<u>roh</u>·tee·see

queue [BE] v **περιμένω στην ουρά**
peh·ree·<u>meh</u>·noh steen oo·<u>rah</u>

quick **γρήγορος** <u>ghree</u>·ghoh·rohs

quiet adj **ήσυχος** <u>ee</u>·see·khohs

R

racket (tennis, squash) **ρακέτα**
rah-<u>keh</u>-tah

radio n **ραδιόφωνο** rah-THee-<u>oh</u>-foh-noh

railway station [BE] **σιδηροδρομικός**
σταθμός see-THee-rohTH-roh-mee-<u>kohs</u>
stahth-<u>mohs</u>

rain n **βροχή** vroh-<u>khee</u>; v **βρέχει** <u>vreh</u>-khee

raincoat αδιάβροχο
ah-THee-<u>ahv</u>-roh-khoh

rapids ρεύμα ποταμού <u>rehv</u>-mah
poh-tah-<u>moo</u>

rare (unusual) **σπάνιος** <u>spah</u>-nee-ohs

rash n **εξάνθημα** eh-<u>ksahn</u>-thee-mah

ravine ρεματιά reh-mah-<u>tiah</u>

razor ξυραφάκι ksee-rah-<u>fah</u>-kee

razor blade ξυραφάκι ksee-rah-<u>fah</u>-kee

ready adj **έτοιμος** eh-<u>tee</u>-mohs

real (genuine) **γνήσιος** <u>ghee</u>see-ohs;
(true) **αληθινός** ah-lee-thee-nohs

receipt απόδειξη ah-<u>poh</u>-THee-ksee

reception (hotel) **ρεσεψιόν**
reh-seh-<u>psiohn</u>

recommend συστήνω sees-<u>tee</u>-noh

reduction έκπτωση <u>ehk</u>-ptoh-see

refund n **επιστροφή χρημάτων**
eh-pees-troh-<u>fee</u> khree-<u>mah</u>-tohn

region περιοχή peh-ree-oh-<u>khee</u>

registration number αριθμός
κυκλοφορίας ah-reeth-<u>mohs</u>
kee-kloh-foh-<u>ree</u>-ahs

religion θρησκεία three-<u>skee</u>-ah

remember θυμάμαι thee-<u>mah</u>-meh

rent v **νοικιάζω** nee-<u>kiah</u>-zoh

repair n **επισκευή** eh-pee-skeh-<u>vee</u>; v
επισκευάζω eh-pee-skeh-<u>vah</u>-zoh

repeat v **επαναλαμβάνω**
eh-pah-nah-lahm-<u>vah</u>-noh

replacement part ανταλλακτικό
ahn-dah-lahk-tee-<u>koh</u>

report v **αναφέρω** ah-nah-<u>feh</u>-roh

restaurant εστιατόριο
ehs-tee-ah-<u>toh</u>-ree-oh

restroom τουαλέτα too-ah-<u>leh</u>-tah

retired συνταξιούχος
seen-dah-ksee-<u>oo</u>-khohs

return ticket [BE] **εισιτήριο με**
επιστροφή ee-see-<u>tee</u>-ree-oh meh
eh-pee-stroh-<u>fee</u>

reverse the charges με χρέωση του
καλούμενου meh <u>khreh</u>-oh-see too
kah-<u>loo</u>-meh-noo

revolting αηδιαστικός
ah-ee-THee-ah-stee-<u>kohs</u>

rib πλευρό plehv-<u>roh</u>

right adj (correct) **σωστός** soh-<u>stohs</u>;
(side) **δεξιός** THeh-ksee-<u>ohs</u>

river ποταμός poh-tah-<u>mohs</u>

road δρόμος THroh-mohs

road assistance οδική βοήθεια
oh-THee-<u>kee</u> voh-<u>ee</u>-thee-ah

road sign πινακίδα pee-nah-<u>kee</u>-Thah

robbery ληστεία lees-<u>tee</u>-ah

rock n **βράχος** <u>vrah</u>-khohs

rock climbing αναρρίχηση
ah-nah-<u>ree</u>-khee-see

romantic ρομαντικός
roh-mahn-dee-<u>kohs</u>

roof n **στέγη** <u>steh</u>-yee

room n **δωμάτιο** THoh-<u>mah</u>-tee-oh

room service υπηρεσία δωματίου
ee-pee-reh-<u>see</u>-ah THoh-mah-<u>tee</u>-oo

rope n **σχοινί** skhee-<u>nee</u>

round adj **στρογγυλός**
strohn-gkee-<u>lohs</u>; n (of golf) **παιχνίδι**
pehkh-<u>nee</u>-THee

round-trip ticket εισιτήριο με επιστροφή ee-see-<u>tee</u>-ree-oh meh eh-pee-stroh-<u>fee</u>

route n **διαδρομή** THee-ahTH-roh-<u>mee</u>

rowing κωπηλασία koh-pee-lah-<u>see</u>-ah

rubbish [BE] **σκουπίδια** skoo-<u>peeTH</u>-yah

rude αγενής ah-yeh-<u>nees</u>

rug χαλί khah-<u>lee</u>

run v **τρέχω** <u>treh</u>-khoh

rush hour ώρα αιχμής <u>oh</u>-rah ehkh-<u>mees</u>

S

safe adj (not dangerous) **ασφαλής** ahs-fah-<u>lees</u>

sailing boat ιστιοπλοϊκό ees-tee-oh-ploh-ee-<u>koh</u>

sales tax ΦΠΑ fee-pee-<u>ah</u>

same ίδιος <u>ee</u>-THee-ohs

sand άμμος <u>ah</u>-mohs

sandals πέδιλα peh-<u>THee</u>-lah

sandy (beach) **με άμμο** meh <u>ah</u>-moh

sanitary napkin σερβιέτα sehr-vee-<u>eh</u>-tah

satin σατέν sah-<u>tehn</u>

saucepan κατσαρόλα kah-tsah-<u>roh</u>-lah

sauna σάουνα <u>sah</u>-oo-nah

scarf κασκόλ kahs-<u>kohl</u>

scissors ψαλίδι psah-<u>lee</u>-THee

scratch γρατζουνιά ghrah-joo-<u>niah</u>

screw n **βίδα** <u>vee</u>-THah

screwdriver κατσαβίδι kah-tsah-<u>vee</u>-THee

sea θάλασσα <u>thah</u>-lah-sah

seafront προκυμαία proh-kee-<u>meh</u>-ah

seat n **θέση** <u>theh</u>-see

second-hand shop κατάστημα μεταχειρισμένων

ειδών kah-<u>tah</u>-stee-mah meh-tah-khee-reez-<u>meh</u>-nohn ee-<u>THohn</u>

sedative ηρεμιστικό ee-reh-mee-stee-<u>koh</u>

see βλέπω <u>vleh</u>-poh

send στέλνω <u>stehl</u>-noh

senior citizen ηλικιωμένος ee-lee-kee-oh-<u>meh</u>-nohs

separately ξεχωριστά kseh-khoh-ree-<u>stah</u>

service n (business) **υπηρεσία** ee-pee-reh-<u>see</u>-ah; (mass) **λειτουργία** lee-toor-<u>yee</u>-ah

service charge χρέωση υπηρεσίας <u>khreh</u>-oh-see ee-pee-reh-<u>see</u>-ahs

sewer υπόνομος ee-<u>poh</u>-noh-mohs

shade (color) **απόχρωση** ah-<u>pohkh</u>-r oh-see; (darkness) **σκιά** skee-<u>ah</u>

shampoo n **σαμπουάν** sahm-poo-<u>ahn</u>

shape n **σχήμα** <u>skhee</u>-mah

shaving cream κρέμα ξυρίσματος <u>kreh</u>-mah ksee-<u>reez</u>-mah-tohs

shelf n **ράφι** <u>rah</u>-fee

ship n **πλοίο** <u>plee</u>-oh

shirt πουκάμισο poo-<u>kah</u>-mee-soh

shock (electric) **ηλεκτροπληξία** ee-leh-ktroh-plee-<u>ksee</u>-ah

shoe παπούτσι pah-<u>poo</u>-tsee

shoe polish βερνίκι παπουτσιών vehr-<u>nee</u>-kee pah-poo-<u>tsiohn</u>

shoe repair επισκευή παπουτσιών eh-pee-skeh-<u>vee</u> pah-poo-<u>tsiohn</u>

shoe store κατάστημα υποδημάτων kah-<u>tah</u>-stee-mah ee-poh-THee-<u>mah</u>-tohn

shop (store) **κατάστημα** kah-<u>tah</u>-stee-mah

shopping mall εμπορικό κέντρο
ehm·boh·ree·<u>koh</u> keh·ntroh

shore n **ακτή** ahk·<u>tee</u>

short adj **κοντός** kohn·<u>dohs</u>

shorts n **σορτς** sohrts

short-sighted [BE] μύωπας <u>mee</u>·oh·pahs

shoulder n (anatomy) **ώμος** <u>oh</u>·mohs

show δείχνω <u>THeekh</u>·noh

shower n **ντουζ** dooz

shower gel αφρόλουτρο για ντουζ
ahf·<u>roh</u>·loot·roh yah dooz

shut adj **κλειστός** klees·<u>tohs</u>

sick adj **άρρωστος** <u>ah</u>·rohs·tohs

side (of road) **μεριά** mehr·<u>yah</u>

sightseeing sight αξιοθέατο
ah·ksee·oh·<u>theh</u>·ah·toh

**sightseeing tour ξενάγηση στα
αξιοθέατα** kseh·<u>nah</u>·yee·see stah
ah·ksee·oh·<u>theh</u>·ah·tah

sign (road) **σήμα** <u>see</u>·mah

silk μετάξι meh·<u>tah</u>·ksee

silver ασήμι ah·<u>see</u>·mee

simple απλός ahp·<u>lohs</u>

single (not married) **ελεύθερος**
eh·<u>lehf</u>·theh·rohs

single room μονόκλινο δωμάτιο
moh·<u>noh</u>·klee·noh THoh·<u>mah</u>·tee·oh

single ticket [BE] απλό εισιτήριο
ahp·<u>loh</u> ee·see·<u>tee</u>·ree·oh

sink (bathroom) **νιπτήρας** nee·<u>ptee</u>·rahs

sit κάθομαι <u>kah</u>·thoh·meh

size n **μέγεθος** <u>meh</u>·yeh·thohs

skates παγοπέδιλα
pah·ghoh·<u>peh</u>·THee·lah

skating rink παγοδρόμιο
pah·ghohTH·<u>roh</u>·mee·oh

ski boots μπότες του σκι <u>boh</u>·tehs too
skee

ski poles μπαστούνια του σκι
bahs·<u>too</u>·niah too skee

ski school σχολή σκι skhoh·<u>lee</u> skee

skiing σκι skee

skin n **δέρμα** <u>Thehr</u>·mah

skirt φούστα <u>foo</u>·stah

sleep v **κοιμάμαι** kee·<u>mah</u>·meh

sleeping bag υπνόσακκος
ee·<u>pnoh</u>·sah·kohs

sleeping car βαγκόν-λι vah·<u>gohn</u>·lee

sleeping pill υπνωτικό χάπι
eep·noh·tee·<u>koh</u> <u>khah</u>·pee

slippers παντόφλες pahn·<u>dohf</u>·lehs

slope (ski) **πλαγιά** plah·<u>yah</u>

slow adj **αργός** ahr·<u>ghohs</u>

small μικρός meek·<u>rohs</u>

smell v **μυρίζω** mee·<u>ree</u>·zoh

smoke v **καπνίζω** kahp·<u>nee</u>·zoh

**smoking area περιοχή για
καπνίζοντες** peh·ree·oh·<u>khee</u> yah
kahp·<u>nee</u>·zohn·dehs

snack bar κυλικείο kee·lee·<u>kee</u>·oh

sneakers αθλητικά παπούτσια
ath·lee·tee·<u>kah</u> pah·<u>poo</u>·tsiah

**snorkeling equipment εξοπλισμό
για ελεύθερη κατάδυση**
eh·ksohp·leez·<u>moh</u> yah eh·<u>lehf</u>·theh·ree
kah·<u>tah</u>·THee·see

snow v **χιονίζει** khioh·<u>nee</u>·zee

soap n **σαπούνι** sah·<u>poo</u>·nee

soccer ποδόσφαιρο poh·<u>THohs</u>·feh·roh

socket πρίζα <u>pree</u>·zah

socks κάλτσες <u>kahl</u>·tsehs

sofa καναπές kah·nah·<u>pehs</u>

sole (shoes) **σόλα** <u>soh</u>·lah

something κάτι <u>kah</u>·tee

sometimes μερικές φορές meh·ree·<u>kehs</u>
foh·<u>rehs</u>

soon **σύντομα** <u>seen</u>-doh-mah

soother [BE] **πιπίλα** pee-<u>pee</u>-lah

sore throat **πονόλαιμος** poh-<u>noh</u>-leh-mohs

sort n **είδος** ee-<u>THohs</u>; v **διαλέγω** THiah-<u>leh</u>-ghoh

south adj **νότιος** <u>noh</u>-tee-ohs

souvenir **σουβενίρ** soo-veh-<u>neer</u>

souvenir store **κατάστημα σουβενίρ** kah-<u>tahs</u>-tee-mah soo-veh-<u>neer</u>

spa **σπα** spah

space n (area) **χώρος** <u>khoh</u>-rohs

spare (extra) **επιπλέον** eh-peep-<u>leh</u>-ohn

speak **μιλώ** mee-<u>loh</u>

special requirement **ειδική ανάγκη** ee-THee-<u>kee</u> ah-<u>nahn</u>-gkee

specialist **ειδικός** ee-THee-<u>kohs</u>

specimen **δείγμα** <u>THeegh</u>-mah

speed v **τρέχω** <u>treh</u>-khoh

spend **ξοδεύω** ksoh-<u>THEH</u>-voh

spine **σπονδυλική στήλη** spohn-THee-lee-<u>kee stee</u>-lee

spoon n **κουτάλι** koo-<u>tah</u>-lee

sport **αθλητισμός** ahth-lee-teez-<u>mohs</u>

sporting goods store **κατάστημα αθλητικών ειδών** kah-<u>tahs</u>-tee-mah ath-lee-tee-<u>kohn</u> ee-<u>THohn</u>

sports massage **αθλητικό μασάζ** ahth-lee-tee-<u>koh</u> mah-<u>sahz</u>

sports stadium **αθλητικό στάδιο** ahth-lee-tee-<u>koh stah</u>-THee-oh

square **τετράγωνος** teht-<u>rah</u>-ghoh-nohs

stadium **στάδιο** <u>stah</u>-THee-oh

stain n **λεκές** leh-<u>kehs</u>

stairs **σκάλες** <u>skah</u>-lehs

stale **μπαγιάτικος** bah-<u>yah</u>-tee-kohs

stamp n (postage) **γραμματόσημο** ghrah-mah-<u>toh</u>-see-moh

start v **αρχίζω** ahr-<u>khee</u>-zoh

statement (legal) **δήλωση** <u>THee</u>-loh-see

statue **άγαλμα** <u>ah</u>-ghahl-mah

stay v **μένω** <u>meh</u>-noh

sterilizing solution **αποστειρωτικό διάλυμα** ah-pohs-tee-roh-tee-<u>koh</u> THee-<u>ah</u>-lee-mah

sting n (insect) **τσίμπημα** <u>tsee</u>-bee-mah

stolen **κλεμένος** kleh-<u>meh</u>-nohs

stomach n **στομάχι** stoh-<u>mah</u>-khee

stomachache **στομαχόπονος** stoh-mah-<u>khoh</u>-poh-nohs

stop n (bus) **στάση** <u>stah</u>-see; v **σταματώ** stah-mah-<u>toh</u>

store guide [BE] **οδηγός καταστήματος** oh-THee-<u>ghohs</u> kah-tahs-<u>tee</u>-mah-tohs

stove **κουζίνα** koo-<u>zee</u>-nah

straight ahead **ευθεία** ehf-<u>thee</u>-ah

strange **παράξενος** pah-<u>rah</u>-kseh-nohs

straw (drinking) **καλαμάκι** kah-lah-<u>mah</u>-kee

stream n **ρυάκι** ree-<u>ah</u>-kee

street **δρόμος** <u>THroh</u>-mohs

string n (cord) **σπάγγος** <u>spah</u>-gohs

student **φοιτητής** fee-tee-<u>tees</u>

study v **σπουδάζω** spoo-<u>THah</u>-zoh

style n **στυλ** steel

subtitled **με υπότιτλους** meh ee-<u>poh</u>-teet-loos

subway **μετρό** meh-<u>troh</u>

subway station **σταθμός μετρό** stahth-<u>mohs</u> meh-<u>troh</u>

suggest **προτείνω** proh-<u>tee</u>-noh

suit (men's) **κουστούμι** koos-<u>too</u>-mee; (women's) **ταγιέρ** tah-<u>yehr</u>

suitable **κατάλληλος** kah-<u>tah</u>-lee-lohs

sunburn n **έγκαυμα ηλίου** <u>ehn</u>-gahv-mah ee-<u>lee</u>-oo sunglasses **γυαλιά ηλίου** yah·liah ee·lee·oo

sunshade [BE] **ομπρέλλα** ohm·breh·lah

sunstroke **ηλίαση** ee·lee·ah·see

sun tan lotion **λοσιόν μαυρίσματος** loh·siohn mahv·rees·mah·tohs

sunscreen **αντιηλιακό** ahn·dee·ee·lee·ah·koh

superb **έξοχος** eh·ksoh·khohs

supermarket **σουπερμάρκετ** soo·pehr·mahr·keht

supervision **επίβλεψη** eh·peev·leh·psee

surname **επίθετο** eh·pee·theh·toh

sweatshirt **φούτερ** foo·tehr

swelling **πρήξιμο** pree·ksee·moh

swimming **κολύμβηση** koh·leem·vee·see

swimming pool **πισίνα** pee·see·nah

swimming trunks **μαγιό** mah·yoh

swimsuit **μαγιό** mah·yoh

switch n **διακόπτης** THiah·koh·ptees

swollen **πρησμένος** preez·meh·nohs

symptom **σύμπτωμα** seem·ptoh·mah

T

table **τραπέζι** trah·peh·zee

tablecloth **τραπεζομάντηλο** trah·peh·zoh·mahn·dee·loh

tablet **χάπι** khah·pee

take **παίρνω** pehr·noh

take a photograph **βγάζω φωτογραφία** vghah·zoh foh·tohgh·rah·fee·ah

take away [BE] **πακέτο για το σπίτι** pah·keh·toh yah toh spee·tee

tall **ψηλός** psee·lohs

tampon **ταμπόν** tahm·bohn

tax n **φόρος** foh·rohs

taxi **ταξί** tah·ksee

taxi driver **ταξιτζής** tah·ksee·jees

taxi rank [BE] **πιάτσα ταξί** piah·tsah tah·ksee

teaspoon **κουταλάκι** koo·tah·lah·kee

team n **ομάδα** oh·mah·THah

teenager **έφηβος** eh·fee·vohs

telephone n **τηλέφωνο** tee·leh·foh·noh

telephone booth **τηλεφωνικός θάλαμος** tee·leh·foh·nee·kohs thah·lah·mohs

telephone call **κλήση** klee·see

telephone directory **τηλεφωνικός κατάλογος** tee·leh·foh·nee·kohs kah·tah·loh·ghohs

telephone number **αριθμός τηλεφώνου** ah·reeth·mohs tee·leh·foh·noo

tell **λέω** leh·oh

temperature (body) **θερμοκρασία** theh·rmohk·rah·see·ah

temple **ναός** nah·ohs

temporary **προσωρινός** proh·soh·ree·nohs

tennis **τέννις** teh·nees

tennis court **γήπεδο τέννις** yee·peh·THoh teh·nees

tent **σκηνή** skee·nee

terrible **φοβερός** foh·veh·rohs

theater **θέατρο** theh·aht·roh

theft **κλοπή** kloh·pee

there **εκεί** eh·kee

thermal bath **ιαματικό λουτρό** ee·ah·mah·tee·koh loot·roh

thermos flask **θερμός** thehr·mohs

thick **χοντρός** khohn·drohs

thief **κλέφτης** klehf·tees

thin adj **λεπτός** lehp·tohs

think **νομίζω** noh·mee·zoh

thirsty **διψάω** THee·psah·oh

those **εκείνα** eh·kee·nah

throat **λαιμός** leh·mohs

thumb **αντίχειρας** ahn·dee·khee·rahs

ticket **εισιτήριο** ee·see·<u>tee</u>·ree·oh
ticket office **γραφείο εισιτηρίων**
  ghrah·<u>fee</u>·oh ee·see·tee·<u>ree</u>·ohn
tie *n* **γραβάτα** ghrah·<u>vah</u>·tah
tight *adj* **στενός** steh·<u>nohs</u>
tights [BE] *n* **καλσόν** kahl·<u>sohn</u>
timetable [BE] **δρομολόγιο**
  THroh·moh·<u>loh</u>·yee·oh
tire **λάστιχο** <u>lahs</u>·tee·khoh
tired **κουρασμένος** koo·rahz·<u>meh</u>·nohs
tissue **χαρτομάντηλο**
  khahr·toh·<u>mahn</u>·dee·loh
toaster **τοστιέρα** toh·<u>stieh</u>·rah
tobacco **καπνός** kahp·<u>nohs</u>
tobacconist **καπνοπωλείο**
  kahp·noh·poh·<u>lee</u>·oh
toilet [BE] **τουαλέτα** too·ah·<u>leh</u>·tah
toilet paper **χαρτί υγείας** khahr·<u>tee</u>
  ee·<u>yee</u>·ahs
toiletries **καλλυντικά**
  kah·leen·dee·<u>kah</u>
tongue **γλώσσα** <u>ghloh</u>·sah
too (extreme) **πάρα πολύ** <u>pah</u>·rah poh·<u>lee</u>
tooth **δόντι** <u>THohn</u>·dee
toothache **πονόδοντος**
  poh·<u>noh</u>·THohn·dohs
toothbrush **οδοντόβουρτσα**
  oh·THohn·<u>doh</u>·voor·tsah
toothpaste **οδοντόπαστα**
  oh·THohn·<u>doh</u>·pahs·tah
top *adj* **πάνω** <u>pah</u>·noh
torn **σχισμένος** skheez·<u>meh</u>·nohs
tour guide **ξεναγός** kseh·nah·<u>ghohs</u>
tourist **τουρίστας** too·<u>rees</u>·tahs
towards **προς** prohs
tower **πύργος** <u>peer</u>·ghohs
town **πόλη** <u>poh</u>·lee
town hall **δημαρχείο** THee·mahr·<u>khee</u>·oh

toy store **κατάστημα παιχνιδιών**
  kah·<u>tahs</u>·tee·mah peh·khnee·<u>THiohn</u>
traditional **παραδοσιακός**
  pah·rah·THoh·see·ah·<u>kohs</u>
traffic **κίνηση** <u>kee</u>·nee·see
trail **μονοπάτι** moh·noh·<u>pah</u>·tee
trailer **τροχόσπιτο** troh·<u>khohs</u>·pee·toh
train **τρένο** <u>treh</u>·noh
train station **σταθμός των τρένων**
  stahth·<u>mohs</u> tohn <u>treh</u>·nohn
tram **τραμ** trahm
transfer **μεταφέρω** meh·tah·<u>feh</u>·roh
transit *n* **μεταφορά** meh·tah·foh·<u>rah</u>
translate **μεταφράζω** meh·tah·<u>frah</u>·zoh
translation **μετάφραση** meh·<u>tah</u>·frah·see
translator **μεταφραστής**
  meh·tah·frah·<u>stees</u>
trash **σκουπίδια** skoo·<u>peeTH</u>·yah
trash can **κάδος απορριμμάτων**
  <u>kah</u>·THohs ah·poh·ree·<u>mah</u>·tohn
travel agency **ταξιδιωτικό γραφείο**
  tah·ksee·THyoh·tee·<u>koh</u> ghrah·<u>fee</u>·oh
travel sickness [BE] **ναυτία** nahf·<u>tee</u>·ah
traveler's check **ταξιδιωτική επιταγή**
  tah·ksee·THee·oh·tee·<u>kee</u> eh·pee·tah·<u>yee</u>
tray **δίσκος** <u>THees</u>·kohs
tree **δέντρο** <u>THehn</u>·droh
trim *n* **διόρθωμα** THee·<u>ohr</u>·thoh·mah
trolley [BE] (cart) **καροτσάκι**
  kah·roh·<u>tsah</u>·kee
trolley-bus **τρόλλεϋ** <u>troh</u>·leh·ee
trousers [BE] **παντελόνι** pahn·deh·<u>loh</u>·nee
try on **δοκιμάζω** THoh·kee·<u>mah</u>·zoh
T-shirt **μπλουζάκι** bloo·<u>zah</u>·kee
tunnel **τούνελ** <u>too</u>·nehl
turn *v* **γυρίζω** yee·<u>ree</u>·zoh
turn down *v* (volume, heat) **χαμηλώνω**
  khah·mee·<u>loh</u>·noh

turn off v **σβήνω** svee-noh

turn on v **ανάβω** ah-nah-voh

turn up v (volume, heat) **ανεβάζω**
ah-neh-vah-zoh

TV τηλεόραση tee-leh-oh-rah-see

twin bed διπλό κρεβάτι THeep-loh
kreh-vah-tee

typical τυπικός tee-pee-kohs

U

ugly άσχημος ahs-khee-mohs

unconscious αναίσθητος
ah-nehs-thee-tohs

underground [BE] **υπόγειος**
ee-poh-ghee-ohs

underpants [BE] **κυλοτάκι** kee-loh-tah-kee

understand καταλαβαίνω
kah-tah-lah-veh-noh

underpants (ground) **ανώμαλος**
ah-noh-mah-lohs

uneven (ground) **ανώμαλος**
ah-noh-mah-lohs

unfortunately δυστυχώς
THees-tee-khohs

uniform n **στολή** stoh-lee

unique μοναδικός
moh-nah-THee-kohs

unit μονάδα moh-nah-THah

United Kingdom Ηνωμένο Βασίλειο
ee-noh-meh-noh vah-see-lee-oh

United States Ηνωμένες Πολιτείες
ee-noh-meh-nehs poh-lee-tee-ehs

university Πανεπιστήμιο
pah-neh-pees-tee-mee-oh

unlimited mileage απεριόριστα
χιλιόμετρα ah-peh-ree-ohr-ees-tah
khee-lioh-meht-rah

unpleasant δυσάρεστος
THee-sah-reh-stohs

upper (berth) **πάνω (κουκέτα)** pah-noh
(koo-keh-tah)

upstairs επάνω eh-pah-noh

urgent επείγον eh-pee-ghohn

use v **χρησιμοποιώ** khree-see-moh-pee-oh

useful χρήσιμος khree-see-mohs

V

vacancy ελεύθερο δωμάτιο
eh-lehf-theh-roh THoh-mah-tee-oh

vacant ελεύθερος eh-lehf-theh-rohs

vacation διακοπές THee-ah-koh-pehs

vacation resort θέρετρο διακοπών
theh-reh-troh THee-ah-koh-pohn

vaccination εμβόλιο ehm-voh-lee-oh

valid ισχύει ee-skhee-ee

valley κοιλάδα kee-lah-THah

valuable πολύτιμος poh-lee-tee-mohs

value n **αξία** ah-ksee-ah

VAT [BE] **ΦΠΑ** fee-pee-ah

vegetarian χορτοφάγος
khohr-toh-fah-ghohs

vein φλέβα fleh-vah

velvet βελούδο veh-loo-THoh

very πολύ poh-lee

video βιντεοκασέτα
vee-deh-oh-kah-seh-tah

video game παιχνίδι βίντεο
pehkh-nee-THee vee-deh-oh

village χωριό khohr-yoh

visa βίζα vee-zah

visit n **επίσκεψη** eh-pees-keh-psee

volleyball βόλεϋ voh-leh-ee

vomit v **κάνω εμετό**
kah-noh eh-meh-toh

W

wait v **περιμένω** peh•ree•<u>meh</u>•noh
waiter n **γκαρσόν** gahr•<u>sohn</u>
waitress δεσποινίς THehs•pee•<u>nees</u>
wake v **ξυπνώ** kseep•<u>noh</u>
walk v **περπατώ** pehr•pah•<u>toh</u>
walking route διαδρομή περιήγησης
  THee•ah•THroh•<u>mee</u> peh•ree•<u>ee</u>•yee•sees
wall τοίχος <u>tee</u>•khohs
wallet πορτοφόλι pohr•toh•<u>foh</u>•lee
want θέλω <u>theh</u>•loh
warm ζεστός zehs•<u>tohs</u>
washing machine πλυντήριο
  pleen•<u>deer</u>•ee•oh
watch n **ρολόι** roh•<u>loh</u>•ee
watch strap λουρί ρολογιού loo•<u>ree</u>
  roh•loh•<u>yioo</u>
water n **νερό** neh•<u>roh</u>
waterfall καταρράχτης kah•tah•<u>rahkh</u>•tees
waterproof αδιάβροχος
  ah•THee•<u>ahv</u>•roh•khohs
wave n **κύμα** <u>kee</u>•mah
way δρόμος <u>THroh</u>•mohs
wear v **φορώ** foh•<u>roh</u>
weather καιρός keh•<u>rohs</u>
weather forecast πρόβλεψη καιρού
  <u>prohv</u>•leh•psee keh•<u>roo</u>
wedding γάμος <u>ghah</u>•mohs
west δυτικά THee•tee•<u>kah</u>
wetsuit στολή δύτη stoh•<u>lee</u> THee•tee
wheelchair αναπηρική καρέκλα
  ah•nah•pee•ree•<u>kee</u> kah•<u>rehk</u>•lah
wide φαρδύς fahr•<u>THees</u>
wife σύζυγος <u>see</u>•zee•ghohs
window παράθυρο pah•<u>rah</u>•thee•roh
window seat θέση δίπλα στο παράθυρο
  theh•see THeep•lah stoh pah•<u>rah</u>•thee•roh
winery οινοποιείο ee•noh•pee•<u>ee</u>•oh

wireless internet ασύρματο ίντερνετ
  ah•<u>see</u>•rmah•toh ee•nteh•rnet
with με meh
withdraw κάνω ανάληψη kah•noh
  ah•<u>nah</u>•lee•psee
without χωρίς khoh•<u>rees</u>
witness μάρτυρας <u>mahr</u>•tee•rahs
wood (forest) **δάσος** <u>THah</u>•sohs; (material)
  ξύλο <u>ksee</u>•loh
work δουλεύω THoo•<u>leh</u>•voh
worry ανησυχώ ah•nee•see•<u>khoh</u>
worse χειρότερος khee•<u>roh</u>•teh•rohs
wound (cut) **πληγή** plee•<u>yee</u>
write (down) **γράφω** <u>ghrah</u>•foh
wrong λάθος <u>lah</u>•thohs

X

x-ray ακτινογραφία
  ahk•tee•nohgh•rah•<u>fee</u>•ah

Y

yacht γιωτ yoht
yellow κίτρινος <u>keet</u>•ree•nohs
young νέος <u>neh</u>•ohs
youth hostel ξενώνας νεότητας
  kseh•<u>noh</u>•nahs neh•<u>oh</u>•tee•tahs

Z

zoo ζωολογικός κήπος
  zoh•oh•loh•yee•<u>kohs</u> <u>kee</u>•pohs

GREEK–ENGLISH

A

ATM ehee·tee·<u>ehm</u> **ATM**

άγαλμα <u>ah</u>·ghahl·mah **statue**

αγαπημένος ah·ghah·pee·<u>meh</u>·nohs **favorite**

αγαπώ ah·ghah·<u>poh</u> v **love**

αγγειοπλαστική ahn·gee·ohp·lahs·tee·<u>kee</u> **pottery**

Αγγλία ahng·<u>lee</u>·ah **England**

αγγλικά ahng·lee·<u>kah</u> **English language**

αγγλικός ahng·lee·<u>kohs</u> adj **English**

Άγγλος <u>ahng</u>·lohs **English (nationality)**

αγενής ah·yeh·<u>nees</u> **rude**

αγορά ah·ghoh·<u>rah</u> n **market**

αγοράζω ah·ghoh·<u>rah</u>·zoh **buy**

αγόρι ah·<u>ghoh</u>·ree **boy**

αγώνας ah·<u>ghoh</u>·nahs n **match (sport)**

άδεια <u>ah</u>·THee·ah n **permit**

άδεια σκι <u>ah</u>·THee·ah skee **lift pass**

άδειος <u>ahTH</u>·yohs adj **empty**

αδιάβροχο ah·THee·<u>ahv</u>·roh·khoh **raincoat**

αδιάβροχος ah·THee·<u>ahv</u>·roh·khohs **waterproof**

αδύναμος ah·THee·nah·mohs **weak**

αεροδρόμιο ah·eh·roh·<u>THroh</u>·mee·oh **airport**

αεροπλάνο ah·eh·rohp·<u>lah</u>·noh n **plane**

αεροπορική εταιρία ah·eh·roh·poh·ree·<u>kee</u> eh·teh·<u>ree</u>·ah **airline**

αεροπορικώς ah·eh·roh·poh·ree·<u>kohs</u> **airmail**

αηδιαστικός ah·ee·THee·ah·stee·<u>kohs</u> **revolting**

αθλητικά παπούτσια ath·lee·tee·<u>kah</u> pah·<u>poo</u>·tsiah **sneakers**

αθλητικό στάδιο athh·lee·tee·<u>koh</u> <u>stah</u>·THee·oh **sports stadium**

αθλητικός όμιλος athh·lee·tee·<u>kohs</u> <u>oh</u>·mee·lohs **sports club**

αθλητισμός athh·lee·teez·<u>mohs</u> **sport**

αθώος ah·<u>thoh</u>·ohs **innocent**

αιμορραγία eh·moh·rah·<u>yee</u>·ah n **bleed**

αιμορραγώ eh·moh·rah·<u>yoh</u> v **bleed**

αίθουσα συναυλιών eh·thoo·sah see·nahv·lee·<u>ohn</u> **concert hall**

ακολουθώ ah·koh·loo·<u>thoh</u> v **follow**

ακουστικό βαρυκοΐας ah·koo·stee·<u>koh</u> vah·ree·koh·<u>ee</u>·ahs **hearing aid**

ακριβός ahk·ree·<u>vohs</u> **expensive**

ακτή ahk·<u>tee</u> n **shore**

ακτινογραφία ahk·tee·nohgh·rah·<u>fee</u>·ah **x-ray**

ακυρώνω ah·kee·<u>roh</u>·noh v **cancel**

αληθινός ah·lee·thee·<u>nohs</u> **real (genuine)**

αλλά ah·<u>lah</u> conj **but**

άλλα <u>ah</u>·lah **others**

αλλαγή ah·lah·<u>yee</u> n **change**

αλλάζω ah·<u>lah</u>·zoh v **exchange (money)**

αλλεργικός ahl·ehr·yee·<u>kohs</u> **allergic**

αλληλογραφία ah·lee·lohgh·rah·<u>fee</u>·ah n **mail**

άλλο ένα <u>ah</u>·loh eh·nah **extra (additional)**

άλλος ah·lohs **another**

αλουμινόχαρτο ah·loo·mee·noh·khah·rtoh **aluminum foil**

Αμερικανός ah·meh·ree·kah·nohs *n* **American**

αμέσως ah·meh·sohs **immediately**

άμμος ah·mohs **sand**

ανάβω ah·nah·voh *v* **turn on**

αναίσθητος ah·nehs·thee·tohs **unconscious**

ανάκτορα ah·nahk·toh·rah **palace**

αναλυτικός λογαριασμός ah·nah·lee·tee·kohs loh·ghahr·yahz·mohs **itemized bill**

αναπηρική καρέκλα ah·nah·pee·ree·kee kah·rehk·lah **wheelchair**

αναπνευστήρας ah·nahp·nehf·stee·rahs **snorkel**

αναπνέω ah·nahp·neh·oh **breathe**

αναπτήρας ah·nahp·tee·rahs *n* **lighter (cigarette)**

αναρρίχηση ah·nah·ree·khee·see **rock climbing**

ανατολικά ah·nah·toh·lee·kah **east**

αναφέρω ah·nah·feh·roh **mention (report)**

αναχώρηση ah·nah·khoh·ree·see **departure (travel)**

άνδρας ahn·THrahs *n* **male (man)**

ανεμιστήρας ah·neh·mees·tee·rahs *n* **fan (air)**

ανεβάζω ah·neh·vah·zoh *v* **turn up (volume, heat)**

ανέκδοτο ah·nehk·THoh·toh *n* **joke**

ανησυχώ ah·nee·see·khoh **worry**

ανθοπωλείο ahn·thoh·poh·lee·oh **florist**

ανοίγω ah·nee·ghoh *v* **open**

ανοιχτήρι ah·neekh·tee·ree **can opener**

ανοιχτός ah·neekh·tohs *adj* **light (color), open**

ανοιχτότερος ah·neekh·toh·teh·rohs *adj* **lighter (color)**

ανταλλακτικό ahn·dah·lahk·tee·koh **replacement part**

αντιβιοτικό ahn·dee·vee·oh·tee·koh **antibiotic**

αντιηλιακό ahn·dee·ee·lee·ah·koh **sunscreen**

αντισηπτική κρέμα ahn·dee·seep·tee·kee kreh·mah **antiseptic cream**

αντίχειρας ahn·dee·khee·rahs **thumb**

ανώμαλος ah·noh·mah·lohs **uneven (ground)**

αξεσουάρ ah·kseh·soo·ahr **accessory**

αξία ah·ksee·ah *n* **value**

αξιοθέατο ah·ksee·oh·theh·ah·tah **sightseeing sight**

απαγορευμένος ah·pah·ghoh·rehv·meh·nohs **prohibited**

απαραίτητος ah·pah·reh·tee·tohs **essential, necessary**

απασχολημένος ah·pahs·khoh·lee·meh·nohs *adj* **busy (occupied)**

απέναντι ah·peh·nahn·dee **opposite**

απεριόριστα χιλιόμετρα ah·peh·ree·ohr·ees·tah khee·lioh·meht·rah **unlimited mileage**

απλό εισιτήριο ahp·loh ee·see·tee·ree·oh **one-way [single BE] ticket**

απλός ahp·lohs **simple**

από ah·poh **from**

απομίμηση ah·poh·<u>mee</u>·mee·see
imitation

αποβάθρα ah·poh·<u>vahth</u>·rah **platform,
quay**

απόγευμα ah·<u>poh</u>·yehv·mah **afternoon**

απόδειξη ah·<u>poh</u>·THee·ksee **receipt**

απορρυπαντικό ah·poh·ree·
pahn·dee·<u>koh</u> **detergent**

αποσμητικό ah·pohz·mee·tee·<u>koh</u>
deodorant

αποσκευές ah·pohs·keh·<u>vehs</u>
baggage [BE]

αποσκευές χειρός ah·pohs·keh·<u>vehs</u>
khee·<u>rohs</u> **hand luggage**

αποστειρωτικό διάλυμα
ah·pohs·tee·roh·tee·<u>koh</u>
THee·<u>ah</u>·lee·mah **sterilizing solution**

απόχρωση ah·<u>pohkh</u>·roh·see **shade (color)**

απώλεια ah·<u>poh</u>·lee·ah n **loss**

αργά ahr·<u>ghah</u> adv **late**

αργία ahr·<u>yee</u>·ah **public holiday**

αργός ahr·<u>ghohs</u> adj **slow**

αριθμός κυκλοφορίας ah·reeth·<u>mohs</u>
kee·kloh·foh·<u>ree</u>·ahs **registration
number**

αριθμός πτήσεως ah·reeth·<u>mohs</u>
ptee·seh·ohs **flight number**

αριθμός τηλεφώνου ah·reeth·<u>mohs</u>
tee·leh·<u>foh</u>·noo **telephone number**

αριστερός ah·rees·teh·<u>rohs</u> **left** (adj)

αριστερά ah·rees·teh·<u>rah</u> **left** (adv)

αρκετά ahr·keh·<u>tah</u> **enough**

αρραβωνιαστικιά ah·rah·voh·
niahs·tee·<u>kiah</u> **fiancée**

αρραβωνιαστικός ah·rah·voh·
niahs·tee·<u>kohs</u> **fiancé**

αρρώστεια ahr·<u>ohs</u>·tee·ah **illness**

άρρωστος <u>ah</u>·rohs·tohs adj **sick**

αρτοποιείο ah·rtoh·pee·<u>ee</u>·oh **bakery**

αρχάριος ahr·<u>khah</u>·ree·ohs **beginner**

αρχίζω v ahr·<u>khee</u>·zoh **start**

ασανσέρ ah·sahn·<u>sehr</u> n **lift
(elevator)**

ασήμι ah·<u>see</u>·mee **silver**

ασύρματο ίντερνετ ah·<u>see</u>·rmah·toh
ee·nteh·rnet **wireless internet**

ασθενοφόρο ahs·theh·noh·<u>foh</u>·roh
ambulance

ασθματικός ahsth·mah·tee·<u>kohs</u>
asthmatic

ασπιρίνη ahs·pee·<u>ree</u>·nee **aspirin**

αστυνομία ah·stee·noh·<u>mee</u>·ah n **police**

αστυνομικό τμήμα ah·stee·noh·
mee·<u>koh</u> tmee·mah **police station**

ασφάλεια ahs·<u>fah</u>·lee·ah n **fuse;
insurance**

ασφάλεια αποζημίωσης ahs·<u>fah</u>·lee·ah
ah·poh·zee·
mee·oh·sees **insurance claim**

ασφάλεια υγείας ahs·<u>fah</u>·lee·ah
ee·<u>yee</u>·ahs **health insurance**

ασφαλής ahs·fah·<u>lees</u> adj **safe (not
dangerous)**

ασφαλιστική εταιρία ahs·fah·lees·
tee·<u>kee</u> eh·teh·<u>ree</u>·ah **insurance
company**

άσχημος <u>ahs</u>·khee·mohs **ugly**

άτομο με ειδικές ανάγκες <u>ah</u>·toh·moh
meh ee·THee·<u>kehs</u> ah·<u>nahn</u>·gehs
disabled

ατύχημα ah·<u>tee</u>·khee·mah **accident**

αυθεντικός ahf·thehn·dee·<u>kohs</u> **genuine**

αυθεντικότητα ahf·thehn·dee·<u>koh</u>·tee·tah **authenticity**

αϋπνία ah·eep·<u>nee</u>·ah **insomnia**

αυτοκίνητο ahf·toh·<u>kee</u>·nee·toh **car**

αυχένας ahf·<u>kheh</u>·nahs **neck (part of body)**

αφήνω ah·<u>fee</u>·noh v **leave (let go)**

αφορολόγητα είδη ah·foh·roh·<u>loh</u>·yee·tah ee·<u>THee</u> **duty-free goods**

αφρόλουτρο για ντουζ ahf·<u>roh</u>·loot·roh yah dooz **shower gel**

αχθοφόρος ahkh·thoh·<u>foh</u>·rohs **porter**

B

βαμβάκι vahm·<u>vah</u>·kee **cotton**

βαγκόν-λι vah·<u>gohn</u>·lee **sleeping car**

βάζο <u>vah</u>·zoh n **jar**

βάζω <u>vah</u>·zoh v **put**

βαλές vah·<u>lehs</u> **jack**

βαρετός vah·reh·<u>tohs</u> **boring**

βάρκα <u>vahr</u>·kah **boat**

βαρύς vah·<u>rees</u> **heavy**

βασιλιάς vah·see·<u>liahs</u> **king**

βγαίνω <u>vyeh</u>·noh **get out (of vehicle)**

βελούδο veh·<u>loo</u>·THoh **velvet**

βενζινάδικο vehn·zee·<u>nah</u>·THee·koh **gas [petrol BE] station**

βενζίνη vehn·<u>zee</u>·nee **gasoline [petrol BE]**

βερνίκι παπουτσιών vehr·<u>nee</u>·kee pah·poo·<u>tsiohn</u> **shoe polish**

βήχας <u>vee</u>·khahs n **cough**

βήχω <u>vee</u>·khoh v **cough**

βιβλίο veev·<u>lee</u>·oh n **book**

βιβλιοθήκη veev·lee·oh·<u>thee</u>·kee **library**

βιβλιοπωλείο veev·lee·oh·poh·<u>lee</u>·oh **bookstore**

βίδα <u>vee</u>·THah n **screw**

βίζα <u>vee</u>·zah **visa**

βιντεοκασέτα vee·deh·oh·kah·<u>seh</u>·tah **video**

βλάβη <u>vlah</u>·vee **breakdown** n **(car)**

βλέπω <u>vleh</u>·poh **see**

βοήθεια voh·<u>ee</u>·thee·ah n **help**

βοηθώ voh·ee·<u>thoh</u> v **help**

βόλεϋ <u>voh</u>·leh·ee **volleyball**

βόρεια <u>voh</u>·ree·ah **north**

βοτανικός κήπος voh·tah·nee·<u>kohs</u> <u>kee</u>·pohs **botanical garden**

βουνό voo·<u>noh</u> **mountain**

βουρτσίζω voor·<u>tsee</u>·zoh v **brush**

βραδινό vrah·THee·<u>noh</u> **dinner**

βράδυ <u>vrah</u>·THee **evening**

βράζω <u>vrah</u>·zoh **boil**

βράχος <u>vrah</u>·khohs n **rock**

βρετανικός vreh·tah·nee·<u>kohs</u> adj **British**

Βρετανός vreh·tah·<u>nohs</u> **British (nationality)**

βρέχει <u>vreh</u>·khee v **rain**

βροχή vroh·<u>khee</u> n **rain**

βρύση <u>vree</u>·see **faucet**

βρώμικος <u>vroh</u>·mee·kohs adj **dirty**

Γ

γάμος <u>ghah</u>·mohs **wedding**

γάζα <u>ghah</u>·zah **bandage**

γαλάκτωμα για τα μαλλιά ghah·<u>lah</u>·ktoh·mah yah tah mah·<u>liah</u> **conditioner (hair)**

γάντι <u>ghahn</u>·dee n **glove**

γαστρίτιδα ghahs·<u>tree</u>·tee·THah **gastritis**

γεμάτος yeh·<u>mah</u>·tohs adj **full**

γείτονας <u>yee</u>·toh·nahs n **neighbor**

γελώ yeh·<u>loh</u> v **laugh**

γεμιστή yeh·mees·tee **stuffed olive**

γέρικος <u>yeh</u>·ree·kohs **old (person)**

γεύμα <u>yehv</u>·mah **meal**

γέφυρα <u>yeh</u>·fee·rah n **bridge (over water)**

γη ghee n **land**

γήπεδο γκολφ yee·peh·THoh gohlf **golf course**

γήπεδο τέννις <u>yee</u>·peh·THoh teh·nees **tennis court**

γιατρός yah·<u>trohs</u> **doctor**

γιωτ yoht **yacht**

γκαράζ gah·<u>rahz</u> **garage**

γκαρσόν gahr·<u>sohn</u> **waiter**

γκόλφ gohlf **golf**

γκρουπ groop n **group**

γλώσσα <u>ghloh</u>·sah **tongue**

γνωρίζω ghnoh·<u>ree</u>·zoh **know**

γόνατο <u>ghoh</u>·nah·toh **knee**

γονείς ghoh·<u>nees</u> **parents**

γράμμα <u>ghrah</u>·mah **letter**

γραμματόσημο ghrah·mah·<u>toh</u>·see·moh n **stamp (postage)**

γραμμή ghrah·<u>mee</u> n **line (subway)**

γραβάτα ghrah·<u>vah</u>·tah n **tie**

γρασίδι ghrah·<u>see</u>·THee **grass**

γραφείο ghrah·<u>fee</u>·oh **office**

γραφείο ανταλλαγής συναλλάγματος ghrah·<u>fee</u>·oh ahn·dah·lah·<u>yees</u> see·nah·<u>lahgh</u>·mah·tohs **currency exchange office**

γραφείο εισιτίριων ghrah·<u>fee</u>·oh ee·see·tee·<u>ree</u>·ohn **ticket office**

γραφείο πληροφοριών ghrah·<u>fee</u>·oh plee·roh·foh·ree·<u>ohn</u> **information office**

γράφω <u>ghrah</u>·foh **write (down)**

γρήγορα <u>ghree</u>·ghoh·rah adv **fast**

γρήγορος <u>ghree</u>·ghoh·rohs **quick**

γρίππη <u>ghree</u>·pee **flu**

γυαλιά yah·<u>liah</u> **glasses (optical)**

γυαλιά ηλίου yah·<u>liah</u> ee·<u>lee</u>·oo **sun glasses**

γυναικολόγος yee·neh·koh·<u>loh</u>·ghohs **gynecologist**

γυρίζω yee·<u>ree</u>·zoh v **turn**

γωνία ghoh·<u>nee</u>·ah **corner**

Δ

δανείζω THah·<u>nee</u>·zoh **lend**

δάσος THah·sohs n **forest (wood)**

δάχτυλο THakh·tee·loh n **finger**

δείγμα <u>THeegh</u>·mah **specimen**

δείχνω <u>THeekh</u>·noh v **point (show)**

δέντρο <u>THehn</u>·droh **tree**

δεξιός THeh·ksee·<u>ohs</u> adj **right (not left)**

δέρμα <u>THehr</u>·mah n **skin**

δημαρχείο THee·mahr·<u>khee</u>·oh **town hall**

δημοφιλής THee·moh·fee·<u>lees</u> **popular**

δηλητήριο THee·lee·<u>tee</u>·ree·oh n **poison**

δηλητηριώδης THee·lee·tee·ree·<u>oh</u>·THees **poisonous**

δηλώνω THee·<u>loh</u>·noh **declare**

δήλωση <u>THee</u>·loh·see **statement (legal)**

δημόσιος THee·<u>moh</u>·see·ohs **public**

διαμάντι THiah·<u>mahn</u>·dee n **diamond**

διαμέρισμα THee·ah·<u>meh</u>·reez·mah **apartment**

διάβαση πεζών THee·<u>ah</u>·vah·see peh·<u>zohn</u> **pedestrian crossing** διαβατήριο THiah-vah-<u>tee</u>-ree-oh **passport**

διαβητικός THee-ah-vee-tee-<u>kohs</u> **diabetic**

διαδρομή THee-ahTH-roh-<u>mee</u> n **route**

διάδρομος THee-<u>ah</u>-THroh-mohs **aisle seat**

διαζευγμένος THee-ah-zehv-<u>ghmeh</u>-nohs **divorced**

διακοπές THee-ah-koh-<u>pehs</u> **vacation [holiday BE]**

διακόπτης THiah-<u>koh</u>-ptees n **switch**

διαμέρισμα THee-ah-mehr-ees-mah n **flat**

διάρροια THee-<u>ah</u>-ree-ah **diarrhea**

διάσημος THee-<u>ah</u>-see-mohs **famous**

διεθνής THee-eth-<u>nees</u> **international**

διεθνής φοιτητική κάρτα
THee-ehth-<u>nees</u> fee-tee-tee-<u>kee</u> kahr-tah
International Student Card

διερμηνέας THee-ehr-mee-<u>neh</u>-ahs **interpreter**

διεύθυνση THee-<u>ehf</u>-theen-see n **address**

διευθυντής THee-ehf-theen-<u>dees</u> **manager**

δικηγόρος THee-kee-<u>ghoh</u>-rohs **lawyer**

δίκλινο δωμάτιο <u>THeek</u>-lee-noh THoh-<u>mah</u>-tee-oh n **double room**

δίνω <u>THee</u>-noh **give**

διόρθωμα THee-<u>ohr</u>-thoh-mah n **trim**

δίπλα <u>THeep</u>-lah **next to**

διπλό κρεβάτι THeep-<u>loh</u> kreh-<u>vah</u>-tee **twin bed**

δίσκος <u>THees</u>-kohs **tray**

διψάω THee-<u>psah</u>-oh **thirsty**

δοκιμάζω THoh-kee-<u>mah</u>-zoh **try on**

δολάριο THoh-<u>lah</u>-ree-oh **dollar**

δόντι <u>THohn</u>-dee **tooth**

δοσολογία THoh-soh-loh-<u>yee</u>-ah **dosage**

δουλειά THoo-<u>liah</u> **job**

δουλεύω THoo-<u>leh</u>-voh **work**

δρομολόγιο THroh-moh-<u>loh</u>-yee-oh **time table**

δρόμος <u>THroh</u>-mohs **road, street, way**

δυνατός THee-nah-<u>tohs</u> adj **loud**

δυσάρεστος THee-<u>sah</u>-reh stohs **unpleasant**

δύσκολος <u>THee</u>-skoh-lohs **difficult**

δυσπεψία Thes-peh-<u>psee</u>-ah **indigestion**

δυστυχώς THees-tee-<u>khohs</u> **unfortunately**

δυτικά THee-tee-<u>kah</u> **west**

δωμάτιο THoh-<u>mah</u>-tee-oh n **room**

δώρο <u>THoh</u>-roh **gift**

E

ελιά eh-liah **olive**

εμβόλιο ehm-<u>voh</u>-lee-oh **vaccination**

εμπορικό κέντρο ehm-boh-ree-<u>koh</u> keh-ntroh **shopping mall [centre BE]**

εγγύηση eh-<u>gee</u>-ee-see n **guarantee**

εγγυώμαι eh-gee-oh-meh v **guarantee**

έγκαυμα ηλίου <u>ehn</u>-gahv-mah ee-<u>lee</u>-oo n **sun burn**

έγκυος <u>eh</u>-gee-ohs **pregnant**

έδαφος <u>eh</u>-THah-fohs **ground (earth)**

εδώ eh-<u>THoh</u> **here**

εδώ κοντά eh-<u>THoh</u> kohn-<u>dah</u> **nearby**

εθνική οδός ehth-nee-<u>kee</u> oh-<u>THohs</u> **highway, motorway**

εθνικός eth-nee-<u>kohs</u> **national**

εθνικός δρυμός eth-nee-<u>kohs</u> THree-<u>mohs</u> **nature reserve** είμαι ee·meh **be**

είμαι κουφός koo·<u>fohs</u> **deaf**

είδη οικιακής χρήσεως ee·THee·
ee·kee·ah·<u>kees</u> khree·seh·ohs
household articles

ειδική ανάγκη ee·THee·kee ah·<u>nahn</u>·gkee
special requirement

ειδικός ee·THee·<u>kohs</u> **specialist**

είδος ee·<u>THohs</u> **kind (sort)**

εισιτήριο ee·see·<u>tee</u>·ree·oh **fare (ticket)**

εισιτήριο με επιστροφή
ee·see·<u>tee</u>·ree·oh meh eh·pee·stroh·<u>fee</u>
roundtrip [return BE] ticket

εκδρομή ehk·THroh·<u>mee</u> **excursion**

εκεί eh·<u>kee</u> **there, over there**

εκείνα eh·<u>kee</u>·nah **those**

έκθεση ehk·theh·see **exhibition**

έκπτωση ehk·ptoh·see **reduction**

έκτακτη ανάγκη ehk·tahk·tee ah·<u>nah</u>·gee
emergency

ελάχιστος eh·<u>lah</u>·khees·tohs **minimum**

ελεύθερο δωμάτιο eh·<u>lehf</u>·theh·roh
THoh·<u>mah</u>·tee·oh **vacancy**

ελεύθερος eh·<u>lehf</u>·theh·rohs adj **free,
single, vacant**

ελικόπτερο eh·lee·<u>kohp</u>·teh·roh
helicopter

Ελλάδα eh·<u>lah</u>·THah **Greece**

Έλληνας eh·lee·nahs **Greek (nationality)**

ελληνικός eh·lee·nee·<u>kohs</u> adj **Greek**

ένα βράδυ eh·nah vrah·<u>THee</u> **overnight**

ένα τέταρτο eh·nah teh·tah·rtoh **quarter
(quantity)**

ενδιαφέρων en·THee·ah·<u>feh</u>·rohn
interesting

ένεση eh·neh·see **injection**

ενήλικας eh·<u>nee</u>·lee·kahs **adult**

ενοχλώ eh·noh·<u>khloh</u> **disturb**

έντομο ehn·doh·moh **insect**

εντομοαπωθητικό
ehn·doh·moh·ah·poh·thee·tee·<u>koh</u>
insect repellent

έντυπο ehn·dee·poh n **form**

εντυπωσιακός ehn·dee·poh·
see·ah·<u>kohs</u> **impressive**

ενυδατική κρέμα eh·nee·THah·tee·<u>kee</u>
<u>kreh</u>·mah **moisturizer (cream)**

εξάνθημα eh·<u>ksahn</u>·thee·mah n **rash**

εξαργυρώνω eh·ksahr·ghee·
<u>roh</u>·noh v **cash**

εξόγκωμα eh·<u>ksoh</u>·goh·mah n **lump
(medical)**

έξοδος eh·ksoh·THohs n **gate (airport);
exit**

έξοδος κινδύνου eh·ksoh·THohs
keen·<u>THee</u>·noo **emergency, fire exit**

εξοχή eh·ksoh·<u>khee</u> **countryside**

έξοχος eh·ksoh·khohs **superb**

εξπρές ehk·<u>sprehs</u> **express (mail)**

εξυπηρέτηση eh·ksee·pee·<u>reh</u>·tee·see
facility

έξω eh·ksoh adv **out**

έξω eh·ksoh adj **outside**

εξωλέμβιο eh·ksoh·<u>lehm</u>·vee·oh
motorboat

εξωτερικός eh·ksoh·teh·ree·<u>kohs</u>
outdoor

επαναλαμβάνω eh·pah·nah·
lahm·<u>vah</u>·noh v **repeat**

επάνω eh·<u>pah</u>·noh **upstairs**

επείγον eh·<u>pee</u>·ghohn **urgent**

επιμένω eh·pee·<u>meh</u>·noh **insist**

επιβάτης eh·pee·<u>vah</u>·tees **passenger**

επιβεβαιώνω eh·pee·veh·veh·<u>oh</u>·noh **confirm**

επίβλεψη eh·<u>peev</u>·leh·psee **supervision**

επίθεση eh·<u>pee</u>·theh·see *n* **attack**

επίθετο eh·<u>pee</u>·theh·toh **surname**

επικοινωνώ eh·pee·kee·noh·<u>noh</u> *v* **contact**

επιληπτικός eh·pee·leep·tee·<u>kohs</u> **epileptic**

επίπεδο eh·<u>pee</u>·peh·THoh **level (even)**

επίπεδος eh·<u>pee</u>·peh·THohs *adj* **flat**

έπιπλα <u>eh</u>·peep·lah **furniture**

επιπλέον eh·peep·<u>leh</u>·ohn **spare (extra)**

επισκευάζω eh·pee·skeh·<u>vah</u>·zoh *v* **repair**

επισκευή eh·pee·skeh·<u>vee</u> *n* **repair**

επισκευή παπουτσιών eh·pee·skeh·<u>vee</u> pah·poo·<u>tsiohn</u> **shoe repair**

επίσκεψη eh·<u>pees</u>·keh·psee *n* **visit**

επιστροφή χρημάτων eh·pees·troh·<u>fee</u> khree·<u>mah</u>·tohn *n* **refund**

επιταγή eh·pee·tah·<u>yee</u> *n* **check [cheque BE] (bank)**

επιτίθεμαι eh·pee·<u>tee</u>·theh·meh *v* **attack**

επιτόκιο eh·pee·<u>toh</u>·kee·oh **interest rate**

επόμενος eh·<u>poh</u>·meh·nohs **next**

έρχομαι <u>ehr</u>·khoh·meh **come**

ερώτηση eh·<u>roh</u>·tee·see *n* **question**

εστιατόριο ehs·tee·ah·<u>toh</u>·ree·oh **restaurant**

εσωτερική γραμμή eh·soh·theh·ree·<u>kee</u> ghrah·<u>mee</u> **extension (number)**

εσωτερική πισίνα eh·soh·teh·ree·<u>kee</u> pee·<u>see</u>·nah **indoor pool**

εσωτερικός eh·soh·teh·ree·<u>kohs</u> **indoor**

ετικέτα eh·tee·<u>keh</u>·tah *n* **label**

έτοιμος eh·tee·mohs *adj* **ready**

ευθεία ehf·<u>thee</u>·ah **straight ahead**

εύκολος <u>ehf</u>·koh·lohs *adj* **easy**

ευρώ ehv·<u>roh</u> **euro**

Ευρωπαϊκή Ένωση ehv·roh·pah·ee·<u>kee</u> <u>eh</u>·noh·see **European Union**

ευτυχώς ehf·tee·<u>khohs</u> **fortunately**

ευχαριστιέμαι ehf·khah·rees·<u>tieh</u>·meh **enjoy**

ευχάριστος ehf·<u>khah</u>·rees·tohs **pleasant**

εφημερίδα eh·fee·meh·<u>ree</u>·THah **newspaper**

έφηβος <u>eh</u>·fee·vohs **teenager**

έχω <u>eh</u>·khoh **have (possession)**

Z

ζαχαροπλαστείο zah·khah·rohp·lahs·<u>tee</u>·oh **pastry store**

ζεστός zes·<u>tohs</u> **hot, warm (weather)**

ζημιά zee·<u>miah</u> *n* **damage**

ζητώ zee·<u>toh</u> **ask**

ζωγραφίζω zohgh·rah·<u>fee</u>·zoh *v* **paint**

ζωγράφος zohgh·<u>rah</u>·fohs **painter**

ζώνη <u>zoh</u>·nee **belt**

ζώνη για χρήματα <u>zoh</u>·nee yah khree·<u>mah</u>·tah **money-belt**

H

ημερομηνία λήξεως ee·meh·roh·mee·<u>nee</u>·ah <u>lee</u>·kseh·ohs **expiration date**

ημερολόγιο ee·meh·roh·<u>loh</u>·yee·oh **calendar**

ημικρανία ee·mee·krah·<u>nee</u>·ah **migraine**

ηλεκτρικός ee·lehk·tree·<u>kohs</u> **electric**

ηλεκτρονικό εισιτήριο ee·leh·ktroh·nee·<u>koh</u> ee·see·<u>tee</u>·ree·oh **e-ticket**

ηλεκτρονικό ταχυδρομείο ee·lehk·troh·nee·<u>koh</u> tah·hee·dro·<u>mee</u>·oh (ee·meh·eel) **e-mail**

ηλεκτροπληξία ee·leh·ktroh·plee·<u>ksee</u>·ah **shock (electric)**

ηλίαση ee·<u>lee</u>·ah·see **sun stroke**

ηλικιωμένος ee·lee·kee·oh·<u>meh</u>·nohs **senior citizen**

Ηνωμένες Πολιτείες ee·noh·<u>meh</u>·nehs poh·lee·<u>tee</u>·ehs **United States**

Ηνωμένο Βασίλειο ee·noh·<u>meh</u>·noh vah·<u>see</u>·lee·oh **United Kingdom**

ηρεμιστικό ee·reh·mee·stee·<u>koh</u> **sedative**

ήσυχος ee·see·khohs *adj* **quiet**

Θ

θάλασσα <u>thah</u>·lah·sah **sea**

θέατρο <u>theh</u>·aht·roh **theater**

θέλω <u>theh</u>·loh **want**

θέρμανση <u>thehr</u>·mahn·see **heating**

θερμή πηγή thehr·<u>mee</u> pee·<u>yee</u> **hot spring**

θερμόμετρο thehr·<u>moh</u>·meht·roh **thermometer**

θερμοκρασία theh·rmohk·rah·<u>see</u>·ah **temperature (body)**

θερμός thehr·<u>mohs</u> **thermos flask**

θέρετρο διακοπών <u>theh</u>·reh·troh THee·ah·koh·<u>pohn</u> **vacation resort**

θέση <u>theh</u>·see *n* **location (space), seat**

θέση δίπλα στο παράθυρο <u>theh</u>·see THeep·lah stoh pah·<u>rah</u>·thee·roh **window seat**

θηλυκός thee·lee·<u>kohs</u> **female**

θορυβώδης thoh·ree·<u>voh</u>·THees **noisy**

θρησκεία three·<u>skee</u>·ah **religion**

θυμάμαι thee·<u>mah</u>·meh **remember**

θυρίδα thee·<u>ree</u>·THah **luggage locker (lock-up)**

I

ιατρική εξέταση ee·ah·tree·<u>kee</u> eh·<u>kseh</u>·tah·see **examination (medical)**

ίδιος ee·<u>THee</u>·ohs **same**

ιδιωτικό μπάνιο ee·THee·oh·tee·<u>koh</u> bah·nioh **private bathroom**

ιερέας ee·eh·<u>reh</u>·ahs **priest**

ινσουλίνη een·soo·<u>lee</u>·nee **insulin**

ίντερνετ <u>ee</u>·nteh·rnet **internet**

ίντερνετ καφέ <u>ee</u>·nteh·rnet kah·<u>feh</u> **internet cafe**

ιπποδρομία ee·poh·THroh·<u>mee</u>·ah **horse racing**

ιστιοπλοϊκό ees·tee·oh·ploh·ee·<u>koh</u> **sailing boat**

ιστορία ee·stoh·<u>ree</u>·ah **history**

ισχύει ee·<u>skhee</u>·ee **valid**

ίσως ee·sohs **maybe, perhaps**

ιώδειο ee·<u>oh</u>·THee·oh **iodine**

K

κάδος απορριμμάτων <u>kah</u>·THohs ah·poh·ree·<u>mah</u>·tohn **trash can**

καθαρισμός προσώπου kah·thah·reez·<u>mohs</u> proh·<u>soh</u>·poo **facial**

καθαρός kah·thah·<u>rohs</u> **clean**

καθαρτικό kah·thahr·tee·<u>koh</u> **laxative**

καθεδρικός ναός kah·theh·THree·<u>kohs</u>
nah·<u>ohs</u> **cathedral**

καθήκον kah·<u>thee</u>·kohn **duty
(obligation)**

κάθομαι <u>kah</u>·thoh·meh **sit**

καθρέφτης kah·<u>threhf</u>·tees n **mirror**

καθυστέρηση kah·thee·<u>steh</u>·ree·see n
delay

καθυστερώ kah·thee·steh·<u>roh</u> v **delay**

καινούργιος keh·<u>noor</u>·yohs **new**

καιρός keh·<u>rohs</u> **weather**

καλά kah·<u>lah</u> adv **fine (well)**

καλαμάκι kah·lah·<u>mah</u>·kee **straw
(drinking)**

καλάθι kah·<u>lah</u>·THee **basket**

καλός kah·<u>lohs</u> **good**

καλσόν kahl·<u>sohn</u> n **tights**

κάλτσες <u>kahl</u>·tsehs **socks**

κάλυμμα φακού <u>kah</u>·lee·mah fah·<u>koo</u>
lens cap

καλώ kah·<u>loh</u> v **call**

κάμπινγκ <u>kah</u>·mpeeng **camping**

καναπές kah·nah·<u>pehs</u> **sofa**

κανένας kah·<u>neh</u>·nahs adj **none**

κάνω ανάληψη <u>kah</u>·noh ah·<u>nah</u>·lee·psee
withdraw

κάνω εμετό <u>kah</u>·noh eh·meh·<u>toh</u> v **vomit**

κάνω κράτηση <u>kah</u>·noh krah·tee·see v **book**

κάνω πεζοπορία <u>kah</u>·noh
peh·zoh·poh·<u>ree</u>·ah v **hike**

καπέλο kah·<u>peh</u>·loh **hat**

καπνίζω kahp·<u>nee</u>·zoh v **smoke**

καπνοπωλείο kahp·noh·poh·<u>lee</u>·oh
tobacconist

καπνός kahp·<u>nohs</u> **tobacco**

καραντίνα kah·rahn·<u>dee</u>·nah n
quarantine

καράφα kah·<u>rah</u>·fah **carafe**

καρδιά kahr·THee·<u>ah</u> v **heart**

καρδιακό έμφραγμα kahr·THee·
ah·<u>koh</u> ehm·frahgh·mah **heart attack**

καροτσάκι kah·roh·<u>tsah</u>·kee **trolley
(cart)**

καροτσάκια αποσκευών
kah·roh·<u>tsah</u>·kiah ah·pohs·keh·<u>vohn</u>
baggage [BE] carts [trolleys]

κάρτα-κλειδί <u>kahr</u>·tah klee·<u>dee</u> **key card**

καρτποστάλ kahrt·poh·<u>stahl</u> **post card**

κασκόλ kahs·<u>kohl</u> **scarf**

κασσίτερος kah·<u>see</u>·teh·rohs **pewter**

κάστρο <u>kahs</u>·troh **castle**

καταδυτικός εξοπλισμός
kah·tah·THee·tee·<u>kohs</u>
eh·ksoh·pleez·<u>mohs</u> **diving
equipment**

καταλαβαίνω kah·tah·lah·<u>veh</u>·noh
understand

κατάλληλος kah·<u>tah</u>·lee·lohs **suitable**

καταρράχτης kah·tah·<u>rahkh</u>·tees
waterfall

κατάστημα kah·tah·stee·mah **shop
(store)**

κατάστημα με αντίκες kah·<u>tah</u>·
stee·mah meh ahn·<u>tee</u>·kehs **antiques
store**

κατάστημα με είδη δώρων
kah·<u>tahs</u>·tee·mah meh ee·THee
<u>THoh</u>·rohn **gift store**

κατάστημα με υγιεινές τροφές
kah·<u>tahs</u>·tee·mah meh ee·yee·ee·<u>nehs</u>
troh·<u>fehs</u> **health food store**

κατάστημα μεταχειρισμένων ειδών kah·<u>tah</u>·stee·mah meh·tah·khee·reez·<u>meh</u>·nohn ee·<u>THohn</u> **second-hand shop**

κατάστημα αθλητικών ειδών kah·<u>tahs</u>·tee·mah ath·lee·tee·<u>kohn</u> ee·<u>THohn</u> **sporting goods store**

κατάστημα ρούχων kah·<u>tahs</u>·tee·mah <u>roo</u>·khohn **clothing store**

κατάστημα σουβενίρ kah·<u>tahs</u>·tee·mah soo·veh·<u>neer</u> **souvenir store**

κατάστημα υποδημάτων kah·<u>tah</u>·stee·mah ee·poh·<u>THee·mah</u>·tohn **shoe store**

καταστρέφω kah·tah·<u>streh</u>·foh v **damage**

κατάψυξη kah·<u>tah</u>·psee·ksee **freezer**

κατεβαίνω kah·teh·<u>veh</u>·noh **get off (transport)**

κατειλημένος kah·tee·lee·<u>meh</u>·nohs **occupied**

κάτι <u>kah</u>·tee **something**

κάτοχος <u>kah</u>·toh·khohs **owner**

κατσαβίδι kah·tsah·<u>vee</u>·THee **screwdriver**

κατσαρόλα kah·tsah·<u>roh</u>·lah **saucepan**

κάτω <u>kah</u>·toh adj **lower (berth)**

καύσωνας <u>kahf</u>·soh·nahs **heat wave**

καφετέρια kah·feh·<u>teh</u>·ree·ah **cafe**

κέντρο της πόλης <u>kehn</u>·droh tees <u>poh</u>·lees **downtown area**

κεφάλι keh·<u>fah</u>·lee n **head**

κήπος <u>kee</u>·pohs n **garden**

κιθάρα kee·<u>thah</u>·rah **guitar**

κινηματογράφος kee·nee·mah·tohgh·<u>rah</u>·fohs **movie theater**

κίνηση <u>kee</u>·nee·see **traffic**

κινητό kee·nee·<u>toh</u> **cell phone [mobile phone BE]**

κίτρινος <u>keet</u>·ree·nohs **yellow**

κλειδαριά klee·THahr·<u>yah</u> n **lock (door)**

κλειδί klee·<u>THee</u> n **key**

κλειδώνω klee·<u>THoh</u>·noh v **lock (door)**

κλειστός klees·<u>tohs</u> adj **shut**

κλεμένος kleh·<u>meh</u>·nos **stolen**

κλέφτης <u>klehf</u>·tees **thief**

κλήση <u>klee</u>·see n **call**

κλιματισμός klee·mah·teez·<u>mohs</u> **air conditioning**

κλοπή kloh·<u>pee</u> **theft**

κομμωτήριο koh·moh·<u>tee</u>·ree·oh **hair dresser**

κόμβος <u>kohm</u>·vohs **junction (intersection)**

κοιμάμαι kee·<u>mah</u>·meh v **sleep**

κοιλάδα kee·<u>lah</u>·THah **valley**

κοιτάω kee·<u>tah</u>·oh v **look**

κολύμβηση koh·<u>leem</u>·vee·see **swimming**

κοντά kohn·<u>dah</u> adv **near**

κοντός kohn·<u>dohs</u> adj **short**

κορυφή koh·ree·<u>fee</u> n **peak**

κορίτσι koh·<u>ree</u>·tsee **girl**

κοσμηματοπωλείο kohz·mee·mah·toh·poh·<u>lee</u>·oh **jeweler**

κουβέρτα koo·<u>veh</u>·rtah **blanket**

κουζίνα koo·<u>zee</u>·nah **stove**

κουνούπι koo·<u>noo</u>·pee **mosquito**

κουρασμένος koo·rahz·<u>meh</u>·nohs **tired**

κουστούμι koos·<u>too</u>·mee **men's suit**

κουταλάκι koo·tah·<u>lah</u>·kee **teaspoon**

κουτάλι koo·<u>tah</u>·lee n **spoon**

κουτί koo·<u>tee</u> **carton**

κουτί πρώτων βοηθειών koo·<u>tee</u> proh·tohn voh·ee·thee·<u>ohn</u> **first-aid kit**

κράμπα <u>krahm</u>·bah n **cramp**

κραγιόν krah·<u>yohn</u> **lipstick**

κρατώ krah·<u>toh</u> v **keep**

κρέμα ξυρίσματος <u>kreh</u>·mah ksee·<u>reez</u>·mah·tohs **shaving cream**

κρεμάστρα kreh·<u>mahs</u>·trah **hanger**

κρεβάτι kreh·<u>vah</u>·tee **bed**

κρυολόγημα kree·oh·<u>loh</u>·yee·mah n **cold (flu)**

κρύος <u>kree</u>·ohs adj **cold (temperature)**

κρύσταλλο <u>kree</u>·stah·loh n **crystal**

κύμα <u>kee</u>·mah n **wave**

κυλικείο kee·lee·<u>kee</u>·oh **snack bar**

κυλιόμενες σκάλες kee·lee·<u>oh</u>·meh·nehs skah·lehs **escalator**

Κύπρος <u>kee</u>·prohs **Cyprus**

κύριος <u>kee</u>·ree·ohs **main**

κωδικός περιοχής koh·THee·<u>kohs</u> peh·ree·oh·<u>khees</u> **area code**

κωπηλασία koh·pee·lah·<u>see</u>·ah **rowing**

Λ

λάμπα <u>lahm</u>·bah **lamp, light bulb**

λάθος <u>lah</u>·thohs **error, wrong**

λαιμόκοψη leh·<u>moh</u>·koh·psee **neck (shirt)**

λαιμός leh·<u>mohs</u> **throat**

λάστιχο <u>lahs</u>·tee·khoh **tire [tyre BE]**

λειτουργία lee·toor·<u>yee</u>·ah n **mass (church)**

λεκές leh·<u>kehs</u> n **stain**

λεξικό leh·ksee·<u>koh</u> **dictionary**

λεπτό lehp·<u>toh</u> n **minute (time)**

λεπτός lehp·<u>tohs</u> adj **thin**

λέω <u>leh</u>·oh **tell**

λεωφορείο leh·oh·foh·<u>ree</u>·oh **bus**

ληστεία lees·<u>tee</u>·ah **robbery**

λιμάνι lee·<u>mah</u>·nee n **harbor**

λίμνη <u>leem</u>·nee **lake**

λιμνούλα leem·<u>noo</u>·lah n **pond**

λιγότερο lee·<u>ghoh</u>·teh·roh **less**

λιπαντικό lee·pahn·dee·<u>koh</u> **lubricant**

λιπαρός lee·pah·<u>rohs</u> **greasy (hair, skin)**

λιποθυμώ lee·poh·thee·<u>moh</u> **faint**

λίρα <u>lee</u>·rah **pound (sterling)**

λίτρο <u>lee</u>·troh **liter**

λογαριασμός loh·ghahr·yahz·<u>mohs</u> n **check (bill), account**

λοσιόν loh·<u>siohn</u> **lotion**

λοσιόν μαυρίσματος loh·<u>siohn</u> mahv·<u>rees</u>·mah·tohs **sun tan lotion**

λουκέτο loo·<u>keh</u>·toh **padlock**

λουλούδι loo·<u>loo</u>·THee n **flower**

λουρί ρολογιού loo·<u>ree</u> roh·loh·<u>yioo</u> **watch strap**

λόφος <u>loh</u>·fohs **hill**

Μ

μαγιό mah·<u>yoh</u> **swimming trunks, swimsuit**

μαθαίνω mah·<u>theh</u>·noh **learn**

μάθημα ξένης γλώσσας <u>mah</u>·thee mah kseh·nees ghloh·sahs **language course**

μακιγιάζ mah·kee·<u>yahz</u> **make-up**

μακριά mahk·ree·<u>ah</u> adv **far**

μακρύς mak·<u>rees</u> adj **long**

μαλλιά mah·<u>liah</u> **hair**

μανικιούρ mah·nee·<u>kioor</u> **manicure**

μαξιλαροθήκη mah·ksee·lah·roh·<u>thee</u>·kee **pillow case** μαργαριτάρι mahr·ghah·ree·tah·ree **pearl**

μάρτυρας mahr·tee·rahs **witness**

μας mahs **our**

μασάζ mah·sahz *n* **massage**

μάσκα mahs·kah *n* **mask (diving)**

μάτι mah·tee *n* **eye**

μαχαίρι mah·kheh·ree **knife**

με meh **with**

με άμμο meh ah·moh **sandy (beach)**

με υπότιτλους meh ee·poh·teet·loos **subtitled**

με χαλίκια meh khah·lee·kiah **pebbly (beach)**

μεγαλοπρεπής meh·ghah·lohp·reh·pees **magnificent**

μεγάλος meh·ghah·lohs *adj* **big, large**

μέγεθος meh·yeh·thohs *n* **size**

μέδουσα meh·THoo·sah **jellyfish**

μένω meh·noh *v* **stay**

μεριά mehr·yah **side (of road)**

μερίδα meh·ree·THah *n* **portion**

μερικές φορές meh·ree·kehs foh·rehs **sometimes**

μέσα meh·sah **inside**

μεσημεριανό meh·see·mehr·yah·noh *n* **lunch**

μετά meh·tah **after**

μετακομίζω meh·tah·koh·mee·zoh *v* **move (room)**

μέταλλο meh·tah·loh *n* **metal**

μετάξι meh·tah·ksee **silk**

μεταφέρω meh·tah·feh·roh **transfer**

μεταφορά meh·tah·foh·rah *n* **transit**

μεταφράζω meh·tah·frah·zoh **translate**

μετάφραση meh·tah·frah·see **translation**

μεταφραστής meh·tah·frah·stees **translator**

μέτρηση meh·tree·see **measurement**

μετρητά meht·ree·tah *n* **cash**

μετρό meh·troh **subway**

μετρώ meht·roh *v* **measure**

μη καπνίζοντες mee kap·nee·zon·des **non-smoking**

μήκος mee·kohs **length**

μήνας του μέλιτος mee·nahs too meh·lee·tohs **honeymoon**

μήνυμα mee·nee·mah *n* **message**

μηχανή mee·khah·nee **engine**

μια φορά miah foh·rah **once**

μικρός meek·rohs **little, small**

μιλώ mee·loh **speak**

μίνι-μπαρ mee·nee bahr **mini-bar**

μισός mee·sohs **half**

μνημείο mnee·mee·oh **memorial, monument**

μολυσμένος moh·leez·meh·nohs **infected**

μονάδα moh·nah·THah **unit**

μοναδικός moh·nah·THee·kohs **unique**

μονόκλινο δωμάτιο moh·noh·klee·noh THoh·mah·tee·oh **single room**

μονοπάτι moh·noh·pah·tee **path, trail**

μοντέρνος moh·deh·rnohs **modern**

μοτοποδήλατο moh·toh·poh·THee·lah·toh **moped**

μουσείο moo·see·oh **museum**

μουσική moo·see·kee **music**

μουσικός moo·see·kohs **musician**

μουστάκι moos·tah·kee **moustache**

μπαγιάτικος bah-yah-tee-kohs **stale**
μπάνιο bah-nioh **bathroom, lavatory**
μπαρ bahr **bar**
μπάσκετ bah-skeht **basketball**
μπαστούνια του σκι bahs-too-niah too
 skee **ski poles**
μπαταρία bah-tah-ree-ah **battery**
μπέιμπι σίτερ beh-ee-bee see-tehr
 babysitter
μπικίνι bee-kee-nee **bikini**
μπλούζα bloo-zah **blouse**
μπλουζάκι bloo-zah-kee **T-shirt**
μπλου-τζην bloo-jeen **jeans**
μποξ bohks n **boxing**
μπότα boh-tah **boot**
μπότες πεζοπορίας boh-tehs
 peh-zoh-poh-ree-ahs **walking boots**
μπότες του σκι boh-tehs too skee **ski boots**
μπουκάλι boo-kah-lee **bottle**
μπρελόκ breh-lohk **key ring**
μύγα mee-ghah n **fly (insect)**
μυρίζω mee-ree-zoh v **smell**
μυς mees n **muscle**
μύτη mee-tee n **nose**
μύωπας mee-oh-pahs **short-sighted [BE]**
μωρό moh-roh **baby**

N

ναός nah-ohs **temple**
ναυαγοσώστης nah-vah-ghoh-sohs-tees
 lifeguard
ναυαγοσωστική λέμβος
 nah-vah-ghoh-sohs-tee-kee lehm-vohs
 lifeboat
ναυτία nahf-tee-ah **nausea, travel
 sickness**

νέος neh-ohs **young**
νερό neh-roh n **water**
νεύρο nehv-roh **nerve**
νεφρό nehf-roh **kidney**
νιπτήρας nee-ptee-rahs **sink (bathroom)**
νόμιμος noh-mee-mohs **legal**
νομίζω noh-mee-zoh **think**
νόμισμα noh-meez-mah **currency**
νοικιάζω nee-kiah-zoh v **hire, rent**
νοσοκόμα noh-soh-koh-mah n **nurse**
νοσοκομείο noh-soh-koh-mee-oh
 hospital
νόστιμος nohs-tee-mohs **delicious**
Νοτιοαφρικανός
 noh-tee-oh-ahf-ree-kah-nohs **South
 African (nationality)**
νότιος noh-tee-ohs adj **south**
ντεμοντέ deh-mohn-deh **old-fashioned**
ντήζελ dee-zehl **diesel**
ντουζ dooz n **shower**
ντουζίνα doo-zee-nah **dozen**
νύχι nee-khee n **nail**
νύχτα neekh-tah **night**
νυχτερινό κέντρο neekh-teh-ree-
 noh kehn-droh **night club**
νωρίς noh-rees **early**

Ξ

ξαπλώνω ksah-ploh-noh **lie down**
ξενάγηση kseh-nah-yee-see **guided
 tour**
ξενάγηση στα αξιοθέατα
 kseh-nah-yee-see stah
 ah-ksee-oh-theh-ah-tah **sightseeing
 tour**
ξεναγός kseh-nah-ghohs **tour guide**

ξένο συνάλλαγμα kseh·noh see·<u>nah</u>·lahgh·mah **foreign currency**

ξενοδοχείο kseh·noh·THoh·<u>khee</u>·oh **hotel**

ξένος <u>kseh</u>·nohs **foreign**

ξενώνας νεότητας kseh·<u>noh</u>·nahs neh·<u>oh</u>·tee·tahs **youth hostel**

ξεχνώ ksehkh·<u>noh</u> **forget**

ξεχωριστά kseh·khoh·ree·<u>stah</u> **separately**

ξινός ksee·<u>nohs</u> **sour**

ξοδεύω ksoh·<u>THeh</u>·voh **spend**

ξύλο <u>ksee</u>·loh **wood (material)**

ξυραφάκι ksee·rah·<u>fah</u>·kee **razor, razor blade**

O

ομάδα oh·<u>mah</u>·THah n **team**

όμορφος <u>oh</u>·mohr·fohs adj **beautiful, pretty**

ομπρέλλα ohm·<u>breh</u>·lah **sun shade**

οβάλ oh·<u>vahl</u> **oval**

οδηγία oh·THee·<u>yee</u>·ah **instruction**

οδηγός καταστήματος oh·THee·<u>ghohs</u> kah·tahs·<u>tee</u>·mah·tohs **store guide**

οδηγός ψυχαγωγίας oh·THee·<u>ghohs</u> psee·khah·ghoh·<u>yee</u>·ahs **entertainment guide**

οδηγώ oh·THee·<u>ghoh</u> v **drive**

οδική βοήθεια oh·THee·<u>kee</u> voh·<u>ee</u>·thee·ah **road assistance**

οδοντίατρος oh·THohn·<u>dee</u>·ah·trohs **dentist**

οδοντόβουρτσα oh·THohn· <u>doh</u>·voor·tsah **tooth brush**

οδοντόπαστα oh·THohn·<u>doh</u>· pahs·tah **tooth paste**

οικογένεια ee·koh·<u>yeh</u>·nee·ah **family**

οινοποιείο ee·noh·pee·<u>ee</u>·oh **winery**

όνομα <u>oh</u>·noh·mah n **name**

όπερα <u>oh</u>·peh·rah **opera**

οπωροπωλείο oh·poh·roh·poh·<u>lee</u>·oh **greengrocer [BE]**

οργανωμένος ohr·ghah·noh· <u>meh</u>·nohs **organized**

ορχήστρα ohr·<u>khees</u>·trah **orchestra**

οτιδήποτε oh·tee·<u>THee</u>·poh·teh **anything**

οτοστόπ oh·toh·<u>stohp</u> **hitchhiking**

οφείλω oh·<u>fee</u>·loh **have to (obligation)**

οφθαλμίατρος ohf·thahl·<u>mee</u>·aht·rohs **optician**

Π

παγοπέδιλα pah·ghoh·<u>peh</u>·THee·lah **skates**

πάγος <u>pah</u>·ghohs n **ice**

παιδική χαρά peh·THee·<u>kee</u> khah·<u>rah</u> **playground**

παιδικό κρεβάτι peh·THee·<u>koh</u> kreh·<u>vah</u>·tee **crib [cot BE]**

παίζω <u>peh</u>·zoh v **play (games, music)**

παιχνίδι pehkh·<u>nee</u>·THee n **game (toy), round**

παιχνίδι βίντεο pehkh·<u>nee</u>·THee vee·deh·oh **video game**

πακέτο pah·<u>keh</u>·toh **parcel**

πακέτο για το σπίτι pah·<u>keh</u>·toh yah toh <u>spee</u>·tee **take away**

παλιά πόλη pah·<u>liah</u> poh·lee **old town**

παλιός pah·<u>liohs</u> **old (thing)**

πάνα μωρού pah·nah moh·<u>roo</u> **diaper**

Πανεπιστήμιο pah·neh·pees·<u>tee</u>·mee·oh **university**

πάνες μωρού pah·nehs moh·<u>roo</u> **nappies**

πανόραμα pah·<u>noh</u>·rah·mah **panorama**

παντελόνι pahn·deh·<u>loh</u>·nee **pants [trousers BE]**

παντοπωλείο pahn·doh·poh·<u>lee</u>·oh **minimart**

παντόφλες pahn·<u>dohf</u>·lehs **slippers**

παντρεμένος pahn·dreh·<u>meh</u>·nohs **married**

πάνω pah·noh *adj* **top, upper (berth)**

παπούτσι pah·<u>poo</u>·tsee **shoe**

πάρα πολύ pah·rah poh·lee **too (extreme)**

παραγγέλνω pah·rah·<u>gehl</u>·noh *v* **order**

παράδειγμα pah·<u>rah</u>·THeegh·mah **example**

παραδοσιακός pah·rah·THoh·see·ah·kohs **traditional**

παράθυρο pah·<u>rah</u>·thee·roh **window**

παραλαβή αποσκευών pah·rah·lah·<u>vee</u> ah·poh·skeh·<u>vohn</u> **baggage [BE] claim**

παραλία pah·rah·<u>lee</u>·ah **beach**

παραλία γυμνιστών pah·rah·<u>lee</u>·ah yeem·nees·<u>tohn</u> **nudist beach**

παραλυσία pah·rah·lee·<u>see</u>·ah **paralysis**

παράνομος pah·<u>rah</u>·noh·mohs **illegal**

παράξενος pah·<u>rah</u>·kseh·nohs **strange**

παραπάνω pah·rah·<u>pah</u>·noh **more**

παρεξήγηση pah·reh·<u>ksee</u>·yee·see **misunderstanding**

πάρκο <u>pahr</u>·koh *n* **park**

παρκόμετρο pahr·<u>koh</u>·meht·roh **parking meter**

πάρτυ <u>pah</u>·rtee *n* **party (social gathering)**

παυσίπονο pahf·<u>see</u>·poh·noh **painkiller**

παχύς pah·<u>khees</u> *adj* **fat (person)**

πέδιλα peh·<u>THee</u>·lah **sandals**

πεζόδρομος peh·<u>zohTH</u>·roh·mohs **pedestrian zone**

περιμένω peh·ree·<u>meh</u>·noh *v* **hold on, wait**

περιμένω στην ουρά peh·ree·<u>meh</u>·noh steen oo·<u>rah</u> *v* **queue [BE]**

περιέχω peh·ree·<u>eh</u>·khoh **contain**

περιοδικό peh·ree·oh·THee·<u>koh</u> **magazine**

περίοδος peh·<u>ree</u>·oh·THohs **period (menstrual)**

περιοχή peh·ree·oh·<u>khee</u> **region**

περιοχή για καπνίζοντες peh·ree·oh·<u>khee</u> yah kahp·<u>nee</u>·zohn·dehs **smoking area**

περιοχή για πικνίκ peh·ree·oh·<u>khee</u> yah peek neek **picnic area**

περίπτερο peh·<u>ree</u>·pteh·roh **newsstand, kiosk**

περνώ pehr·<u>noh</u> *v* **pass**

περπατώ pehr·pah·<u>toh</u> *v* **walk**

περσίδες pehr·<u>see</u>·THehs **blinds**

πετάω peh·<u>tah</u>·oh *v* **fly**

πετσέτα peh·<u>tseh</u>·tah **napkin**

πέφτω <u>pehf</u>·toh *v* **fall**

πηγαίνω pee·<u>yeh</u>·noh **go**

πιάτσα ταξί piah·tsah tah·<u>ksee</u> **taxi rank [BE]**

πίεση <u>pee</u>·eh·see **blood pressure**

πιθανός pee·thah·<u>nohs</u> **possible**

πινακίδα pee·nah·<u>kee</u>·THah **road sign**

πίνω pee-noh *v* **drink**

πίπα pee-pah **pipe (smoking)**

πιπίλα pee-pee-lah **pacifier [soother BE]**

πισίνα pee-see-nah **swimming pool**

πιστοποιητικό ασφάλειας pees-toh-pee-ee-tee-koh ahs-fah-lee-ahs **insurance certificate**

πιστωτική κάρτα pees-toh-tee-kee kahr-tah **credit card**

πιτσαρία pee-tsah-ree-ah **pizzeria**

πλαγιά plah-yah **slope (ski)**

πλαστική σακούλα plahs-tee-kee sah-koo-lah **plastic bag**

πλατίνα plah-tee-nah **platinum**

πλευρό plehv-roh **rib**

πλημμύρα plee-mee-rah *n* **flood**

πληγή plee-yee **wound (cut)**

πληροφορίες plee-roh-foh-ree-ehs **information**

πληρωμή plee-roh-mee **payment**

πληρώνω plee-roh-noh *v* **pay**

πλοίο plee-oh *n* **ship**

πλυντήριο pleen-deer-ee-oh **washing machine**

πνεύμονας pnehv-moh-nahs **lung**

πόμολο poh-moh-loh *n* **handle**

ποδήλατο poh-THee-lah-toh **bicycle**

πόδι poh-THee **foot, leg**

ποδόσφαιρο poh-THohs-feh-roh **soccer [football BE]**

ποιότητα pee-oh-tee-tah **quality**

πόλη poh-lee **town**

πολυκατάστημα poh-lee-kah-tahs-tee-mah **department store**

πολυτέλεια poh-lee-teh-lee-ah **luxury**

πολύτιμος poh-lee-tee-mohs **valuable**

πονόδοντος poh-noh-THohn-dohs **toothache**

πονοκέφαλος poh-noh-keh-fah-lohs **headache**

πονόλαιμος poh-noh-leh-mohs **sore throat**

πόνος poh-nohs *n* **pain**

πόνος στο αυτί poh-nohs stoh ahf-tee **earache**

πόρτα pohr-tah **door**

πορτοφόλι pohr-toh-foh-lee **wallet**

ποσό poh-soh *n* **amount**

ποσότητα poh-soh-tee-tah **quantity**

ποταμός poh-tah-mohs **river**

ποτέ poh-teh **never**

ποτήρι poh-tee-ree **glass (container)**

ποτό poh-toh *n* **drink**

πουκάμισο poo-kah-mee-soh **shirt**

πράσινος prah-see-nohs **green**

πρέπει preh-pee *v* **must**

πρεσβεία prehz-vee-ah **embassy**

πρεσβύωπας prehz-vee-oh-pahs **long-sighted [BE]**

πρήξιμο pree-ksee-moh **swelling**

πρησμένος preez-meh-nohs **swollen**

πρίζα pree-zah *n* **plug, socket**

πριν preen **before**

πρόβλεψη prohv-leh-psee *n* **forecast**

πρόβλεψη καιρού prohv-leh-psee keh-roo **weather forecast**

πρόβλημα prohv-lee-mah **problem**

πρόγραμμα prohgh-rah-mah *n* **program**

πρόγραμμα θεαμάτων proh-ghrah-mah theh-ah-mah-tohn **program of events** προς prohs **towards**

προσαρμοστής proh·sahr·moh·<u>stees</u> **adaptor**

πρόσβαση <u>prohz</u>·vah·see n **access**

προσγειώνομαι prohz·yee·<u>oh</u>·noh·meh v **land**

προσκαλώ prohs·kah·<u>loh</u> v **invite**

πρόσκληση <u>prohs</u>·klee·see **invitation**

πρόστιμο <u>prohs</u>·tee·moh n **fine (penalty)**

πρόσωπο <u>proh</u>·soh·poh n **face**

προσωρινός proh·soh·ree·<u>nohs</u> **temporary**

προτείνω proh·<u>tee</u>·noh **suggest**

προφέρω proh·<u>feh</u>·roh **pronounce**

προφυλακτικό proh·fee·lah·ktee·<u>koh</u> **condom**

προωθώ proh·oh·<u>thoh</u> **forward**

πρωί proh·<u>ee</u> **morning**

πρωινό proh·ee·<u>noh</u> **breakfast**

πρώτη θέση <u>proh</u>·tee theh·see **first class**

πτήση <u>ptee</u>·see **flight**

πυρετός pee·reh·<u>tohs</u> **fever**

πυροσβεστήρας pee·rohz·vehs·<u>tee</u>·rahs **fire extinguisher**

πυροσβεστική pee·rohz·vehs·tee·<u>kee</u> **fire brigade [BE]**

πυτζάμες pee·<u>jah</u>·mehs **pajamas**

Ρ

ραδιόφωνο rah·THee·<u>oh</u>·foh·noh n **radio**

ρακέτα rah·<u>keh</u>·tah **racket (tennis, squash)**

ραντεβού rahn·deh·<u>voo</u> **appointment**

ράφι <u>rah</u>·fee n **shelf**

ρεματιά reh·mah·<u>tiah</u> **ravine**

ρεσεψιόν reh·seh·<u>psiohn</u> **reception (hotel)**

ρεύμα ποταμού rehv·mah poh·tah·<u>moo</u> **rapids**

ρηχή πισίνα ree·<u>khee</u> pee·<u>see</u>·nah **paddling pool**

ρομαντικός roh·mahn·dee·<u>kohs</u> **romantic**

ρολόι roh·<u>loh</u>·ee n **watch**

ρυάκι ree·<u>ah</u>·kee n **stream**

Σ

σμαράγδι zmah·<u>rahgh</u>·THee **emerald**

σαμπουάν sahm·poo·<u>ahn</u> n **shampoo**

σαγιονάρες sah·yoh·<u>nah</u>·rehs **flip-flops**

σαγόνι sah·<u>ghoh</u>·nee **jaw**

σάκκος <u>sah</u>·kohs **knapsack**

σαλόνι sah·<u>loh</u>·nee **living room**

σάουνα <u>sah</u>·oo·nah **sauna**

σαπούνι sah·<u>poo</u>·nee n **soap**

σατέν sah·<u>tehn</u> **satin**

σβήνω <u>svee</u>·noh v **turn off**

σβώλος <u>svoh</u>·lohs n **lump**

σεζ-λονγκ sehz <u>lohng</u> **deck chair**

σενιάν seh·<u>niahn</u> **rare (steak)**

σερβιέτες sehr·vee·<u>eh</u>·tehs **sanitary towels**

σεσουάρ seh·soo·<u>ahr</u> **hair dryer**

σήμα <u>see</u>·mah **sign (road)**

σημαία see·<u>meh</u>·ah n **flag**

σημαίνω see·<u>meh</u>·noh v **mean**

σημείο see·<u>mee</u>·oh n **point**

σίδερο <u>see</u>·THeh·roh n **iron**

σιδερώνω see·THeh·<u>roh</u>·noh v **iron, press**

σιδηροδρομικός σταθμός see·THee·rohTH·roh·mee·<u>kohs</u> stahth·mohs **rail station**

σκάλα <u>skah</u>·lah **ladder**

σκάλες <u>skah</u>·lehs **stairs**

σκηνή skee·<u>nee</u> **tent**

σκι skee **skiing**

σκιά skee·<u>ah</u> **shade (darkness)**

σκοπός skoh·<u>pohs</u> **purpose**

σκούπα <u>skoo</u>·pah n **broom**

σκουπίδια skoo·<u>peeTH</u>·yah **trash [rubbish BE]**

σκούρος <u>skoo</u>·rohs adj **dark (color)**

σλιπ sleep **briefs**

σόλα <u>soh</u>·lah **sole (shoes)**

σορτς sohrts n **shorts**

σουβενίρ soo·veh·<u>neer</u> **souvenir**

σουπερμάρκετ soo·pehr·<u>mahr</u>·keht **supermarket**

σουτιέν soo·<u>tiehn</u> **bra**

σπα spah **spa**

σπάγγος <u>spah</u>·gohs n **string (cord)**

σπάνιος <u>spah</u>·nee·ohs adj **rare (unusual)**

σπασμένος spahz·<u>meh</u>·nohs **broken**

σπάω <u>spah</u>·oh v **break**

σπήλαιο <u>spee</u>·leh·oh n **cave**

σπίρτο <u>speer</u>·toh n **match (to start fire)**

σπονδυλική στήλη spohn·THee·lee·<u>kee</u> <u>stee</u>·lee **spine**

σπουδάζω spoo·<u>THah</u>·zoh v **study**

σταματώ stah·mah·<u>toh</u> v **stop**

στάδιο <u>stah</u>·THee·oh **stadium**

σταθμός μετρό stahth·<u>mohs</u> meh·<u>troh</u> **subway [underground BE] station**

σταθμός λεωφορείων stahTH·<u>mohs</u> leh·oh·foh·<u>ree</u>·ohn **bus station**

στάση <u>stah</u>·see **exposure (photos), stop (bus)**

στάση λεωφορείου <u>stah</u>·see leh·oh·foh·<u>ree</u>·oo **bus stop**

στέγη <u>steh</u>·yee n **roof**

στέλνω <u>stehl</u>·noh **send**

στενός steh·<u>nohs</u> adj **narrow, tight**

στήθος <u>stee</u>·THohs **breast**

στόμα <u>stoh</u>·mah n **mouth**

στομάχι stoh·<u>mah</u>·khee n **stomach**

στομαχόπονος stoh·mah·<u>khoh</u>·poh·nohs **stomach ache**

στολή stoh·<u>lee</u> n **uniform**

στολή δύτη stoh·<u>lee</u> THee·tee **wetsuit**

στρογγυλός strohn·gkee·<u>lohs</u> adj **round**

στυλ steel n **style**

στυλό stee·<u>loh</u> n **pen**

συμπεριλαμβάνεται seem·beh·ree·lahm·<u>vah</u>·neh·teh **included**

σύζυγος <u>see</u>·zee·ghohs **husband, wife**

συκώτι see·<u>koh</u>·tee **liver**

σύμπτωμα <u>seem</u>·ptoh·mah **symptom**

συναγερμός πυρκαγιάς see·nah·yehr·<u>mohs</u> peer·kah·<u>yahs</u> **fire alarm**

συναντώ see·nahn·<u>doh</u> **meet**

συνέδριο see·<u>neh</u>·THree·oh **conference**

συνταγή γιατρού seen·dah·<u>yee</u> yaht·<u>roo</u> **prescription**

συνταγογραφώ seen·dah·ghoh·ghrah·<u>foh</u> **prescribe**

συνταξιούχος seen·dah·ksee·<u>oo</u>·khohs **retired**

σύντομα <u>seen</u>·doh·mah **soon**

συντριβάνι seen·dree·<u>vah</u>·nee **fountain**

συστάσεις see·<u>stah</u>·sees **introductions**

συστήνω see·<u>stee</u>·noh **introduce, recommend**

συχνός seekh·<u>nohs</u> adj **frequent**

σφηνωμένος sfee·noh·<u>meh</u>·nohs **jammed**

σφράγισμα <u>sfrah</u>·yeez·mah **filling (dental)**

σφυρί sfee·<u>ree</u> **hammer**

σχέδιο <u>skheh</u>·THee·oh *n* **plan**

σχήμα <u>skhee</u>·mah *n* **shape**

σχισμένος skheez·<u>meh</u>·nohs **torn**

σχοινί skhee·<u>nee</u> *n* **rope**

σχολή σκι skhoh·<u>lee</u> skee **ski school**

σωσίβιο soh·<u>see</u>·vee·oh **lifejacket**

σωστός sohs·<u>stohs</u> *adj* **right (correct)**

T

ταμπόν tahm·<u>bohn</u> **tampon**

τάβλι <u>tah</u>·vlee **backgammon**

ταγιέρ tah·<u>yehr</u> **women's suit**

ταΐζω tah·<u>ee</u>·zoh *v* **feed**

ταινία teh·<u>nee</u>·ah **movie**

ταξί tah·<u>ksee</u> **taxi**

ταξίδι tah·<u>ksee</u>·THee **journey**

ταξίδι με πλοίο tah·<u>ksee</u>·THee meh <u>plee</u>·oh **boat trip**

ταξιδιωτική επιταγή tah·ksee·THee·oh·tee·<u>kee</u> eh·pee·tah·<u>yee</u> **traveler's check [traveller's cheque BE]**

ταξιδιωτικό γραφείο tah·ksee·THyoh·tee·<u>koh</u> ghrah·<u>fee</u>·oh **travel agency**

ταξιτζής tah·ksee·<u>jees</u> **taxi driver**

ταυτότητα tahf·<u>toh</u>·tee·tah **identification**

ταχυδρομείο tah·kheeTH·roh·<u>mee</u>·oh **post office**

ταχυδρομική επιταγή tah·kheeTH·roh·mee·<u>kee</u> eh·pee·tah·<u>yee</u> **money order**

ταχυδρομικό κουτί tah·kheeTH·roh·mee·<u>koh</u> koo·<u>tee</u> **mailbox [postbox BE]**

τεμάχιο teh·<u>mah</u>·khee·oh **piece**

τελειώνω teh·lee·<u>oh</u>·noh *v* **end**

τελευταί ος teh·lehf·<u>teh</u>·ohs **last**

τελεφερίκ teh·leh·feh·<u>reek</u> **cablecar**

τέλος <u>teh</u>·lohs *n* **end**

τελωνειακή δήλωση teh·loh·nee·ah·<u>kee</u> THee·loh·see **customs declaration (tolls)**

τελωνείο teh·loh·<u>nee</u>·oh **customs (tolls)**

τέννις <u>teh</u>·nees **tennis**

τετράγωνος teht·<u>rah</u>·ghoh·nohs **square**

τζετ-σκι jeht skee **jet-ski**

τζόγκινγκ joh·geeng **jogging**

τζόγος <u>joh</u>·ghohs **gambling**

τηλεκάρτα tee·leh·<u>kahr</u>·tah **phone card**

τηλεόραση tee·leh·<u>oh</u>·rah·see **TV**

τηλεφώνημα tee·leh·<u>foh</u>·nee·mah **phone call**

τηλεφωνικός θάλαμος tee·leh·foh·nee·<u>kohs</u> thah·lah·mohs **telephone booth**

τηλεφωνικός κατάλογος tee·leh·foh·nee·<u>kohs</u> kah·<u>tah</u>·loh·ghohs **telephone directory**

τηλέφωνο tee·<u>leh</u>·foh·noh *n* **phone**

την teen **per**

τιμή συναλλάγματος tee·<u>mee</u> see·nah·<u>lahgh</u>·mah·tohs **exchange rate**

τιμή εισόδου tee·<u>mee</u> ee·<u>soh</u>·THoo **entrance fee**

τιρμπουσόν teer·boo·<u>sohn</u> **corkscrew**

τοίχος <u>tee</u>·khohs **wall**

τοπικός toh·pee·<u>kohs</u> **local**

τοστιέρα toh-stieh-rah **toaster**

τουαλέτα too-ah-leh-tah **restroom [toilet BE]**

τούνελ too-nehl **tunnel**

τουρίστας too-rees-tahs **tourist**

τουριστική θέση too-ree-stee-kee theh-see **economy class**

τουριστικός οδηγός too-ree-stee-kohs oh-THee-ghohs **guide book**

τραβώ το καζανάκι trah-voh toh kah-zah-nah-kee **flush**

τραμ trahm **tram**

τράπεζα trah-peh-zah **bank**

τραπέζι trah-peh-zee **table**

τραπεζομάντηλο trah-peh-zoh-mahn-dee-loh **tablecloth**

τραυματισμένος trahv-mah-teez-meh-nohs **injured**

τρένο treh-noh **train**

τρέχω treh-khoh v **run, speed**

τρόμπα troh-mbah n **pump**

τρόλλεϋ troh-leh-ee **trolley-bus**

τρύπα tree-pah **hole (in clothes)**

τρώω troh-oh **eat**

τσάντα tsahn-dah **handbag**

τσίμπημα tsee-bee-mah n **bite, sting (insect)**

τσίμπημα κουνουπιού tseem-bee-mah koo-noo-piooh **mosquito bite**

τυπικός tee-pee-kohs **typical**

τύχη tee-khee **luck**

υγρό πιάτων eegh-roh piah-tohn **dishwashing detergent**

υπεραστικό λεωφορείο ee-peh-rahs-tee-koh leh-oh-foh-ree-oh **long-distance bus**

υπεραστικό τηλεφώνημα ee-pehr-ahs-tee-koh tee-leh-foh-nee-mah **long-distance call**

υπέρβαρο ee-pehr-vah-roh **excess baggage [BE]**

υπηκοότητα ee-pee-koh-oh-tee-tah **nationality**

υπηρεσία ee-pee-reh-see-ah n **service (administration, business)**

υπηρεσία δωματίου ee-pee-reh-see-ah THoh-mah-tee-oo **room service**

υπηρεσία πλυντηρίου ee-pee-reh-see-ah pleen-dee-ree-oo **laundry service**

υπνόσακκος ee-pnoh-sah-kohs **sleeping bag**

υπνωτικό χάπι eep-noh-tee-koh khah-pee **sleeping pill**

υπόγειος ee-poh-ghee-ohs **underground [BE]**

υπολογιστής ee-poh-loh-yee-stees **computer**

υπόνομος ee-poh-noh-mohs **sewer**

ύφασμα ee-fahs-mah **fabric (cloth)**

ύψος ee-psohs **height**

φακός fah-kohs **flashlight, lens**

φακός επαφής fah-kohs eh-pah-fees **contact lens**

υπηρεσία φαξ ee-pee-reh-see-ah fahks **fax facility**

φάρμα fahr-mah n **farm**

φάρμακα fahr·mah·kah **medication**

φαρδύς fahr·THees **loose (fitting), wide**

φάρος fah·rohs **lighthouse**

φέρνω fehr·noh **bring**

φέρυ-μπωτ feh·ree boht **ferry**

φεστιβάλ fehs·tee·vahl **festival**

φεύγω fehv·ghoh v **leave (depart)**

φιλμ feelm n **film (camera)**

φίλη fee·lee **girlfriend**

φιλί fee·lee n **kiss**

φιλοδώρημα fee·loh·THoh·ree·mah **gratuity**

φίλος fee·lohs **friend, boyfriend**

φίλτρο feel·troh n **filter**

φιλώ fee·loh v **kiss**

φλέβα fleh·vah **vein**

φλεγμονή flegh·moh·nee **inflammation**

φλυτζάνι flee·jah·nee **cup**

φοβερός foh·veh·rohs **terrible**

φοβισμένος foh·veez·meh·nohs **frightened**

φοιτητής fee·tee·tees **student**

φόρεμα foh·reh·mah n **dress**

φόρος foh·rohs **duty (customs), tax**

φορώ foh·roh v **wear**

φούρνος foor·nohs **oven**

φούρνος μικροκυμάτων foor·nohs mee·kroh·kee·mah·tohn **microwave (oven)**

φούστα foo·stah **skirt**

φούτερ foo·tehr **sweatshirt**

ΦΠΑ fee·pee·ah **sales tax**

φράγμα frahgh·mah n **lock (river, canal)**

φράση frah·see n **phrase**

φράχτης frahkh·tees n **fence**

φρέσκος frehs·kohs adj **fresh**

φτάνω ftah·noh **arrive**

φτηνός ftee·nohs **cheap, inexpensive**

φτιάχνω τις βαλίτσες ftee·ahkh·noh tees vah·lee·tsehs v **pack (baggage)**

φυλακή fee·lah·kee n **prison**

φύση fee·see **nature**

φυτό fee·toh n **plant**

φως fohs n **light (electric)**

φώτα foh·tah **lights (car)**

φωτογραφία foh·tohgh·rah·fee·ah v **photo**

φωτογραφική μηχανή foh·tohgh·rah·fee·kee mee·khah·nee **camera**

φωτοτυπικό foh·toh·tee·pee·koh **photocopier**

X

χαμηλώνω khah·mee·loh·noh v **turn down (volume, heat)**

χαλί khah·lee **rug**

χαλκός khahl·kohs **copper**

χάπι khah·pee **tablet**

χάρτης khahr·tees n **map**

χαρτί khar·tee **paper**

χαρτί κουζίνας khah·rtee koo·zee·nahs **kitchen**

χαρτί υγείας khahr·tee ee·yee·ahs **toilet paper**

χαρτομάντηλο khahr·toh·mahn·dee·loh **tissue**

χαρτομάντηλο khah·rtoh·mahn·dee·loh **handkerchief**

χείλη khee·lee **lips**

χειροκίνητος khee·roh·<u>kee</u>·nee·tohs **manual (car)**

χειρότερος khee·<u>roh</u>·teh·rohs **worse**

χιλιόμετρα khee·<u>lioh</u>·meh·trah **mileage**

χιονίζει khioh·<u>nee</u>·zee *v* **snow**

χλιαρός khlee·ah·<u>rohs</u> **lukewarm**

χόμπυ <u>khoh</u>·bee **hobby (pastime)**

χοντρός khohn·<u>drohs</u> **thick**

χορεύω khoh·<u>reh</u>·voh *v* **dance**

χορτοφάγος khohr·toh·<u>fah</u>·ghohs **vegetarian**

χρειάζομαι khree·<u>ah</u>·zoh·meh *v* **need**

χρέωση υπηρεσίας <u>khreh</u>·oh·see ee·pee·reh·<u>see</u>·ahs **service charge**

χρήματα <u>khree</u>·mah·tah **money**

χρησιμοποιώ khree·see·moh·pee·<u>oh</u> *v* **use**

χρήσιμος <u>khree</u>·see·mohs **useful**

χρονική περίοδος khroh·nee·<u>kee</u> peh·<u>ree</u>·oh·THohs **period (time)**

χρυσός khree·<u>sohs</u> *n* **gold**

χρώμα <u>khroh</u>·mah *n* **color**

χρωστώ khroh·<u>stoh</u> **owe**

χτένα <u>khteh</u>·nah *n* **comb**

χτενίζω khteh·<u>nee</u>·zoh *v* **comb**

χτες khtehs **yesterday**

χώρα <u>khoh</u>·rah **country (nation)**

χωριό khohr·<u>yoh</u> **village**

χωρίς khoh·<u>rees</u> **without**

χώρος <u>khoh</u>·rohs *n* **space (area)**

χώρος κάμπινγκ <u>kah</u>·mpeeng <u>khoh</u>·rohs **campsite**

χώρος στάθμευσης <u>khoh</u>·rohs stahth·mehf·sees **car park [BE]**

χώρος στάθμευσης <u>khoh</u>·rohs stahth·mehf·sees **parking lot**

Ψ

ψαλίδι psah·<u>lee</u>·THee **scissors**

ψάρεμα <u>psah</u>·reh·mah **fishing**

ψάχνω <u>psahkh</u>·noh **look for**

ψηλός psee·<u>lohs</u> **tall**

ψύλλος <u>psee</u>·lohs **flea**

Ω

ώμος <u>oh</u>·mohs *n* **shoulder (anatomy)**

ώρα αιχμής <u>oh</u>·rah ehkh·<u>mees</u> **rush hour**

ώρες λειτουργίας <u>oh</u>·rehs lee·toor·<u>yee</u>·ahs **opening hours**